Lois McMaster Bujold

CRITICAL EXPLORATIONS IN SCIENCE FICTION AND FANTASY
(a series edited by Donald E. Palumbo and C.W. Sullivan III)

ALSO EDITED BY JANET BRENNAN CROFT

Tolkien and Shakespeare: Essays on Shared Themes and Language (McFarland, 2007)

Lois McMaster Bujold

Essays on a Modern Master of Science Fiction and Fantasy

Edited by JANET BRENNAN CROFT

CRITICAL EXPLORATION IN SCIENCE FICTION AND FANTASY, 37
Donald E. Palumbo *and* C.W. Sullivan III, *series editors*

McFarland & Company, Inc., Publishers
Jefferson, North Carolina, and London

Quotations from *Barrayar, Brothers in Arms, A Civil Campaign, Cetaganda, Cordelia's Honor, CryoBurn, Diplomatic Immunity, Komarr,* "Labyrinth," *Memory, Mirror Dance,* "The Mountains of Mourning," *Shards of Honor, The Vorkosigan Companion, The Vor Game,* and *The Warrior's Apprentice* are used with the kind permission of Baen Books.

Quotations from *The Sharing Knife, Volume Four: Horizon, Paladin of Souls* and *The Curse of Chalion* are used with the kind permission of HarperCollins Publishers.

ISBN 978-0-7864-6833-1
softcover : acid free paper ∞

LIBRARY OF CONGRESS CATALOGUING DATA ARE AVAILABLE

BRITISH LIBRARY CATALOGUING DATA ARE AVAILABLE

On the cover: touchdown (iStockphoto/Thinkstock)

Manufactured in the United States of America

*McFarland & Company, Inc., Publishers
Box 611, Jefferson, North Carolina 28640
www.mcfarlandpub.com*

Table of Contents

Introduction

Forward Momentum

JANET BRENNAN CROFT

Lois McMaster Bujold belongs to a very select group of authors: those whose work I find compelling and rewarding enough to reread in their entirety every few years.

The pleasures I find in reading Bujold are akin to those I experience in, for example, reading J.R.R. Tolkien's legendarium or viewing the television series of Joss Whedon: immersion in complex worlds inhabited by well-rounded and realistically-portrayed people whom the reader gets to know over the course of a sustained, lengthy, and multi-part narrative; plots that arise from, illuminate, and influence character; actions that have real consequences that aren't ignored or glossed over in the next installment, but become a part of who that person is and how the world works; deep themes handled with grace, good will, intelligence, and just the right amount of humor; and stories that have applicability to our own situations and personal lives.

In the Miles Vorkosigan books, the reader is confronted with serious questions about what it means to be human in our fast-approaching, potentially post-human future. Is a mutant human? Is a genetically engineered quaddie or hermaphrodite or super-soldier human? Is a clone human? Is a person who is cryo-frozen and comes back from the dead still human, or a person born from a uterine replicator? Is a rich man who's had his brain implanted in a clone human? And if one is human, what are one's responsibilities towards all the other humans out there? Particularly if one is a human with power or influence or great gifts or great challenges, how should one construct one's identity, live one's life, and find one's proper work in the world?

In the *Chalion* fantasy series, Bujold adds questions of human relations with the divine to the mix. In the actions of people called upon by the gods of the Chalion universe, we consider power, responsibility, sacrifice, love, family, the impact of religion on society and on individuals, human fallibility, and human transcendence. And in *The Sharing Knife* series, what happens when the gods are absent and people have to find their own way without them?

1

Bujold consistently addresses great issues and problems on a human level, where they are faced by quirky, prickly, and very real characters. She writes in a compulsively readable style and has an insidiously fiendish plotting ability. But it's these problems and themes that she addresses so compellingly, in the persons of her very real characters, that make her worthy of serious critical attention.

And Why *Hasn't* She Gotten This Attention?

John Lennard addresses this issue in his essay which concludes this volume: "[A]cademic failures to recognize Bujold's literary talent and superb teachability seem glaring," he writes, but "in some ways academic reluctance to engage with [her] is predictable." Her resistance to neat classification leaves her "equally unpalatable to the critical left and devotees of the technosublime"; and "she fails to serve the agendas of minority writing" in part by being "far less amenable" to "recruitment in the gender wars" than other female SF writers. Sylvia Kelso analyzed the situation in an exchange of letters with Bujold, telling her that on the one hand "you don't fit the feminist SF critics' canon, because, 1. You usually have a male protagonist, 2. You don't do feminist Utopias, 3. You don't do alternate sexualities, and in especial lesbians, and 4. you aren't overtly politicized," and on the other, "you don't fit the male canon either in the community or in the critical industry" ("Letterspace" 392–3).

The very breadth of her *oeuvre* also reinforces her resistance to pigeon-holing and therefore easy critical approaches. While Bujold has called her own work "hopelessly, stubbornly, mulishly in-genre" (Bujold and Kelso, "Letterspace" 388), under the broad umbrella of science fiction or fantasy, Bujold crosses and combines genres with a fine disregard for the "rules." The Miles series blithely skips from picaresque space opera to wrenching psychodrama to police procedural to romance to military SF to prison escape to comedy of manners and back, sometimes in the same book, and *The Sharing Knife* series has been taken to task for being both too romance-focused and too "political" at different times in its writing. Additionally, series fiction, as Bujold herself points out, is not as frequently studied by academics as it might be, since it is difficult to teach within the time constraints of a semester, especially with a series as long as the Miles books ("Topias").

A background in hospital work and a familiarity with embryology has led her to view individual humans as falling somewhere along any number of different scales, never purely this or that. As a result of this, her conscious rejection of simplified visions of gender and gender relations becomes another problem for critics; she resists classification as feminist or antifeminist, being unapologetically humanist. And then there is the unfashionable bedrock of her work — biology: life, death, and the reproductive imperative, in all their permutations and interactions with technology. As Aral Vorkosigan says, "All true wealth is biological" (*Mirror Dance* 278), and Bujold herself rewrites his statement to claim that "all true story is biological" ("Sherwooding"). Lennard points out in his discussion of *The Sharing Knife* in particular that "feminist readings are possible but biological ones comprehend them and extend more widely still," and this is true for all of her works.

Another quality that may baffle the critics is Bujold's almost Golden Age writing style — straightforward, nothing too flashy on the surface, a style one might associate more with Isaac Asimov, for example, than with Ursula K. Le Guin. (In a field where James Tiptree, Jr. is invoked as the *locus classicus* of the pen name gender blunder, being told by a young male fan that one "writes like a man" is a bit of a conversation-stopper [Introduction vii]. As Bujold mused, how *does* one respond?) Amy H. Sturgis says in her essay in this volume that Bujold's style is deliberately and consciously "traditional, almost transparent." But anyone familiar with her works soon learns to recognize Bujold's unique voice and the distinguishing tics and tricks she deploys in all of her writing; she "writes like [herself], and like no one else" (Bujold, Introduction vii).

Bujold's writing is also always character-centered and character-driven; we explore societies and watch them change through the eyes of characters rather than in some vast overview setting out the author's political and artistic agenda. Bujold insists that "[t]he politics portrayed in my works exist almost wholly to brace the psychological plot and are set around the problems of characterization, which are central" ("Letterspace" 395). Even the humor (especially in the Miles books) can be problematic for critics who expect total seriousness of focus on big issues; Sylvia Kelso points out in her essay in this volume that while "most of the Vorkosigan books are fast-moving adventures" where "serious issues are confronted," still, "over-the-top comedy is often hovering quite close." For example, the subversive glee Dono Vorrutyer takes in launching his gender change on an unsuspecting Barrayar in *A Civil Campaign* encourages a shallow reading as farce, especially with Ivan Vorpatril as the bemused narrator — yet the first openly acknowledged sex change on Barrayar may turn out to be an unsuspected carnivalesque upending of society.

Like Barrayar confronted with Donna/Dono, critics generally haven't seemed to know quite what to do with Bujold. As she herself puts it, "any theory of SF must now account for me" ("Letterspace" 396); and yet, so few critics have made the attempt. But as this volume shows, her work can be profitably and quite rewardingly approached using many of the standard theoretical tools in the critic's kit. However, just as I've found with Tolkien, one must not expect one critical approach to explain everything; Bujold's writing contains multitudes, and the critic must be prepared to let a few bits and pieces stubbornly stick out from under the lid of his neat little box.

This Collection

Like Bujold's works, this collection is broad-ranging. The aim was for scholarly yet readable prose — thought-provoking and challenging but always accessible. (Somewhat in the spirit of Bujold's own observation that "an academic reading is just an over-empowered reader response" ["Letterspace" 399].) Our authors are both established and emerging scholars; some have written on Bujold before, some haven't, and they represent much of the Anglophone world that makes up Bujold's primary fan base.

The first two items examine Bujold as a writer. What interests her as an author and why? What is her history as a writer? How does she work? We begin with an interview commissioned for this volume, conducted by Sandra J. Lindow, which engages with some of her recent themes and interests. Bujold's discussion of *CryoBurn*, at the time of the interview the most recent Miles book, reinforces the point made above: "all true story is biological," and stories about death and the struggle to cheat the reaper are biological at their core. Amy H. Sturgis's essay then examines Bujold's long engagement with the phenomenon of fan fiction, first as a "nursery for baby writers" like herself who grew up watching, reading, and "appropriating" cultural products like *Star Trek* and the Sherlock Holmes canon, then as a source for understanding reader preferences in style and content and as a living example of Bujold's own elaboration of reader-response theory wherein the reader is the "unsung collaborator."

The bulk of this collection deals with the Miles books, her best-known works, which are simply bristling with hooks for different critical approaches. The first group of papers focuses on aspects of Miles's family situation, starting before he is even born to his remarkable parents, Cordelia and Aral. Regina Yung Lee examines the intersection of power, legitimacy, patriarchy, and technology in Cordelia's unsettling effect on the ossified power structures of Barrayar, paying particular attention to the team Cordelia assembles for her daring and insubordinate raid on the palace occupied by Vordarian the Pretender. Sandra J. Lindow, in an update of her 2001 paper for *Foundation*, addresses the moral examples of Cordelia and Aral and what Miles learns and puts into practice from the integration of their ethical perspectives of care and justice and Aral's distinction between honor and reputation. My own paper deals with the family plot of name-giving — the attempt to control and classify the child by naming it — and how Miles and Mark both use and fight against these imposed boundaries to reach their own goals of identity and purpose. Andrew Hallam builds on the concepts in the two preceding papers and returns to the Cordelia–Vordarian–Kareen confrontation with a quite different approach integrating concepts of home, the uncanny, doubling, the abstract and the concrete.

The next group of papers situates Miles within his broader society. Virginia Bemis analyzes Miles's life narrative using the critical techniques of disability studies, charting Miles's moral development as he lives with his disabilities and develops an ethic of service to others marginalized by society. Linda Wight examines Miles's complex performance and critique of masculinity in *The Warrior's Apprentice*, where his military leadership style is tempered by his instinctive empathy and drive to build relationships. Shannan Palma looks at issues of both disability and masculinity, and how they lead to fitting and misfitting in society, using the characters of Miles, Mark, and Bothari in particular. And Sylvia Kelso takes a double Bakhtinian approach to the cyborg body of Simon Illyan and the failure of his eidetic memory chip, using his theories of the grotesque body and of carnival to make sense of Illyan's and Miles's parallel disintegations and reintegrations.

Our final two papers situate Bujold's fantasy novels within the broader body of her work, and show how the genre allows her to expand on certain themes in ways the Miles books in particular do not. David D. Oberhelman looks at how Bujold uses the history of the Spanish Reconquest of the Moorish states of southern Al-Andalus for the first two books of the *Chalion* series, flipping not just the geography of the primary world but also the religious situation on its head; the Quintarian version of the Reconquista leads back to an earlier broader religious tolerance rather than to forced conversion and Inquisition as it did in Spain. John Lennard brings the volume to a close with his analysis of the deep critique of religion and religiosity running throughout all of Bujold's works, both SF and fantasy, but more clearly foregrounded as an essential element of the recent *Chalion* and *The Sharing Knife* fantasies.

Our aim is to increase readers' appreciation of Bujold and to point the way for new scholarly study. Much remains to be explored; we have only scratched the surface of the possibilities of approaches using disability and masculinity, the cyborg, and gender analysis in this volume, and just barely addressed questions of genre, reader response, source study, personal identity and work, and the effects of technological change. We hope to see these topics explored in the future, while we try to keep up with Bujold as she continues to pull us along in the wake of her own explorations.

And now, if you'll excuse me, I'm due for another re-read.

WORKS CITED

Bujold, Lois McMaster. *A Civil Campaign*. Riverdale, NY: Baen, 1999.

_____. Introduction. In *Women at War*. Lois McMaster Bujold and Roland J. Green, eds. New York: Tor, 1995. vii.

_____. *Mirror Dance*. Riverdale, NY: Baen, 1994.

_____. "Sherwooding on genre, gender, representation." 11 Aug. 2011. Email to the Official LMB mailing-list. 12 April 2012. http://lists.herald.co.uk/ pipermail/lois-bujold/2011-august/080062.html.

_____. "Topias." *Locus* 68:1 (January 2012): 6–7, 54.

_____, and Sylvia Kelso. "Letterspace: In the Chinks Between Published Fiction and Published Criticism." In *Women of Other Worlds: Excursions Through Science Fiction and Feminism*. Helen Merrick and Tess Williams, eds. Melbourne: University of Western Australia Press, 1999. 385–409.

Kelso, Sylvia. "The Decay of the Cyborg Body in Bujold's *Memory*." In the present volume.

Lennard, John. "(Absent) Gods and Sharing Knives: The Purpose of Lois McMaster Bujold's Fantastic Ir/Religions." In the present volume.

Sturgis, Amy H. "From Both Sides Now: Bujold and the Fan Fiction Phenomenon." In the present volume.

A Note on Editions
and Abbreviations

Bujold's books have been printed in many different editions — standard paperback, trade paperback, hardback, omnibus, reissue, international — all with different paginations. As there is no "standard" edition, I have kept the references in each paper to the editions used by the authors. I have, however, standardized the titles to the original individual novel or short story units of publication rather than the omnibus titles. Thus "Mountains of Mourning" will always be referenced as Mountains, whether the author quotes from *Borders of Infinity*, *Young Miles*, *Dreamweaver's Dilemma*, or even the version on the Baen website. Additionally, each section of *Dreamweaver's Dilemma* and *The Vorkosigan Companion* will be referenced by section title.

Standard Abbreviations for Bujold's Books

Alliance = *Captain Vorpatril's Alliance*
Barrayar = *Barrayar*
Beguile = *Sharing Knife: Beguilement*
Borders = "Borders of Infinity"
Brothers = *Brothers in Arms*
Campaign = *Civil Campaign*
Cetaganda = *Cetaganda*
Chalion = *Curse of Chalion*
CryoBurn = *CryoBurn*
Ethan = *Ethan of Athos*
Falling = *Falling Free*
Game = *The Vor Game*
Gifts = "Winterfair Gifts"
Horizon = *Sharing Knife: Horizon*
Hunt = *Hallowed Hunt*

Immunity = *Diplomatic Immunity*
Infinity = *Borders of Infinity* (bridging material only)
Komarr = *Komarr*
Labyrinth = "Labyrinth"
Legacy = *Sharing Knife: Legacy*
Memory = *Memory*
Mirror = *Mirror Dance*
Mountains = "Mountains of Mourning"
Paladin = *Paladin of Souls*
Passage = *Sharing Knife: Passage*
Shards = *Shards of Honor*
Spirit = *Spirit Ring*
Warrior = *The Warrior's Apprentice*

Collections

Cordelia's Honor includes *Shards* and *Barrayar*
Miles Errant includes Borders, *Brothers,* and *Mirror*
Miles in Love includes *Komarr, Campaign,* and Gifts
Miles, Mutants, and Microbes includes *Falling,* Labyrinth, and *Immunity*
Miles, Mystery and Mayhem includes *Cetaganda, Ethan,* and Labyrinth
Young Miles includes *Warrior,* Mountains, and *Game*

Love and Death in the Vorkosiverse

An Interview with Lois McMaster Bujold

SANDRA J. LINDOW

Sandra J. Lindow interviewed Bujold exclusively for this volume in July 2011. The book mentioned at the end is *Captain Vorpatril's Alliance*, Baen Books, 2012.

SL: You have said in conversation that your fantasy series are more profitable than your science fiction despite the awards. What brings you back to Miles Vorkosigan after several years?

LMB: Actually, now the dust has settled, it looks as if all Bujold books sell pretty much the same. Advances have equalized, actual sales are always a moving target. (Evergreens, yay! E-books, hmm....) So there is nothing on the economic side to force a choice between fantasy and science fiction, not that I need allow myself to be forced these days. Fan pressure is more of an issue, if I listen to it.

What brought me back to Miles were contractual issues separate from money. Really, I think the organic end of the Miles series came (and went) with *A Civil Campaign* (1999) and Miles's betrothal, always the proper ending for a comedy. However, I needed an option-filler to expedite the move from Baen to HarperCollins/Eos (and to keep my fences mended, since I had no idea back then how Eos would work out for me over time, nor whether I would want to do more Vorkosiverse later.) Hence *Diplomatic Immunity* (2002), where I was able to come up with a second happy organic closure for the series, still thematically cohering with the book, with the birth of Miles's children.

Then, shortly after Jim Baen's death in 2006, Baen editor Toni Weisskopf called me with a request for another Miles book, as she was pulling things together at the company in the wake of that event. I had worked with Toni for almost as many years as I had worked with Jim, and I wanted to support the cause, as Baen had certainly supported me over the years, through thick and thin. (And there were several daunting thins, along the way.) I was in the middle of the second pair of *The Sharing Knife* books at that point, but promised to do a Miles book, content unspecified, for Toni next, for which we would sign the contract then. The notion of something exploring the demographics of mass cryonics had been kicking around in the back of my mind for literally decades, so this (after a couple of false plot starts — cloning, I'd *done* cloning) became the setting and subject of *CryoBurn*. The picture of Miles's initial hallucinatory encounter with a young street kid had also been in my head for years, no plot or setting attached, but it was hook enough to hang the story-start on.

The rest of the inspiration for Jin Sato's character came from Gerald Durrell's memoir *My Family and Other Animals*, which I first read, gosh, in the late 1960s, and had been recently reminded of by the excellent BBC-TV adaptation. (Jin also has, come to think, a touch of the poor street kid in the dimly-remembered movie *Salaam Bombay!*, only much less depressing.)

Also, after listening (always a mistake) to all the outraged and wounded SF fans kvetching about the romance central to *The Sharing Knife* tetralogy, I set out to write something that was properly SFnal, all tech and politics and no romance. I almost succeeded — it's not got *much* rat in it — but no one seemed to appreciate the effort.

The end of *CryoBurn* was thematically inherent in the subject matter (and drawn from my own life experience). Also, it provided yet another organic close for the series, if not so happy a one this time. I'm running out of endings, here.

In the past your Vorkosigan series as well as Falling Free *focused on personal issues related to disability and different ability. In* CryoBurn *(2010) Miles seems to have a mature handle on his rather complex health issues. Are you moving away from disability as a focus?*

This question presupposes that I ever *had* disability as a focus in the first place. It seems to invite the notion that I begin a book with an Issue, which everything else is got up to illustrate, cherry-picked editorial fashion; since much political science fiction is apparently devised in just this way, as intentional allegory and persuasion, I suppose it's a natural mistake.

In fact, I almost always begin books with characters (or they arrive very shortly, else the book-idea promptly augers into the ground); whatever issues the characters may have come along for the ride. It is simply an aspect of Miles's own maturity that his handle on his dodgy health has grown firmer. If a character is supposed to learn and grow over time, it only makes sense that their major lessons *stay learned*.

So Dag's lost hand, or Miles's multiple health problems, or Cazaril's demonic pseudo-cancer, do not comprise the sums of their characters nor the reasons for their existences, but are just plot-things that happen to them and with which they must deal, daily or otherwise. The letters I get from readers themselves struggling with assorted handicaps indicate they prefer this approach; so I feel no need to change it.

Also: the two qualities that science fiction and fantasy readers seem to most uncompromisingly demand from their protagonists is that they be (1) very smart, and (2) underdogs. If characters from Class 1 are not to too-quickly work themselves out of Class 2, the writer has to slow them down somehow. This is especially a problem with Miles, who has so many non-underdoggish advantages. (Not to mention his appalling energy.)

What appealed to me most in CryoBurn *is the community of interesting unregistered citizens that grows up around the supposedly abandoned cryo facility, what Paul Goodman has described as* communitas, *a support structure that exists inside, outside, or in the interstices of organized civic structures. Communitas is an important aspect of all your books. Will you explain this further?*

Well ... partly it's just worldbuilding. Characters require stories which require settings. Settings need to vary realistically, or at least plausibly or convincingly. (Not to mention entertainingly.) I've set scenes in space stations, palaces, hill cabins, interstellar jumpships, mansions, slums, castles, research laboratories, stables, prison camps, temples, hospitals, clinics, monasteries, lakes, woods, mountains, rivers, land, sea, air ... every sort of place that I can get my head around gets a turn in the barrel.

Settings, in turn, are populated, unless they are deserts or other wildernesses, by their natural and economic ecosystems of people. Whom I then have to make up and, if I am especially unlucky that day, *name*.

The bootleg cryonics facility in *CryoBurn* came from the need for Jin to be from somewhere. A little thought and poking into the question of, "And what would street people be all about on Kibou-daini?" brought me very quickly to the problem of the poor being shut out of medical care, and the question of what that would look like when the care in question was cryo-freezing. The necessities of the technology shaped the feasible answers. Some anecdotes from an acquaintance who used to work with street people in Minneapolis, my own life observations, and my youthful experiences working in an urban hospital supplied evocative details that I could pry open and rummage around in to find the rest.

I've noticed that CryoBurn *is darker and less comic than your earlier work. Do you perceive it that way? Is this a sign of the times? In your 1997 Kaleidoscope interview you described a "toxically utilitarian" worldview where the value of a*

human being is defined by economic utility. Has your perception of the world
changed since the 90s? To my mind, government has gotten less reliable and cor-
porations have gotten even more dangerous. What is your experience?

Well, the underlying theme of *CryoBurn* is death, and all the multitude
of ways people dodge or deal with it, ending in the inescapable Fact of it,
mute. If some people find this a dark theme, just wait; one grows more used
to it over time. Part of the loss-of-comedy comes from Miles's own increased
maturity; we lose the farcical edge that came from his earlier ability to make
interesting and appalling mistakes, because he doesn't make those sorts of
mistakes anymore, in part because he isn't as frantically "on the make" as he
used to be. So any perceived darkness is only a sign of my times, if
that. I thought the book had quite a bit of humor, myself; some reviewers
considered the book slight and trivial (a subset of the usual "I wanted it to
have been a different book" crowd), so your perception is not universally
espoused.

I still find defining people by their economic utility to be toxic; but that
has been with us forever, part of human nature, not tied to the times. I don't
think either the world or people in it have changed much about that. Alas.

To my way of thinking, both governments and corporations are human
mental constructs; they are what we make them. It's not as if they exist separately from the persons who comprise them. They are, at most, consensus
realities, like money or sports scores or religions; we *make them up*; they exist,
like the fairies in *Peter Pan*, because we continue to agree to believe in them.

Getting back to the *communitas* question, whenever these structures fail
to serve the people in and around them, people make up new structures in
the interstices, sure. Some are parasitical (criminal organizations), some are
benign (various kinds of self-organized social groups), some can grow and
replace the original structure in a quasi-revolutionary manner.

Any human organization whatsoever is always in danger of being hijacked
by the sociopaths, because the sociopaths are always with us; the organization
will always have a tipping-point where the toxic people start to outnumber
or outmaneuver the nontoxic ones, and then things will slide down the tubes.
I suppose one might try to consciously construct one's organizations to be
more sociopath-resistant or robust; any organization that survives over an
extended period of time likely already has some of these aspects naturally
evolved within it.

The one thing that I think makes a solid difference to people's real lives,
both for good and for ill, is changing technologies and people's changing
access to them. Technology defines the ambit of the possible. The rest is, as
it were, a software problem.

Getting back to disability, might it be possible to consider being cryofrozen as the ultimate disability? In CryoBurn, *disability then takes on an economic utility twist—freezing the less-able now, letting the future deal with them later, this being the ultimate in placing an economic value on the life of a human being. Thus, when their freezing contract runs out and no one renews it, some individuals are successfully revived only to still be elderly and even more marginalized than before. Could this have been part of your consideration when writing?*

Death is too universal to be classified as a disability. It's more of a norm. Granted, when one is young, death can indeed seem to be something that only happens to someone else, but one gets over that.

To be a disability proper, the problem needs to be something that most people don't have, that society and one's surroundings are not usually set up to cope with. The fact that no one can flap their arms and fly is thus not classified as a disability; the constructed world accommodates. The fact that some people can't walk *is* so classified, because they are a minority and the world is set up, default, to serve the needs of the mobile majority.

One certainly can't call the frozen dead on Kibou-daini a minority, whatever else they may be. (Now, that's a *real* Silent Majority....) Nor could one call them underserved. And as dead people go, they are *way* more present than the usual graveyard dust.

What I wanted to do with *CryoBurn* was look, even if only glancingly, at as many aspects of mass cryonics as I could fit within the parameters of the story. How many things can go wrong?— oh, let us count the ways! Or right, for that matter. But the economic-utility parts are only one such angle. Other angles include generation gaps, the emotional effects and coping mechanisms of living with this tech, and competition for resources.

(That said, if anyone wants to discern any tart observations about health care distribution in the here-and-now from all this, feel free.)

Do note, not all of the cryocorps in the story are corrupt; just the ones Miles meets, because he's going for them preferentially, and he has a keen nose for trouble. Stories only happen when things go wrong, after all.

To me CryoBurn *seems closer to our real world than earlier books in the Vorkosigan series. I see the out-of-control capitalism demonstrated by* CryoBurn's *cryogenic care facilities as quite believable. You have described writing as "strip-mining" your life; would you be willing to talk about what inspired you to write about cryo-facilities?*

Most proximately, it was from meeting a fellow–Midwestern SF fan of mine who was also involved in Alcor, the company that is attempting to freeze people right now in hopes that future medicine might be able to revive them.

He sent me a very interesting packet of materials from his organization, back in the early 90's. I thought, perusing them, that this was all very well for the tiny minority, but what if *everybody* wanted in on the act? What happens then? At present, the cryonics movement seems to consist of sincere geekly people, but what if, after some generational flow, it fell into the hands of the sort of corporate minds written about in the excellent *The Smartest Guys in the Room*? What would mass cryonics really do to a culture or an economy? And to the people in them? And most of all, why on earth would the future *want* us in all our messy masses? *CryoBurn* is my exploration of some plausible outcomes.

It's not a new vision, though in prior eras it was confined only to fantastical nightmares: as I have Miles quote from *The Epic of Gilgamesh* (which I read back in my late teens, having been directed to it by the same quote in the John Brunner tale *The Traveller in Black*): "I shall bring up the dead to take food with the living, and the living shall be outnumbered by the host of them." This does not exactly constitute welcoming the proposed family reunion with open arms.

There is a deal of generational crisis embedded in this vision. (Said crisis seemed new to me when I first encountered it in my youth, but I now realize it to be another on-going universal.) How are young people ever to get their turn at the world if the old people never let it go? Thus did the Alcor ideas hit a baby boomer who remembers the frustrations of the Sixties (because I didn't do them right, presumably.)

One should also toss in, I suppose, the most of my 20s, when I worked in patient care in a large university hospital. I calculated it out recently; I figure I must have encountered something over 14,000 patients during that period, however briefly, plus staff; just because I was oblivious at the time as to what a mine of human observation I was accumulating, doesn't mean it wasn't all going into the bag.

Cordelia, Miles's mother, at one point says, "Tests are a gift and great tests are a great gift." Is this the organizing principle for your fantasy series as well?

Great tests are certainly the key to gripping fiction, of any genre. I don't think one needs to look further than that.

You have mentioned that in much of your work, your inciting action is "What is the worst thing I can do to this guy?" I noticed that in CryoBurn, *although Miles is drugged and nearly kidnapped in the first chapter, the worst really doesn't happen until the very end when Miles is told of the death of his father, Count Aral Vorkosigan. Is this the setup for the next book where Miles must deal with the complicated public issues of trying to fill his father's much larger shoes?*

No. It's another *end of the series*, dammit. Again.

I have no idea if it will hold.

Mark Twain, in one of his inimitable anecdotes, describes the effect of a certain preacher pleading, movingly, for relief for the sufferings of the benighted; in his mind, Twain upped and upped his proposed contribution — and then, as the preacher continued and continued, dropped it back down and down again. "*Still* he went on. When the collection plate finally came around, I took ten cents out of it."

I should like to find some graceful way to stop before people start taking dimes out of my plate.

Is there anything else that's new that you want to touch on?

Every decade or so, it seems, I need to remake myself as a writer. I feel about a book and a half overdue for this process just now. I should like to do something that's actually new, not just more new-old, which is all anybody ever asks for. No, I don't know what.

Meanwhile, however, succumbing to much fannish pressure and the witch-light lure of what seemed a bright idea at the time, at the end of 2009 I embarked on an Ivan book. (It avoids messing up my ending by being a prequel, hah!) It got off to a flying start, but was then interrupted by many distractions — home repair, book promotion, mundane medical issues — and died in the middle of my road, blocking traffic. Thank heavens I hadn't yet taken it to contract, or I should really have gone mad in white linen. Having finally staked, Buffy-style, everything between the em-dashes, I have recently restarted it (July 2011 as I write this), but I don't yet know how it will run. It does seem to have acquired the critical mass to demand its own completion; I can't just tow it into the ditch and abandon it, apparently. So we'll see.

From Both Sides Now
Bujold and the Fan Fiction Phenomenon
AMY H. STURGIS

Before earning four Hugo Awards, three Nebula Awards, the Mythopoeic and Skylark Awards, and a number of additional honors, as well as a devoted audience among science fiction, fantasy, and romance readers, author Lois McMaster Bujold was a fan. As she explains in her essay entitled "Here's Looking at You, Kid...," "I was a reader and fan first, and a fan fiction writer pretty much simultaneously with my start at trying to write original fiction."

Bujold does not seek to hide what she calls her "fling with fandom" ("Answers" 201); on the contrary, she credits it as a kind of apprenticeship, one that not only nurtured her growth as a writer but also prepared her to relate to fan readers once her professional fiction became popular. Today she is a self-proclaimed fan-friendly author who has used the insights gained from fan fiction to develop strong ties to her fan community; to wrestle in particular with the question of sex and readership in fiction; and to articulate her theory of the "unsung collaborator," which has been credited with re-inventing the reader-response theory of literature ("How I Met the Inklings").

Bujold the Fan

Both Bujold and her childhood friend, Lillian Stewart Carl, who also grew up to become a professional fiction writer, have recounted in a variety of essays and interviews Bujold's youthful experience as a fan. Beyond the aforementioned "Here's Looking at You, Kid...," some of the most insightful of these discussions include Bujold's "Answers," Carl's "Through Darkest Adolescence with Lois McMaster Bujold, or Thank You, But I Already Have a Life," and Carl's interview, "A Conversation with Lois McMaster Bujold."

From these accounts and others one can reconstruct a portrait of Bujold the young science fiction/fantasy/mystery fan as she gravitated to the works of authors such as Robert Heinlein, Poul Anderson, J.R.R. Tolkien, and Arthur Conan Doyle, and television series such as *The Twilight Zone, The*

Man from U.N.C.L.E., and the original *Star Trek*. She also kept abreast of the larger science fiction community, subscribing to the magazine *Analog Science Fiction and Fact*, becoming an active member of the COSFS, the Central Ohio Science Fiction Society, and attending genre conventions.

Bujold's transition from being a mere consumer of genre texts to an active transformer of them is the kind of journey explored and analyzed by scholars of fan culture and transformative media, including pioneers of the field such as Henry Jenkins, Camille Bacon-Smith, Joan Marie Verba, Constance Penley, Cheryl Harris, Alison Alexander, and Matt Hills, among others. Fan fiction itself is far from new, of course; to give a common example, one could say that the medieval authors who embellished and explored preexisting Arthurian legends were early fan fiction producers. Contemporary fan fiction has been dated from the publication of the first *Star Trek* fanzine, *Spockanalia*; that very publication in particular inspired Bujold to write fan fiction and co-produce a *Star Trek* zine of her own, *StarDate*.

When looking back at the *StarDate* experience, Bujold is quick to point out that creating the fan publication served as a training ground for future professionals. Of the other fans besides Bujold who contributed fiction and art to the zine, two became writers and another became an artist by trade. In retrospect, Bujold notes, "it's interesting to see all of us baby artists getting our first fling there" ("Answers" 201).

Although it marked Bujold's first experience with genre-related publication, *StarDate* was not the first time Bujold's fan appreciation for texts had led to her write. At the tender age of fifteen, Bujold read both *The Lord of the Rings* and *The Faerie Queene* twice, and then felt moved to attempt fantasy of her own. The resulting project, never completed, was in Bujold's words a "Tolkienesque epic" with "the dubious distinction of having been written in Spenserian verse" ("Conversation" 32).

StarDate was not Bujold's final foray into fan fiction, either. While in college, she penned a tribute to Arthur Conan Doyle's great detective, her very own Sherlock Holmes mystery. While it failed to launch her career in Holmesian pastiche writing, it did mark the first incarnation of a gutsy heroine named Cordelia Naismith, who would later become reborn as Cordelia Naismith Vorkosigan in Bujold's highly successful Vorkosigan series. "The Adventure of the Lady on the Embankment" finally saw print — minus its now-missing final pages — in the 1996 collection *Dreamweaver's Dilemma: A Collection of Short Stories and Essays*.

The fact that Bujold is candid about her early participation in fandom, and even allowed her Holmes story to be published in a collection alongside professional works long after her reputation as an award-winning author was secure, says much about her attitude toward the fan experience as a legitimate and much-needed training ground of sorts. "It's very tough for an apprentice to get the kind of experience that they need to go on to grow into the full-fledged artist," she explains in "Answers." She credits fanzine projects such as *StarDate* with serving as "a nursery for baby writers," including herself (202).

Bujold the Author

If her fan fiction experience represented an apprenticeship for Bujold, then it is unsurprising that echoes of the texts that inspired her fannish creativity resound in her original works. As a fan she was moved to write by works of science fiction (the original *Star Trek*), fantasy (*The Lord of the Rings* and *The Faerie Queene*), and mystery (the Sherlock Holmes canon). Although the crossing, blending, and transcending of genres is one of the trademarks of her writing, Bujold's fiction falls broadly into the category of science fiction and fantasy, often informed by mystery.

As an author, Bujold is known foremost for her bestselling and widely translated Vorkosigan series (1986–present), which is comprised of more than a dozen novels, novellas, and short stories. This saga fits squarely into the science fiction genre (and the subgenres of military, political, and sociological science fiction), but many of its stories are framed around classic "whodunit" scenarios. Perhaps the best example of this is the Hugo and Nebula Award–winning "The Mountains of Mourning" (1989), which casts protagonist Miles Vorkosigan in the role of detective uncovering the truth behind an infanticide when the murdered baby's mother appeals to Count Vorkosigan's court for justice. The rich world-building tradition of classic fantasy informs Bujold's other series, the three-novel *Chalion* series (2001–2005) and the four-novel *Sharing Knife* series (2006–2009), as well as her stand-alone novel *The Spirit Ring* (1993).

Another object of Bujold's early fannish appreciation also has left a lasting footprint on her original writing. Bujold has mentioned repeatedly her love of the "spy-fi" television series *The Man from U.N.C.L.E.* (1964–1968), which mixed high-tech, futuristic gadgetry with international power politics to create a show filled with action-packed espionage. Nearly all of Bujold's stories, even those in the decidedly pastoral *Sharing Knife* series, contain an element of political subterfuge in their plots. The Vorkosigan series in particular shares the spy-fi marriage of science fictional technology and high-stakes political espionage Bujold encountered as a teenager while following the adventures of the agents of U.N.C.L.E., the United Network Command for Law and Enforcement.

In the Vorkosigan series, Bujold offers an almost-overt nod to her inspiration through the character of Simon Illyan, the slight, cool, and quietly heroic lieutenant who eventually rises to become the trusted chief of Imperial Security on the Vorkosigans' homeworld of Barrayar. Illyan's natural gifts are complemented by an eidetic memory chip implanted in his brain, which provides him perfect recall. The vicious sabotaging of this chip eventually leads to his forced though highly honorable retirement, during which he proves that at least one highly intelligent lady, Alys Vorpatril, finds him quite attractive.

The image Bujold paints of the intelligent, aloof, uber-capable Illyan is a clear match to that of the slight, cool, and quietly heroic agent Illya Kuryakin in *The Man from U.N.C.L.E.* Although Kuryakin had no memory chip in his brain, his dispassionate logic and calm menace lent him a computer-like — or Spock-like, to speak in *Star Trek* terms — gravity, and made actor David McCallum an instant sex symbol for viewers, especially those who were "brainy teens headed to college" (Walker and Sturgis 205). Bujold, of course, was one of those "brainy teens" at the time, as was her friend Lillian Stewart Carl, who implies that Bujold is self-conscious and intentional in her homage: "Television produced *The Man from U.N.C.L.E.* and Illya Kuryakin, an example of the sidekick being more interesting than the hero. (It's no accident that the head of Imperial Security on Barrayar is named Illyan)" ("Darkest" x).

It seems, then, that the genres that inspired Bujold's creativity as a fan became the genres in which she has been most productive as a writer of original fiction. And one might say that her fannish sensibility has not altogether disappeared, as is evident in the loving tribute to *The Man from U.N.C.L.E.*'s Illya Kuryakin that is the Vorkosigan series' Simon Illyan. There is yet another way in which Bujold's experience as a fan has influenced her career as an author, however. She makes her debt to fan fiction itself explicit in her 2006 essay "Writing Sex."

In "Writing Sex," Bujold details the challenge posed by her *Sharing Knife* series. More than any other of her works, *The Sharing Knife* novels are centered on a romance, specifically the one that blossoms between the widowed and middle-aged Lakewalker Dag and the young, inexperienced farmer girl Fawn, whose unplanned pregnancy ends tragically at the start of the first novel. In her previous fiction, Bujold could leave much to the readers' imagination for sexual scenes, fading to a discreet black before involved description became necessary. In *The Sharing Knife* books, however, as Bujold explains, "the characters' various sexual problems were quite central to the plot" ("Writing Sex"). This left her with the question of how to write intimate scenes without boring a substantial number of readers past caring or shocking and scaring away a different portion of the audience.

As she maps her reasoning for the approach she ultimately chose, Bujold notes a turning point in her life as a reader that now informs her life as a writer. She knew what did not work for her: previously she had found written pornography to be "profoundly anti-erotic," and, later, graphic sexual scenes in two science fiction novels proved to be so "repellent" to her that she never completed the books or read any other publications by their authors. It took a friend loaning her several fanzines to help Bujold discover what did work for her. These zines contained slash fan fiction. In Bujold's words, "the light dawned in more ways than one" ("Writing Sex").

Slash, or homoerotic, fan fiction takes its name from the manner in which writers denote a sexual pairing by placing a slash mark between the names of the involved characters (Kirk/Spock, for example). If the printed fanzine *Spockanalia* ushered in the modern era of fan fiction in 1967, the modern era of slash fan fiction officially began with the publication of Diane Marchant's "A Fragment Out of Time" in the 1974 *Star Trek* fanzine *Grup III*. The contemporary slash phenomenon itself predates Marchant's story, however, as Jennifer Guttridge's *Star Trek* slash story "The Ring of Soshern" may have been in private circulation among fans as early as 1968, and UK fan author "B" shared a friendship-turned-slash series with fellow *Star Trek* fans sometime in the late sixties and early seventies.[1]

As Bujold stayed up all night to read the loaned slash zines, she felt a "riveted interest" that no other literature had evoked in her. From this experience, she built an understanding of what traditional pornography did for some, and "figured out fetish and how it works" ("Writing Sex"). In the end, she took away several lessons from this. One, for instance, is the folly of assuming that one's own sexual "turn-ons" are equally true for the rest of humanity (or, more to the point, one's readership). Just because the author likes it does not mean the audience will. Another is an appreciation of the fact that the romantic and the erotic are not the same thing.

In *The Sharing Knife* series, she translated insights gained from her fan fiction reading into practice, muting sexual scenes so they read as proportionate to non-desensitized readers and focusing on achieving an "explicit" tone rather than "graphic" content ("Writing Sex"). In short, she crafted the series to try to avoid the pitfalls of other texts that had left her uncomfortable or unmoved in the past, and to try to recapture the "riveted" interest fan fiction had evoked in her. The fact that Bujold in 2006 not only remembers her first reading of slash zines more than twenty years earlier, but also acknowledges the insights they gave her into her own psyche and the successful professional writing of sex scenes, says much about the respect and seriousness with which Bujold approaches fan writing.

Bujold and the Fans

Fan fiction is a controversial issue for authors. For example, one of the most recent, not to mention highly publicized and ill-tempered, eruptions of the question occurred in May 2010. Diana Gabaldon, best known for her romance/historical fantasy *Outlander* series, made a post entitled "Fan Fiction and Moral Conundrums" on her official blog on May 3, noting her policy against fan fiction: "OK, my position on fan-fic is pretty clear: I think it's immoral, I know it's illegal, and it makes me want to barf whenever I've inadvertently encountered some of it involving my characters."[2] George R.R. Martin, most famous for his epic fantasy series *A Song of Ice and Fire*, published a post in support of Gabaldon's policy ("Someone Is Angry on the Internet") four days later on his LiveJournal, blaming fan fiction for, among other things, the fact that H.P. Lovecraft lived in poverty, ate poorly, and died an early death.

Several popular science fiction writers such as John Scalzi and Charlie Stross spoke out against "Gabaldon's recent declaration of war on fanfic" (Stross). Horror author Nick Mamatas posted a specific rebuttal to Martin in his own LiveJournal, pointing out factual errors in Martin's understanding both of copyright and of Lovecraft's life story, arguing that Lovecraft's work survived and grew popular in large part due to his fans and their writings. Mamatas suggested that detractors of fan fiction "should avoid rewriting history by trying to show Lovecraft as a negative example of the power of fanfic when ultimately, Lovecraft's reputation is what it is today partially *because* of fanfic." Neither side backed down.

In her blog post "Fan the Flames," science fiction and fantasy writer Catherynne M. Valente took stock of the debate, framing it in terms of age divisions: "This argument is already over. It is a generational one. You've got a whole host of authors coming into their own who grew up with fanfic as a fact of life, or even committed it themselves. Who have been messing about with creative commons since forever. A whole generation who sees fanfic as, not a nuisance, but a mark of success, a benchmark[...]."

This may be the case; there is anecdotal evidence to support this from the likes of successful younger writers such as science fiction author Cory Doctorow and fantasy author Maggie Stiefvater. If it is, then Lois McMaster Bujold, who falls between the ages of Gabaldon and Martin (whom Valente described as representing that "certain generation of authors" who "will always hate and fear fanfic"), is ahead of her time. She both acknowledges her own experience with fan fiction, and she encourages her fans to be creative.

Her personal policy on consuming fan fiction based on her publications has changed somewhat over the years. Due to legal concerns about story rights — that is, the desire to avoid a situation in which fans might sue her for stealing their ideas — she now follows her agent's advice and no longer reads fan fiction inspired by her own writings. On a post to her mailing list in 1997, she notes this decision came "most reluctantly" ("Post"). In 2005's "Here's Looking At You, Kid...," she expresses regret at this self-imposed restriction, explaining that these legal and financial issues are "why I have stopped reading fanfic of my own works, fascinating as I find it."

She does, however, continue to earn her fan-friendly reputation, encouraging her fans to "Feel free to write amongst yourselves" ("Post"). Her official and authorized website, *The Bujold Nexus*, includes links to fan fiction, fan art, fan music (or "filk"), and other fan creations on its front page. Her greatest support to the fan community, one could argue, is the credibility she lends to fan activities by recognizing her own background as a fan and by taking seriously the insights available from fan fiction.

Bujold and the "Unsung Collaborator"

Bujold may not read fan fiction related to her own works any longer, but she does read fan fiction inspired by other texts ("Here's Looking"). In fact, her reading of fan fiction helps to inform her theory of what writers and readers do together in order to make literature, a theory she explains in her 1989 essay "The Unsung Collaborator."

In this work, Bujold describes a book not as an object, but as a process, one that requires both the author's and reader's input in order to reach completion. Writer and reader share the work; one creates a framework of story, and the other fills in its ellipses. Bujold likens the author to the architect who draws the plans for a structure, and the reader to the contractor who "does the actual sweat-work of building" ("Unsung" 176). Without one or the other, construction does not happen. For success, writers and readers both must be willing to invest effort.

Scholars of literary theory would identify Bujold's argument as a variation on the theme of reader-response criticism, represented by pioneering figures such as Louise Rosenblatt and Stanley Fish, among others. Bujold's essay, however, was not published in a scholarly journal, but in a science fiction fanzine, *Lan's Lantern*. It is aimed not at literary theorists and their fellow academics, but rather at genre readers themselves.

Reader-response criticism approaches a text by exploring and analyzing the various reactions it evokes in different readers. In "Here's Looking At You, Kid...," Bujold notes that examining fan fiction sheds new light on this enterprise: "What I really find fascinating in fanfic is that it's a natural reader-response laboratory." By noting what missing scenes fan fiction writers choose to add, which back stories they choose to flesh out, and which plot discrepancies or oversights they choose to correct — not to mention the styles through which fan authors choose to express themselves and the ways they harness preexisting story elements to focus on their own interior concerns — one can, Bujold explains, "see inside readers' heads, that otherwise inaccessible stage where all this art takes place." In other words, fan fiction makes manifest or acts out the otherwise private and thus opaque process audience members go through as they consume and digest a text.

Bujold further details her theory of the "unsung collaborator" in her 1999 convention address given as the Guest of Honor Speech at MileHiCon and at SwanCon, "When World-Views Collide." She argues that the writer's and reader's world-views touch every time a book is read. Four outcomes are possible: the world-views might match; the world-views might collide; the world-views might miss each other completely; or the reader's world-view might expand with new information or insights, so that he or she leaves the work changed.

It follows that the "little story-petrie-dishes" ("Here's Looking") provided by fan fiction offer useful windows into the results of such outcomes. To put it another way, a work of fan fiction might illustrate the comfort and pleasure that comes from matching world-views, the fury and frustration of colliding world-views, or the growth and satisfaction of an expanded world-view. On the other hand, it might represent "active misreading," the altering or editing of a text by which the consumer reconciles world-views that miss each other entirely, reworking the author's message until it makes "more sense" ("When World-Views"). Again, fan fiction takes audience members' reactions out of their inaccessible and mysterious home inside readers' heads and puts them on the page (or monitor) where authors may contemplate and learn from them.

How does Bujold's theory of the "unsung collaborator" affect the style of her writing? The goal of the author, she suggests, is to attract active readers, these unsung collaborators who are willing to meet the text halfway and do their part to make it come alive. Bujold proposes two ways to judge style in this context. First, and unsurprisingly, the style of a work should fit its content

("Unsung" 178). While she gives examples of unusual styles working to good effect due to unique subject matter (Roger Zelazny's first-person, present-tense delivery of "Twenty-four Views of Mount Fuji," for instance), her own remains traditional, almost transparent.

The second "yardstick" by which Bujold proposes to judge a writer's style is one she admits "I have not heard suggested before[...]: Does the style act to exclude readers?" ("Unsung" 178). She asserts that writing might exclude readers in one of two ways. First, it might be crude, and therefore it might turn away sensitive (and active) readers. Bujold strictly rations profanity in her fiction, following her own advice. This rule also relates to her choices about muting intimate interludes in stories so that, to readers who have not been desensitized to graphic sexual content, they will seem in balance with surrounding scenes.

Second, Bujold argues that an author's style might be "hyper-stylistic, self-absorbed" ("Unsung" 178). If it is, she says, this betrays a writer's elitist assumptions about who makes up an audience that matters, and it alienates many worthy readers. While appreciating the poetry of precise wordcraft, Bujold attempts to make her style as invisible as possible, so that the words themselves do not get in the way of "the story, characters, images, and ideas" ("Unsung" 178). In this sense, she tries to craft inclusive, not exclusive, fiction.

Her ability to bend and blend genres also assists Bujold in writing works that will please the greatest number of readers while excluding the fewest. This goal, like her theory of the "unsung collaborator" itself, comes in part from Bujold's study of fan fiction and the example set by fan fiction writers as the kind of active readers and "invisible partners" she desires ("Unsung" 179).

By terming fan fiction "a natural reader-response laboratory," then, Bujold implies that fan fiction is more than simply an opportunity for fledgling writers to practice and hone their skills. It is a valid response for consumers of texts as they work through the repercussions of meeting the author's world-view with their own. The fan fiction phenomenon also offers a useful object of study for the professional writer; in Bujold's words, it provides "not just food for thought about my craft, but a banquet" ("Here's Looking").

Conclusion

"All writers work off a springboard of prior models which they have internalized," Bujold writes in "Here's Looking At You, Kid..."; "the boundary between 'original' and 'derivative' can get fuzzy." It seems that Lois McMaster

Bujold has been crossing and recrossing boundaries throughout her career as she has maintained a lifelong relationship with the fan fiction phenomenon. Bujold began writing as a fan, and her fannish interests have left their mark on her original fiction. Her experience as a fan fiction writer prepared her not only to create professional fiction, but also to relate to the many fans who read and enjoy it — including those who in turn have been inspired to write fan fiction about it.

Being a consumer of fan fiction has allowed Bujold to gain insights that have informed everything from her strategies about the writing of sex scenes to her understanding of the very nature of literature itself. Perhaps most significantly, the credit (and thus credibility) she gives to fan fiction encourages others to take it seriously both as a legitimate reader response and as a fruitful subject of study.

NOTES

1. See Sinclair and Verba for different accounts.
2. This post was deleted from Gabaldon's blog as of May 9, 2010. It is excerpted in Meadows.

WORKS CITED

Bacon-Smith, Camille. *Enterprising Women: Television Fandom and the Creation of Popular Myth*. Philadelphia: University of Pennsylvania Press, 1992.

Bujold, Lois McMaster. "Answers." *Dreamweaver's Dilemma: A Collection of Short Stories and Essays*. Suford Lewis, ed. Framingham, MA: The NESFA Press, 1996. 197–228.

_____. "Here's Looking at You, Kid..." 15 December 2005. *The Bujold Nexus*. 12 April 2012. http://www.dendarii.com/fanfic.html.

_____. "How I Met the Inklings." 6 August 2006. Guest of Honor Speech at Mythcon 37. *The Bujold Nexus*. 12 April 2012. http://www.dendarii.com/inklings.html.

_____. Post to the Lois McMaster Bujold Mailing List. 16 October 1997. Quoted at *The Lois McMaster Bujold Fan Fiction Archive*. 12 April 2012. http://www.dendarii.co.uk/FanFic/.

_____. "The Unsung Collaborator." 1989. *Dreamweaver's Dilemma: A Collection of Short Stories and Essays*. Suford Lewis, ed. Framingham, MA: The NESFA Press, 1996. 175–179.

_____. "When World-Views Collide." 1999. Guest of Honor Speech at MileHiCon and SwanCon. *The Bujold Nexus*. 12 April 2012. http://www.dendarii.com/collide.html.

_____. "Writing Sex." 12 December 2006. *The Bujold Nexus*. 12 April 2012. http://www.dendarii.com/sex.html.

The Bujold Nexus. 14 January 2012. http://www.dendarii.com/.

Carl, Lillian Stewart. "A Conversation with Lois McMaster Bujold." *The Vorkosigan Companion*. Lillian Stewart Carl and John Helfers, eds. Riverdale, NY: Baen Books, 2008. 29–64.

_____. "Through Darkest Adolescence with Lois McMaster Bujold, or Thank You, But I Already Have a Life." *Dreamweaver's Dilemma: A Collection of Short Stories and Essays*. Suford Lewis, ed. Framingham, MA: The NESFA Press, 1996. ix–xiv.

Doctorow, Cory. "In Praise of Fanfic." 16 May 2007. *Locus Magazine*. 24 January 2012. http://www.locusmag.com/Features/2007/05/cory-doctorow-in-praise-of-fanfic.html.

Harris, Cheryl, and Alison Alexander, eds. *Theorizing Fandom: Fans, Subcultures, and Identity.* Cresskill, NJ: Hampton, 1998.

Jenkins, Henry. *Textual Poachers: Television Fans and Participatory Culture.* New York: Routledge, 1992.

Mamatas, Nick. "George R.R. Martin Is Wrong About Lovecraft." 8 May 2010. *LiveJournal.* 12 April 2102. http://nihilistic-kid.livejournal.com/1470621.html.

Martin, George R.R. "Someone Is Angry On the Internet." May 7, 2010. *LiveJournal.* 26 January 2012. http://grrm.livejournal.com/151914.html.

Meadows, Chris. "Novelist Diana Gabaldon Causes Fanfic Furor." 5 May 2010. *TeleRead: News & views on e-books, libraries, publishing and related topics.* 12 April 2012. http://www.teleread.com/copy-right/novelist-diana-gabaldon-causes-fanfic-furor/.

Penley, Constance. *NASA/Trek: Popular Science and Sex in America.* New York: Verson, 1997.

Sinclair, Jenna. "A Short History of Early K/S, or How The First Slash Fandom Came to Be." Original date unknown. 2002. *Beyond Dreams Press.* 26 January 2012. http://www.beyonddreamspress.com/index2.htm.

Stiefvater, Maggie. Untitled reply to blog comment. 21 December 2008. *LiveJournal.* 24 January 2012. http://m-stiefvater.livejournal.com/89143.html?thread=2078775#t2078775.

Stross, Charlie. "FAQ: Fanfic." 5 May 2010. *Antipope.* 12 April 2012. http://www.antipope.org/charlie/blog-static/2010/05/faq-fanfic.html.

Valente, Catherynne M. "Fan the Flames." 20 May 2010. *LiveJournal.* 12 April 2012. http://yuki-onna.livejournal.com/582169.html.

Verba, Joan Marie. *Boldly Writing: A Trekker Zine History, 1967–1987.* Minnetonka: FTL Productions, 1996.

Walker, Cynthia W., and Amy H. Sturgis. "Sexy Nerds: Illya Kuryakin, Mr. Spock, and the Image of the Cerebral Hero in Television Drama." *Common Sense: Intelligence as Presented on Popular Television.* Lisa Holderman, ed. Lanham, MD: Lexington Books, 2008. 201–216.

Legitimacy and Legibility

Rereading Civil Discourse Through Feminist Figurations in Cordelia's Honor

REGINA YUNG LEE

"I was an astrocartographer. Then a Survey captain. Then a soldier, then a POW, then a refugee. And then I was a wife, and then I was a mother. I don't know what I'm going to be next."—Lois McMaster Bujold, *Barrayar* (442)

"When did society ever ask fathers to choose between being men and citizens?"—Luce Irigaray, *Sexes and Genealogies* (18)

"Sexual difference is one of the major philosophical issues, if not the issue, of our age," says philosopher Luce Irigaray (*An Ethics of Sexual Difference* 13), not because it constitutes the only or most important form of difference, but because it must be addressed first, providing a basis from which other differences emerge into civil life. In *Cordelia's Honor*, recognition of this difference becomes a kind of passage, not toward any single purpose or ending, but from a dystopic equilibrium into something else. Cordelia's actions are a speculative venture that explores the necessities and possibilities of fulfilling Irigaray's recommendation in *Thinking the Difference* for "creat[ing] a politics of sexual difference that encompasses the most private life between persons as well as the organization of society or societies as a whole" (xvi). In order to create these new forms of public and private participation, Irigaray suggests two immediate responses: changing the civil law "to give both sexes their own identities as citizens," which alters (or institutes) the functional definition of women through the law, and "changing the forms of symbolic mediation," which requires new figures and figurations of womanhood in order for the woman to emerge as a person, that is, as a representable and recognizable subject who can viably participate in both the household and civic life. As Irigaray puts it, "[w]hen did society ever ask fathers to choose between being men and citizens? We don't have to give up being women to be mothers" (*Sexes and Genealogies* 18). This statement leads not only to a reformulation of the relationship between women and motherhood, but also the relationship between women and civic discourse.

Of particular interest from this perspective is Lois McMaster Bujold's two-novel prologue to the Vorkosigan series, *Shards of Honor* (1986) and the Hugo award-winning *Barrayar* (1991), reissued by Baen as *Cordelia's Honor* in 1999. The duology depicts the meeting and courtship of Betan Survey Captain Cordelia Naismith and Barrayaran Lord Aral Vorkosigan, Cordelia's harried introductions to the legitimating structures of Barrayaran patriarchy, and her desperate attempt to rescue her unborn son from being murdered as a pawn in the upheaval surrounding Vordarian's Pretendership, and ends with the birth of series protagonist Miles Naismith Vorkosigan. Cordelia's arrival on Barrayar marks the advent of a difference; because of her previous experiences, she can engage with Barrayar's univocal constructs in the certain knowledge that its singularity of vision is artificial.

For philosopher Judith Butler,[1] the refiguration of the excluded person and the creation of that person's civic identity cannot simply reverse a public exclusion; the system itself is structurally incapable of encompassing such difference. Instead, these legitimating structures must be questioned until they crack: "It is not a matter of a simply entry of the excluded into an established ontology, but an insurrection at the level of ontology, a critical opening up of the questions, What is Real? Whose lives are real? How might reality be remade?" (Butler 31). Any alteration at this level requires catastrophic change: at its most volatile, it leads through revolutionary politics into civil war. This is the arc of *Cordelia's Honor,* culminating in a public execution whose profound impacts on civil life stem from the center of the household itself. The narrative's subtle, near-invisible reclamation of the embattled alterities of embodiment and culture is nothing less than a pervasive technologically-mediated resistance to the embedded systems of legitimation which the characters struggle to subvert.

Cordelia is not only an agential (and therefore alien) woman, Survey Captain, wife, and mother. In the epigraph above, the crucial space of speculation in her answer reveals her world-changing ability to articulate a placeholder for as-yet unimaginable futures. Her recognition of Barrayar's deep civil inequities underwrites all her subsequent choices and actions. When Aral is made Regent, she requires that he bring her vision into law, that as Regent he "[r]emake this world into one Miles can survive in. And Elena. And Ivan. And Gregor" (*Barrayar* 567). This stringent directive, the coeval survival of the mutant, the woman, the scion, and the emperor, necessitates an insurrection in the operations of legitimacy on the planet. However, the world Cordelia requests is not one Aral can imagine; that is, the future she requires from Aral is one only she can see. Therefore, it must be Cordelia who takes up the work of transformative legitimations, establishing a chance for life in, through, and for herself, as the first of many unimaginable others. She must seize the present and render it into the future she so unequivocally requires. When Cordelia moves to retake Miles's replicator, mobilizing against all orders and in defiance of the law, she makes her name's word an action, engendering a difference in kind in the definitions of personhood on Barrayar. What the cyborg birth between woman and uterine replicator create together is the necessary first difference, first in a sequence from which all other differences proliferate. Through Cordelia's radical speculative futures, all presently-illegible alienated bodies become birthed into a speculative legitimacy, awaiting their actualization into the future tense. To deform philosopher Gilles Deleuze's *enculage* of his various subjects,[2] Cordelia takes legitimation from below, and makes it her own — not for her own sake, not only for herself, but for the sake of her fellow monstrous regiment, and all the different futures she has seen and named.

Mutants and Cannibals:
A Brief History of Barrayar

At the beginning of *Shards of Honor*, Barrayaran society is nearing the end of several important transitions, originating in the abrupt introduction of Barrayar into galactic society eighty years ago, as well as the first Cetagandan invasion, which brought galactic weapons technology to the planet. The tense political situation on Barrayar, with its secret military police and dying Emperor, mix synergistically with these exceedingly unstable social mores to form tense overlapping sets of cultural stigmas, which link legal status to perfection, with normative physical and cultural breeding defined by the bodies of aristocratic military men. In the wake of a poison-gas attack on Aral and Cordelia, their unborn child must be transferred from her uterus to a uterine replicator as the poison eats through his bones; the child will be born fragile and stunted, a teratogenic mutant in a society that hates visible difference above all else. On Barrayar, woman and mutant and disabled are near-interchangeable terms, code words for less-viable alternatives to the able-bodied masculine aristocrat; these bodies are nonstandard texts, illegible and invisible within extant readings of subjectivity. In this ideological system, any kind of unrecognizable body reads as impure and unnatural — that is, as monstrous. Barrayaran belief in blood purity and physical perfection fuels a deep cultural revulsion against visible mutation. In "a society that loathes and fears the mutations that have been its deepest agony" (*Barrayar* 583), Miles would inevitably be killed, for as a mutant, he is deprived of the legal status of legitimate personhood. In a sense, Miles cannot be born into this world, for his birth would not secure personhood, legitimacy, or legibility; he could exist, but not strive or even live for very long.[3] For Miles to thrive, a whole new form of life must emerge. As she fights to clear a path for her son's survival, Cordelia's unexpected revolutionary gift to her adopted planet will be the slow dissolution of these perilous limits to personhood and life itself.

Barrayar's military-patriarchal legal discourse has a stranglehold on its societal norms, rendering deviance fatal. As Aral euphemistically puts it, "[i]t's our society. It tends to be ... rather hard on anyone who can't keep up" (*Barrayar* 281). The schism between societal requirements and definitions of personhood erupt into punitive violence throughout the duology. This weaponization of bodies under their cooption by state military necessities dominates the action at every scale. Barrayar's too-sudden reintroduction to galactic life fostered a permanent militarization; since another invasion could happen at any moment, Barrayaran bodies held little intrinsic value beyond their strategic and tactical importance to the Imperium. This constant state of emergency combines with a cultural horror of physical mutation to produce an obsessive focus on inalienably legitimate bodies. This exclusivity of recognition, the alienable reading of personhood, authorizes perpetual violence and inequality towards those construed as non-persons, illegitimate alien others such as women, children, mutants, madmen, bastards, and cyborgs, all defined negatively as lacking personhood because they lack legibility under the law.

To be legitimate is to be lawfully-begotten, literally born into the law. In the Barrayaran context, only the aristocratic Vor have the privilege of non-ambiguous relationships to the law and inalienable access to personhood: the Vor scion holds innate significance, with access to agential action and legal recourse in cases of personal injury. The *Oxford English Dictionary* specifies that legitimate status is granted by another in possession of the law; thus, it rests outside of the object, action, or person itself: "[e]tymologically, the word expresses a status which has been conferred or ratified by some authority." Related adjectival uses rest on a lack of ambiguity before the law. In the Barrayaran context, only the aristocratic Vor have the privilege of non-ambiguous relationships to the law and inalienable access to personhood, with its concomitant political and social acceptance. Their bodies hold innate significance, with access to agential action and legal recourse. And since the Vor are legitimated through their names, products of long genetic obsessions, the Vor Lord's living body is the standard for legitimacy in the public realm. His body is thus a metonym of the law, connecting legibility to legitimation. The power of definition is necessarily exclusive, constructing the marginal status of women, bastards, cyborgs, and mutants on Barrayar.[4] For these very ambiguous and therefore illegitimate persons, the concept of legitimacy is closely linked to what Judith Butler would call "precarious life," in which personhood remains destabilized both legally and socially because that personhood is alienable, removable by the word of another legitimate body. Thus, these persons' rights to legitimate personhood rest uneasily in the category of the alienable, or as the OED puts it, "[c]apable of being alienated, or transferred to the ownership of another." Thus, if something requires legitimation, it is also alienable; for the people who fall outside of unambiguous relation to society before the law, their personhood is pervaded with this alienation.

The status of difference on Barrayar includes two possibilities: invisibility, a kind of social death, or true death, a kind of mere killing — for only fully legitimate people have access to the law's protection, and may therefore be murdered, a crime whose every occurrence is a horrific tragedy.[5] On Barrayar within the law there is no true difference possible: all bodies are variously closer to or farther from the one legitimate heir, the body for whom the law is perfectly legible, without question or delay. Both Judith Butler and Donna Haraway discuss human value formation according to this attribution of personhood, which is defined by the ethical characterization of its destruction: the other is rendered non-person when its "murder" is downgraded to "slaughter" or "killing," when its death is not grievable, and when its look is not returned. This "fantasy of mastery" (Butler 29), expressed in the simultaneous disavowal of vulnerability and paranoid attempts to neutralize the perceived threat of the alien, forms the terms which grant personhood on Barrayar: healthy sons form strong armies for a state of permanent emergency, an arrangement Cordelia thinks of as breeding lambs for slaughter (*Shards of Honor* [*Shards*] 69). These ways in which certain lives have been rendered "more grievable than others" (Butler 30) frame the terms of Aral and Cordelia's first conflict, over whether the brain-damaged Ensign Dubauer should live:

> "My combat knife is quite sharp. Used quickly, it would cut his throat almost painlessly. Or should you feel it is your duty as his commander, I'll lend you the knife and you may use it."
> [...]
> She stood and looked at him very steadily. "It must be like living among cannibals, to be a Barrayaran" [*Shards* 13].

In an image which returns several times, Cordelia terms Barrayar's profligacy with the life of its citizens a kind of cannibalism, with especial reference to the young men its wars so rapaciously consume.[6] The intrusive presence of the brain-damaged Lieutenant Dubauer interrupts Aral's smooth elision between functional life, determined by use, and a kind of innate value for life, which Cordelia treats as Dubauer's by right. This claim is one she forcibly guarantees with her parole, staking her name's word as a pledge of her conviction. Cordelia's name's word asserts personhood for the deviant, creating their legitimate personhood from within the parole she offers to both Dubauer and Aral. This is a trade she continues to make for others as long as her word remains recognized, her word for their lives, until even her own illegible word empties out into unilateral unsanctioned action.

Bujold's authorial Afterword frames Cordelia and Aral's dual care of Dubauer as a test-run for their later care of Miles: "I already knew [...] that Aral and Cordelia would have a physically handicapped son in Barrayar's intensely militaristic culture, thought I did not yet know how it would come about. Though I was not really aware of it when I was writing Chapter One, Ensign Dubauer is clearly the first statement of this theme" ("Afterword" 592). Cordelia's commitment to inalienable legitimacy only intensifies in the wake of her pregnancy, specifically once it is clear that her son will be born with visible deformities. Out of both prejudice and political expediency, Aral's father first requests, then attempts to incite, then demands that they abort "[t]hat thing in the can" which Cordelia calls her son (*Barrayar* 418). In a fury over the destruction of his hopes for an unambiguous heir, Aral's father Count Piotr withdraws his name from Miles, destroying the unbroken lineage of the Vorkosigans as a sign of his deep disgust:

> "You're so set on change, here's a change for you. I don't want my name on that thing. I can deny you that, if nothing else."
> [...]
> "Call him Miles Naismith Vorkosigan, then," said Cordelia, feigning calm over a sick and trembling belly. "My father will not begrudge it" [*Barrayar* 418–419].

In Barrayaran naming conventions, the male heir carries both his grandfathers' first names; Miles should have been Piotr Miles Vorkosigan, and Piotr's denial signals his refusal to accept the child as a member of the house. The transfer of naming conventions from Piotr to Cordelia[7] attests to a larger movement, a metonym which places the entire category of Barrayaran personhood at stake in the ensuing action. By withdrawing his name, Piotr condemns Miles to a form of public bastardy, indelibly marked by the absence of patriarchal legitimation. But Cordelia's granting reveals her alternate paradigm, a form of legitimation which transfigures Barrayaran patriarchy. Cordelia's action in this moment takes a deeply private familial matter and refigures it as a true civic alteration. When Miles Naismith Vorkosigan is born, a part of his heritage will manifest itself solely and thoroughly in his mother's name. He inherits her name's word, establishing a paradigm for the conferral of personhood that encompasses difference, legitimating him not as a link in an unbroken chain of physically perfect male successors, but as a mutant born to an alien woman, all agential subjects under the law.

Cordelia is no mere unbiased observer in the imminent derangement of her life. Instead of remaining remote, unencumbered, passing judgment on Barrayar from some objective god's-eye view, Cordelia finds herself tied to and surrounded by the complex outworkings of conflicts between her attitudes toward personhood, reproduction, and Barrayaran law. It is these troublesome interpolations which will determine the intermixture of weaponized politics, social history, and embodied violence which define her formative encounters with Barrayaran bodies. Her stance is what feminist scholar Donna Haraway calls non-innocent, or unEdenic: painfully aware of her implication within the regimes she critiques, as she tries to become a good wife and mother in a society where the categories of wife, mother, and mutant child are all inimical to personhood. In Haraway's terms, Cordelia's witness must be *modest*, "not simply oppositional. Rather, s/he is suspicious, implicated, knowing, ignorant, worried, and hopeful" (*Modest_Witness* 3) — that is, Cordelia's deep implication, once acknowledged, can be used to create a clear observation of her new social structures, sharpened as much by love as by fury.

In Cordelia's case, her modest witness focuses on the closed class of the Vor; her social implication as a Vor wife on Barrayar allows her to get close to its most secret places, its backcountry caves and Imperial sewers, passages beneath otherwise impassable difficulties. Piotr Vorkosigan's resistance fighters used the Dendarii Range's caves as part of their strategic maneuvers, taking advantage of the caves' seeming openness to lure the Cetagandan invaders down into an impermeable underground system. Using her social illegibility as strategic cover and a form of witness, Cordelia's subterranean resistance, foreshadowed through her deceptive use of those same Dendarii caves, likewise gains surprising power from being able to juxtapose the tactical marginality of military resistance and the domestic spaces of the Imperial Residence's innermost rooms.

Rewriting Legibility: Three Othered Women

While in one sense, only male Vor are legitimate persons in Barrayaran society, its structures of legitimation also grant a marginalized status to women, based on a series of layered expectations for legibility within set social structures. Even in Barrayar's newly galactic societies, the only legitimate form of womanhood is publicly mute, located at the nexus of a set of social constraints. These sets result in a legible, legitimated woman necessarily marginalized as

a "frill," lovely and useless, despite the material advantages and physical protection granted to this hypervisible ornamentality. The legitimate form of
womanhood on Barrayar is figured as functional, within a set of severe social
constraints: biologically necessitated, yet politically invisible, or else too visible
to be effective as a measure of social transformation. For wholesale rejection
of these strata of legibility results in total social exclusion, as the subject
becomes obscured through the union of, for example, physical strength and
feminized body. The institutionalization of essential differences precludes this
woman's legibility as well, remanding her again to the margins of civil discourse. Thus, each woman's legibility, fixed through external forces, delegit-
imates any attempt to unfix or change her status; that is, she cannot alter her
frameworks without rendering herself illegible to society, stifling the changes
she attempts to make. Cordelia's surface legibility, as high Vor wife, both
implicates her in existing social strata and shields her from their full destructiveness, a duality she will deploy to enact her word during her raid on the
Imperial Residency. However, her position is unique, if not unprecedented.[8]
Three othered women provide instantiations of these illegitimate forms of
personhood: Lady Alys Vorpatril through her social leverage, which she
deploys to both subvert expectations of feminine activity and support nonaristocratic worth; Cordelia's bodyguard Droushnakovi through her indeterminate status as both soldier and servant, which renders her socially illegible at
nearly every turn, and Princess Kareen through her cryptic conformity, which
disguises her murderous agency almost to the last.

Initially lightly bound through ties of social position and familial proximity, Alys and Kareen become tightly linked to Cordelia through increasing
spirals of political maneuvers, culminating in assassination, murder, and motherhood. Alys and Kareen's stories intertwine with one another, at once an
expression of the various ways a Vor woman may hold and wield power, and
a demonstration of the ways the Vor woman's powers fail, how they must be
subverted in order to create a world in which her children may one day thrive
without (or sometimes live without) her. Whereas Druoushnakovi is so far
outside the legitimating structure she has no recognizable influence on her
status, Alys and Kareen can observe, understand, judge, and mourn, but they
cannot change the terms of that legitimation. Their power comes from the
social structures into which they have been interpellated; to dismantle those
is paradoxically to disarm themselves, delimit their narrow margins then cut
them off.

As a socially-adept and well-respected noblewoman, Alys Vorpatril's
legitimacy depends on her social legibility; she wields considerable power,
but it comes from others' understanding of her high position within estab-

lished parameters for high Vor actions. Alys's own extreme social legibility compels others' mimicry within the social sphere; her influence lies in her excessive visibility, and the performances of social maneuvers it can guarantee. Master of all the forms of courtly fashion, taste, and manner, she is an arbiter whose approval can change a small nonaristocratic wedding into an enthusiastically Vor-approved social event. But her taste and brilliance are untrammeled by naïveté; she is an expert at deploying societal stratagems in high Vor contexts in order to gain her own ends, as precise and astute as any ImpSec officer or member of the Council of Counts.[9] Cordelia almost immediately recognizes that Alys's "social enthusiasms concea[l] an acid judgment" (*Barrayar* 332).

However, the source of Alys's considerable power in Vor society rests on her remaining eminently — even aggressively — legible within its established forms of legitimation. *Cordelia's Honor* thus opens a series with considerable Shakespearian intertexts by paralleling the problematization of language and social legitimacy presented in *King Lear*.[10] Just as Regan, Goneril, and the early Gloucester ensconce themselves in an overly rigid subjectivity by making themselves legible in socially-determined prescriptions, the institutions which grant Alys her clout also underwrite it, and their destruction would result in the loss of her ability to compel. She must remain of perfect breeding, in good taste, with impeccable manners, else risk losing all of her credibility in high Vor society, the locus and basis of her existing power. Alys can promote or defend a new idea, give it entry into that privileged women's space, but cannot overturn those borders of legitimation without losing all of her own. Although Alys can and does underwrite the clean uptake of a social revolution through her calm acceptance and promotion into the societal courtesies she helped form, she cannot be its instigator, else she risks the collapse of the structures which grant her the power to compel.

In direct contrast to Alys, Droushnakovi is a social outlier so significant, she destroys or invalidates social constructs simply by existing. Droushnakovi models a feminine subjectivity so alien to Barrayaran legitimating structures that she is perceived only as a parody of subjectivity, acting and speaking nonsense. Devoted to Princess Kareen as a demure lady-in-waiting, Droushnakovi was paradoxically also trained by ImpSec's fearsome Captain Negri to act as the last physical barrier between Kareen, Gregor, and any attacker. She comes to Cordelia prepared to learn how to be part of a new generation of previously oxymoronic female soldiers and, while stymied by Cordelia's disavowal of the soldier state, continues nevertheless to confound the binaries between woman and physical prowess. Droushnakovi's tactical skills make her the focus of the social backlash against women daring to take on the agential actions of military might. Her daily relationship to modes of legitimacy and power, especially as shadowed by the cyborg Koudelka and queered by the monstrous Bothari, are formed like theirs in modes of extreme visibility and maximum transgression. However, because Droushnakovi weathers an inordinate amount of social backlash, it is difficult to read her outside of the pre-polarized dichotomies which are the condition of her service.

Droushnakovi's presence thus demonstrates the artificiality of Barrayaran femininity, and links its power to its pervasive normativity. Her collapse of gendered binaries renders her public activity and private love-life a fraught and difficult series of stutter-steps and mediated progressions. Because her body is read against and not within these terms, against the class and military hierarchies which structure her service, Droushnakovi's actions are always already illegible. She renders these conflicts open to view, yet must rely on the legitimating structures of her orders and commanders to continue to occupy her very visibly interstitial position. Her excessive transgressiveness and concomitant lack of legibility require that she still be legitimated through others; her own word remains, for now, illegible.

The Princess Kareen is the ultimate in legitimate social bodies. While Alys's actions constitute a social/discursive body made legitimate through her excessive legibility and Droushnakovi's actions are awkwardly legitimized by practical necessity while being radically disapproved of for their social illeg-ibility, Kareen is rendered legitimate and legible by her genetic purity and aristocratic bloodline, guaranteed as the wife of Crown Prince Serg. However, her actual worth is subjugated to others' recognition, becoming a position which she can neither create nor claim for herself. This legitimating factor requires and compels that others sacrifice everything to protect her procreative abilities, yet render her paradoxically both murderable (as a valuable procre-ator) and killable (since she has no intrinsic value) in one blow. Kareen per-fectly embodies the precarious placement of the legitimated woman in Barrayaran society, accepting her personal erosions of agency and subjectivity in order to protect her son. Her integration into the legitimating structures grants her a highly conditional and tenuous prominence, an importance with-out agency.

This erasure of woman's value stems from the Barrayaran elision of the female body and her function as biological and social mediator. The current Emperor, the politically astute and critically ill Ezar, has no faith in Kareen's ability to protect herself or her son after his death. Kareen is not even present at the meeting which decides Aral's Regency; her positioning within the strait-ened confines of motherhood trumps any other political identifiers. Kareen's most important function is to act as a physical medium of transmission for the genetic material between royal generations; her body warrants its validity by providing a legitimate Vorbarra son. Once she has done so, Kareen's power shifts; her position compels protection by others, but is neither caused nor guaranteed by her personhood. It is Kareen who provides Cordelia the key to understanding her position within the Vor, when she speaks for herself, out of her long experience as consort and wife, but never as visible agential person:

> "I'm having trouble understanding this ... venereal transmission of power. Do you have some claim to the Imperium in your own right, or not?"
>
> "That would be for the military to decide," she shrugged. Her voice lowered. "It is like a disease, isn't it? I'm too close, I'm touched, infected.... Gregor is my hope of survival. And my prison."
>
> "Don't you want a life of your own?"
>
> "No. I just want to live" [*Barrayar* 335–336].

Kareen's response demonstrates the severity of her implication in the forms of power she wields, all focused through her Imperial motherhood. Her refusal to take up political power provocatively frames her ambivalence *as* political acumen: as Princess, and therefore pure incarnation of Barrayaran womanhood, she must be invisible, her personhood rendered entirely through the ultimate necessity of her protection. Cloaked in the expectations of an entire planet, her power to compel is limited to protection, but encompasses it fully: her Imperial status mandates the devotion of others. But beneath her cryptic camouflage roils a complex set of desires, indicting her thorough embeddedness in Vor metrics of survival, yet indicating the prize of her dreadful silence: she vanishes. Through a determined campaign of apolitical intent, Kareen renders her Imperial legitimacy an unreadable defense, thereby maintaining a slender armored space of her own.

For these three othered women, born into Barrayaran society and deeply internalizing an agency that is of the state and thereby impotent to overturn it, any actual rebellion is instantly recognized in its legibility and met with harsh discipline. It takes Cordelia, a woman whose commitment to the inherent legitimacy of others compels her to operate outside the rigidity of the hegemonic legitimating structures, to bring about change, to speak difference into being. Cordelia's legitimating gaze, her transformative ability to understand legitimation from a project of difference, allows her to see the valid personhood of the man and the woman, and the monster, psychotic, alien, cyborg, and mutant. These bastardized bodies, rejected by the law, are rerendered or reiterated as subjects through her empathic understanding. For Droushnakovi, Alys, and Kareen, their positioning grants values and powers which cannot themselves overturn the systems which legitimate or reject them wholesale. However, as with her Shakespearian namesake, Cordelia wields both illegibility and illegitimacy to transform the structures legitimate personhood themselves, preparing the way for a world in which people are legitimated by their mere presence, their very existence.

Civil Disobedience: Refiguring the Republic

As we have seen with these three othered women, to exist completely contra to or completely within the set of legible, legitmating positions does not automatically grant the power to overturn them. Some other way must be found, some way taken which leads to what philosopher Elizabeth Grosz terms "[a] difference capable of being understood outside the dominance or regime of the One, the self-same, the imaginary play of mirrors and doubles, the structure of binary pairs in which what is different can be understood only as a variation or negation of identity" (170). This difference, unthinkable within the current regimes, must take form on Barrayar in order for Cordelia's desired futures to begin. But in order to open a way toward difference, the current "regime of the One" must cease. When Vordarian's forces seize her gestating son, still housed in his uterine replicator, Cordelia must engage Barrayar's brutal strategies for changing the rule of law, and endorse a killing to engender the new law.

Cordelia must transgress all legitimacies and leave legibility behind to save her son Miles, for whom the law has no place, before or after his replicator birth. Having attempted to speak for Miles's life and been denied his rescue by her husband Aral, Cordelia chooses to enact her required legitimation through the subterranean conduits of her alien tactics. Her civil disobedience, as she takes up the law in her own name, must come about because civility is already shattered, its center lost. It is only in the margins that she finds the potential for creating the world she absolutely requires, the one in which Miles might live because his death would be a grievable murder rather than an expedient killing. Cordelia's unlawful action begins at the radical split between herself and Aral, whose tactical military commitments prevent him from condoning Cordelia's proposed rescue mission.

In the aftermath of Piotr's vicious reinforcement of Aral's killing denial, Cordelia turns to the thoroughly illegible Droushnakovi, agreeing to a desperate deal: one mutant child for one disposed Princess, one desperate attempt to rescue both Miles and Kareen. Abandoned by the law, Cordelia extends her parole, transmuting her name's word into action as she plans her desperate dual-rescue. Without a second thought, Cordelia calls on the mad soldier

Bothari, a true illegitimate son of Barrayar, a brutal psychopath and her Barrayaran alter-id. She calls on his hands to enforce her will: "She and Bothari were twins, right enough, two personalities separately but equally crippled by an overdose of Barrayar" (*Barrayar* 497). This close parallel shadows their later psychic overlaps, even as it indicates the gulf between them. Their trauma-filled relationship has enacted Cordelia's deepest fears about Barrayar, yet Bothari holds himself ready at her word, revoking all other names except hers. When the group kidnaps the cybernetic Lieutenant Koudelka on their way out of Tanery Base, their band of monsters is complete: soldier woman, alien mother, mad bastard killer, cyborg. Working together at Cordelia's instigation, her monstrous regiment sets out to invade the capital, their every move something unimaginable till now.

This invasion of the capital precipitates a union of socially rejected things, leaving all the bastards to save one another, and thereby themselves. In the company of her fellow monsters, Cordelia charts a course toward rooms hung with green silk, where expediency and desire meet in the contested body of the legitimate heir to the Imperial throne. With her honor guard of fellow illegibles, Cordelia sets out through the disregarded sewers and back doors, striving to bring her mutant son to term, guaranteeing his life through blood and fire. From these ashes she will create a new world. Cordelia's team functions in the liminal spaces of society, setting traps in the deep crevasses, traveling underground to her contested destinations. This mode of operation, a covert attack from the least expected place, mirrors the larger investments of Cordelia's actions. In the caves and sewers, the inaccessible mountain passes, in the covert operations and sequestered rooms she carries her plans to fruition. In centralizing these abject spaces, which Julia Kristeva considers the inescapable fate of women, Cordelia wields the power of the margin to rewrite the letter of the law.

The monsters come face to face with the generator of their illegitimacy when Cordelia, Bothari, and Droushnakovi are captured by Vordarian, inside the Imperial Residence. This conflict extends beyond its principals to cradle the future of the Imperium, as its two speculations finally, spectacularly, collide:

> "What have you done with my son, Vordarian?"
> Vordarian said through his teeth, "An outworlder frill will never gain power on Barrayar by scheming to give a mutant the Imperium. That, I guarantee" [*Barrayar* 549].

In a haunting echo of her private conversation with the Vorkosigans, Cordelia asks Vordarian twice for her son, but is refused: once on the grounds of her being a "frill," and again on the grounds that he will "protect and preserve the real Barrayar" (549). In one sentence Vordarian unites all the fears of the Barrayaran patriarchy into one dismissive threat, laminating the Imperial succession to his schema of truth. His words form a powerful mantra, equating mutant, alien, and woman ("frill," with all its echoes of ornamental inconsequentiality) with the idea of widespread civic misrule. But when Cordelia directs the same question to Kareen, she answers honestly. The ritual nature of the question and answer, with Kareen's as a tiebreaking third, suggest a verbal mirror dance; these are public declarations with political effects. Cordelia understands that by showing Kareen that her son is considered killable rather than grievable, Kareen will abandon her silent, invisible paragon status and come back to life again. This process is opaque to Vordarian, clear demonstration of the incomprehensibility of both Cordelia's strategy and Kareen's response in the terms of Vordarian's "real Barrayar." That Vordarian turns aside to consult a military leader only drives home the finality of his incomprehension: he seeks command and clarity from recognizable lines of power and authority, while ignoring the mother-murderer being birthed behind him. Kareen's final action is a declaration of utter loathing, an emphatic rejection of any Barrayar Vordarian could ever imagine:

> Cordelia read the murderous undertones ringing like a bell; Vordarian, apparently, only heard the breathiness of some girlish grief. He glanced at the shoe, not grasping its message, and shook his head as if to clear it of static. "You'll bear another son someday," he promised her kindly. "Our son."
> *Wait, wait, wait,* Cordelia screamed inside.
> "Never," whispered Kareen. She stepped back beside the guard in the doorway, snatched his nerve disruptor from his open holster, aimed it point blank at Vordarian, and fired [*Barrayar* 550].

These competing futures play out within the text: where Cordelia hears a death knell, Vordarian hears only static. His casual assertion, that Kareen can act only as canal or conduit, is a threat, not a reassurance: his statement carries with it the weight of all Vordarian's speculative futures, the perpetuation of his Imperial lineage, and its metonymic example as the future of all Barrayar, a singular line devoid of difference. Brilliant but mistimed, Kareen's action falls short of her goal: one guard skews her aim, another kills her. But the speed and strength of her rejection signal both her long suppression by the current regime, and her burning desire to destroy it. Vordarian's fatal, total incomprehension of Kareen's desire is reemphasized in his pure repetition: he will exchange one son for another and declare it acceptable to her, a casual, forcible reinscription of his continued legitimacy. But Kareen's last act, performed in her own voice in full view of others, constitutes a conviction, a public demand for Vordarian's death. It is Kareen with her point-blank refusal, fueled by love and fury, who abruptly and irrevocably rejects what she once epitomized.

Cordelia's execution of Kareen's last will brings about the transformation in the symbolic figurations of the woman, the monster, the mother, and the future of Barrayar: she beheads Vordarian as established ritual, ending his functionalization of people as use values while inverting the legitimating structure, transfiguring what was once murder into killing and what was once killing into murder. But even as she commits the traditional execution which ushers in a new age, Cordelia introduces difference through her distributed agents, warping even victory as her execution of Vordarian becomes something inimical to Vordarian and his "true Barrayar," a vision he cannot relinquish. Having rejected Cordelia's offer, choosing instead a perpetual war, Vordarian shows himself truly inimical to the future of difference on Barrayar. Striving toward that other world, Cordelia has Bothari use Koudelka's swordstick, in the presence of Droushnakovi and the incubating Miles:

> "Now that Kareen is dead, how long will you keep fighting?"
> "Forever, he snarled whitely. "I will avenge her — avenge them all —"
> *Wrong answer,* Cordelia thought, with a curious light-hearted sadness.
> "Bothari." He was at her side instantly. "Pick up that sword." He did so. She set the replicator on the floor and laid her hand briefly atop his, wrapped around the hilt. "Bothari, execute this man for me, please," Her tone sounded weirdly serene in her own ears, as if she'd just asked Bothari to pass the butter. Murder didn't really require hysterics [*Barrayar* 554].

The hysterical narrative of motherhood twists and fractures as Cordelia's wandering womb leads her to the very heart of violent civil discourse, which she then changes by ending it. Cordelia's vicious satisfaction that "Kareen encompasses you at last, you bastard" (563), their doubled presences around Vordarian's severed head, marks a true complication of what feminization comes to mean on Barrayar, even as Cordelia's proxy-bloodied hands implicate her into its violent methodologies. The uterine replicator is metonymic for that paradigm shift, even as the swordstick clearly implicates Cordelia into the bloody annals of Barrayaran history.

In her Afterword, Bujold shapes this seemingly climactic moment purely in terms of ultimate sacrifice for the sake of the unborn child, calling her novel "a book about the price of becoming a parent, particularly but not exclusively a mother" (595). But if murder no longer requires hysterics, then this execution also marks an ending to the stakes of Vordarian's legitimacy. Cordelia's civil disobedience for the sake of her mutant child refigures itself as legitimate within the widened meaning of that desirable future. She walks the same arc as those previous heroes, freeing citizens from a restrictive regime, yet carries a speculative presence whose futurities widen beyond the comprehension of current Barrayaran histories. The uterine replicator represents all of these possible futures, the ones outside of Vordarian's dismissals, to which he is deaf, on which he turns his back, and which eventually kill him. The replicator, present at Cordelia's other hand throughout Vordarian's execution, forms a protective shell around her refigurations of legitimacy, civil discourse, and motherhood, in which altered versions of genealogy can take root, grow strangely, and eventually be birthed into a world in which they can strive and grow. The uterine replicator's left-handed presence is a very small metonym for these very large changes in civil discourse, which splits when Cordelia so radically amputates the single-stream futurity of Vordarian's patriarchal speculations.

(N)ovum: The Uterine Replicator

The revolution Cordelia brings seems small at first: seventeen uterine replicators carrying the bastard children of the Barrayaran military, a galactic attempt to hold Barrayar responsible for its war crimes in the abortive Escobaran invasion. The uterine replicator's unfolding narrative on Barrayar demonstrates the surprising power and seeming simplicity of a parable, a small allegorical demonstration given only for those with eyes to see. The machine wombs reveal that on Barrayar, the mother's body is as much an ideological function as a biological entity, bounded by social recognition or repudiation. Within this abstract schema, the woman is little more than a blood-and-bone uterus, and the uncanny frisson caused by the uterine replicator remains its literal externalization of her truncated personhood. This automation of women's work can only overwhelm woman's position, deleteriously affecting her worth, if she was already constructed, like the factory workers during the industrial revolution, as a form of automated work. If this machine womb is to avoid the reinstitutionalization of the pregnant body into the extant structures of legitimacy and legibility, it must be made to figure and mean differently. Yet, inside the imposed illegibility of childbirth, from which the legitimating structure that regulates futurity averts its gaze, the uterine replicator is freed to work the subtle yet crucial changes that will slowly reconfigure Barrayaran society in the wake of Cordelia's more overt revolution.

Although many Barrayarans felt that the uterine replicator's mere existence and near-infallibility[11] would make women superfluous or unnecessary,[12] this concern demonstrates that women have already been exiled from intrinsic worth into functionality. Within that function-state, she is rendered only in and through the terms of her reproductive functionality within society, and neither she nor others can conceive of any other way. By taking on that function-state, and carrying its attendant affective weight, the uterine replicator creates a space (a parenthetical disruption of the legitimating structures holding women as non-agents) in which feminine agency can come to be.[13] By taking on the abject ideological status of blank functionality, and assuming (or curving around protectively against) the weaponized position of pregnancy as pure state production, the uterine replicator can take on the previously required burdens of abasement and silence as it takes up the metabolic load and dangerous physicalities of gestation and birth. The uterine replicator takes these upon its mechanical self, freeing the woman to become some unimaginable else — a novum so pure she cannot yet be described. However, the uterine replicator can only take up; it cannot bring about the transformation in legitimating structures required to begin birthing difference. This is the task to which the uterine replicator releases its women, to become people in ways radically unimaginable from within previous paradigms of personhood and legitimation.

Significantly, the narrative repeatedly parallels the replicators' introduction and integration into Barrayaran society with Cordelia's own integration — it is as if the replicators materialize her subversive re-formation of the dominant ideology. It is Cordelia who requires the reception of the machine wombs with their contents intact, refusing to silence the mothers' rapes or destroy their genetically-validated evidence. It is Cordelia who takes the replicators in. Cordelia's aegis, her shield of protection over the uterine replicators, is one of illegibility, combining the strangeness of alien technology, the marginality of women's work, the reluctance to confront war crimes, and the mucky biological labor of reproduction. Therefore, unlike the mythological aegis, the strength of this protective cloak or shield depends on its being perceived as weakness, a cryptic strategy of camouflage adopted by predator and prey alike. Here, illegibility provides strength as the trivialization of female personhood, a central problem Cordelia works to overturn, is precisely what enables her subversive activity to pass beneath the notice of the legitimating structure. Despite their overt associations with war, no one recognizes the replicators as an infiltration which will restructure the mechanics of childbearing and therefore destabilize the hereditary legitimations upon which Barrayaran society is based. The replicators' disregarded, noncombatant status renders the devices functionally invisible to the Barrayaran military complex; only a few of the medical personnel demonstrate any professional interest in what is seen as primarily a women's matter. Therefore, the machines have seemingly nothing to do with the current contingent of politicos and policy-makers within the increasingly unsettled capital city. This functional invisibility is the replicators' way in past the vigilance and surveillance guarding the state from any sort of paradigm shift. Within their armored matrices lie the quiet beginnings of some new legitimacy, poised for the imminent disruption of its birth.

As infiltrating technology at the service of a speculative futurity, the uterine replicator can be understood as both ovum, the technology that re-births reproduction, and as novum, literary scholar Darko Suvin's word for a new logical entity which bends the entire narrative around itself. Although his stringent categorization requires that all works of science fiction center on the novum, this concept is valuable here not as a genre-establishing argument, but as an accurate name for the metonymic and causal relationships that place this reproductive technology at the center of the novel's speculations on legit-imated difference. According to Suvin, "SF is distinguished by the narrative dominance of a fictional novelty (*novum*, innovation) validated both by being continuous with a body of already existing cognitions and by being a 'mental experiment' based on cognitive logic." Besides a clear reliance on the scientific method, with its complex relations to purity, objectivity, and witness, what Suvin's definition points out is the centrality of the novum to the overall narrative arc. Despite a lack of detail on the functioning technologies of the uterine replicator, with which Suvin would certainly take issue, the duology's latter half is structured by the replicator, not only as an ideological carrier, but as a technological speculum, allowing a vision of a society in which women's bodies are not reduced to a mutely functional state of production. This initial speculation opens the way toward many more, a prelude to rewriting legitimate personhood through multitudes, myriad differences proliferating into time.

A speculum, says philosopher Donna Haraway, "can be any instrument for rendering a part accessible to observation" (*Modest_Witness* 197). In her analysis, the digital image of the fetus visualizes the terms of origin, embodiment, technoscience, and control as sites of contestation and control in the public and political realms. In *Cordelia's Honor*, the speculum moves beyond the fetus to its housing: not to the placenta or the uterus, but to the uterine replicator, which exposes and explodes the functionalization of women's bodies. The uterine replicator is a speculative, specular machine, a pathbreakingly important technological innovation which births change into the entire Imperium by revealing its delegitimation of personhood at the most intimate level. The replicator's construction and function within the series allows a kind of kinship with one of Haraway's most famous constructs: the cyborg, dangerous illegitimate that she is. With her uterus across the room and her swordstick at the ready, the cyborg figures as an appropriate experimental site for ontological war machines and ideological time bombs: in allowing machine intervention into otherwise biological processes, the technology destabilizes the "naturalness" of functionalizing women, revealing the process as an ideological construct, hardened into social strictures.

No one yet knows what Barrayar's women might become when no longer relegated to medium of transmission between legitimate heirs. In the wake of the uterine replicators dual displacements — the deconstruction of hidden ideology and the literal replacement of the female body in the reproduction cycle — Barrayaran female ontology must necessarily move into a new space. The de-dehumanization of women is not itself humanization: women must progress into the unknown, speculate their own visions of what they could become. Three decades after the events of *Cordelia's Honor*, Cordelia discusses the central importance of the replicators on Barrayar with her second son Mark:

> "The whole Vor system is founded on the women's game, underneath. The old men in government councils spend their lives arguing against or scheming to find this or that bit of off-planet military hardware. Meanwhile, the uterine replicator is creeping in past their guard, and they aren't even conscious that the debate that will fundamentally alter Barrayar's future is being carried on right now among their wives and daughters. [...] The Vor system is about to change on its blindest side, the side that looks to — or fails to look to — its foundation. Another half generation from now, it's not going to know what hit it."
>
> Mark almost swore her calm academic voice concealed a savagely vengeful satisfaction. But her expression was as detached as ever [*Mirror Dance* 296–97].

This passage forms one of the series' clearest statements on the replicators' enduring importance. This revolution from within, at the tiniest, most disregarded levels, indicates the mixed success of Cordelia's speculative project within her lifetime, yet points to an eventual, inevitably successful refiguration of all possible futures, invisible from here. Within less than two generations, the mechanical womb will gain traction planetwide, not through the lingeringly patriarchal channels of state, but through the uterine replicators' widespread acceptance into Barrayaran cultures, at the levels of daily life as well as long-term social engineering. Cordelia's version of this revolution sites itself in the cracks and gutters of extant social power structures, in the liminal space shared by both outlaws and pioneers. She brings the machine to the planet, and in doing so, makes these open options a kind of blossoming, instead of another layer of ontological control. The machine wombs are ideological war machines: the children born of these replicators will themselves birth a new Barrayar into being.

Conclusion

Readers of the series know how things work out: frail Miles grows up to change history both within and outside of the Barrayaran Imperium, often to the detriment of someone else's philosophies on his personhood and right to civic participation, and sometimes at considerable cost to his own. And, some thirty-odd years after the events surrounding Vordarian's Pretendership, Miles will move into his grandfather's old rooms at Vorkosigan House.[14] This reclamation of a place previously "jammed with military memorabilia, thick with the formidable scent of old books, old leather, and the old man" (*Memory* 422), while tied to a far more recent storyline, still serves as a quiet finale to Piotr's thundering denouncements of his heir and line.

Cordelia seeks to legitimate people like her son, whose legal and social claims to full personhood on Barrayar remain in doubt. In contravention of the adjectival form, Cordelia seeks to legitimate the non-person, those whom Barrayar would deem only killable — not murderable, since they are not persons. She does not wish to claim their legitimacy through herself, but to release it to their own innate claim; in doing so, she would transfer the category of personhood from legitimation, requiring an outside warrant, authorization, justification, or guarantee, into an inalienable innate value. What she accomplishes through her confrontations with legitimacy will alter its meaning for those whose value was alienable, rendering these questionable persons' illegibilities a test of the law's ability to grant legitimacy.

With her self-possession, her band of fellow social misfits, and her machine womb, it is Cordelia who ends Vordarian's Pretendership with her own mediated hands, hands which then guide the young Emperor's as he lights the last remembrance for Barrayar's diseased past. Cordelia and her band of monsters will demonstrate the current legitimating structure's complete inability to account for them as people. In effect, through her multiplied angles of vision, gained in the caustic intimacy of her personal experience, Cordelia legitimates the other through her comprehensive, recognizant gaze. It is her gift, and she excels at it, which Aral claims and cannot deny, even when her active legitimation results in direct contravention not only of his word, but of all words, rendering them illegible through her own legitimating word. Along the way, social genius Alys Vorpatril solidifies the redefinitions of bravery, expanding them from the military soldier to include the blood and betrayal of giving birth, while Droushnakovi moves from woman soldier to non–Vor social icon as her daughters infiltrate and disperse through rough terrain. And Kareen: the Princess, whose cryptic camouflage has hidden everything about her, finally reveals that her single desire is for self-possession, and that she will kill to have it.

Although Cordelia's position within the series is not central, her influence is pervasive: through her eyes, the transparency of Barrayar's alienating structures of legitimate personhood vanish, thereby losing their insidiously pervasive power. Cordelia will unfurl her illegitimate subjectivity through an insurrection on both public and private scales, to create a world in which her children can survive. In the midst of her reclamations she alters the parameters of legitimate personhood on her adoptive planet, disrupting its tacit univocal strictures through her creation of multiple articulate subjective stances, their speculative futures made visible through the fetus gestating in the machine womb. In doing so they open a way toward new forms of legitimacy, written in civil codes which can account for difference without denigration.

NOTES

Parts of the research for this work were completed during fellowships from the Social Sciences and Humanities Research Council of Canada. I remain deeply grateful to Albert Braz, Harvey Quamen, and Jonathan Rey Lee for their invaluable guidance during this paper's long gestation.

1. I must stress that I make little claim in this paper toward reconciling Irigaray and Butler's larger bodies of work, since there is considerable disagreement between them on the meaning and validity of sexual difference, especially in the public sphere.

2. This alteration in the method of meaning-making, from a casual dominance to a kind of generous transfiguration, is appropriate, given Deleuze's creative, transformational readings of philosophers from Spinoza to Bergson.

3. One of Miles's first cases as an Imperial officer is the prosecution of an infanticide in a rural Dendarii mountain community, as chronicled in the short story "The Mountains of Mourning." Count Vorkosigan deliberately sends his son to personally illustrate the tangible changes concerning killability and inalienable legitimate personhood, since the infant girl had been murdered for bearing a visible mutation.

4. The tense state of race relations on Barrayar is somewhat apparent throughout the Vorkosigan series, through examples including language hierarchies and references to inhabitants of the Dendarii backcountry. Specific examples include the complex case of Duv Galeni, as well as the young ensigns of Greek origin who are so badly used by General Metzov in *The Vor Game*.

5. Within this strictly bounded moment, Judith Butler's work on the murderable versus the merely killable exists in congruence with the larger project of establishing sexual difference as the first among many differences on Barrayar. However, I must stress that there is considerable disagreement between these two philosophers, who have been locked in orbit for some time, engaging with each other, failing of resolution, yet creative and productive within their strongly conflicted intellectual commitments.

6. Cordelia's use of the word in this exchange places emphasis on its connotations of barbaric savagery, which she, a citizen of supposedly more-enlightened Beta Colony, implies

is a Barrayaran relic, with no place in the modern galaxy. This reading of Beta Colony as a bastion of enlightenment also requires acceptance of its subtly invasive formations of its own citizens. Beyond Beta Colony's intense regulation of procreation, a process not without danger to the civil status of women, Cordelia's experience of Betan psychotherapy after the Escobaran invasion is particularly chilling. However, a reading of Beta Colony's complex social structures, and the implications of Cordelia's "reversion" to Barrayaran interrogation techniques in order to escape it, would occupy its own chapter. Suffice to say that this initial dichotomy between Beta and Barrayar swiftly disintegrates as Cordelia and Aral's relationship develops.

7. I find it interesting to note that throughout this confrontation Cordelia is wearing her Betan Astronomical Survey trousers with a Barrayaran flowered smock (*Barrayar* 411), a clear indication of her mixed allegiances and alien origins.

8. The enigmatic presence of Aral Vorkosigan's maternal grandmother is worth noting here: little is known, except that she was in the Betan Department of Interstellar Trade, and that she married into the Vorbarra family through Prince Xav. But her earlier advent may have provided an important correlational precedent in both familial and societal histories. The maternal inheritance of her galactic presence, and her arrival immediately after Barrayar's Time of Isolation, may have established a clear synchronicity (but not a causative one) between the Betan woman's arrival and the widespread destruction of previously-held social tenets. However, this interpolation into Vorkosigan family and political histories is nearly pure speculation.

9. Some thirty years after the events of the duology, the depths of Alys's strategic and tactical gifts are revealed during Miles Vorkosigan's campaign to have Dono Vorrutyer and Rene Vorbretten voted into the Council of Counts. Alys's pivotal letter instigates a significant amount of political action in *A Civil Campaign,* providing methods to secure valuable votes and guarantee strategic absences where needed. Her role within ImpSec, an arrangement seemingly of long standing, is also revealed toward the end of that book.

10. There are a number of possible literary antecedents for a redhead named Cordelia. However, besides L.M. Montgomery's fanciful orphan's *nom de plume* (a triumphant example of a transplant who transforms her environment into one where she can thrive) there is the youngest daughter in William Shakespeare's *King Lear.* This Cordelia holds a nuanced understanding of the ways political manipulation can grant or withhold meaning from words, as evinced in the play's opening scene, when her silent noncompliance is the only gift she can give her father, after the depredations against meaning and language undertaken by her sisters Regan and Goneril. The blurring between Cordelia and the Fool throughout the play only further strengthens their dual hold on speaking transformative uncivil truths into Lear's unwilling ears, driving him to madness and despair, yet reclaiming language as meaningful in the collapse of civil legitimations during the aftermaths of Lear's death. Literary critic Frank Kermode calls this transformation "a monstrously difficult birth" (1302), tying Cordelia's refusal to participate in current regimes of language, her transfigurations of truthfulness and civility, her generation of intrinsic worth without reference to the state, as embodied in Lear, and her ultimate part in the renewal of meaning ("Speak what we feel, not what we ought to say") at the end of the play (*Lear* V, iii, 325).

11. *Cordelia's Honor* retains an uneasy but tantalizing silence about the urgent ideological dangers of this uterine externalization, choosing to give the replicator a positive cast: not only futurity, but safety, health, and home, with implications of Betan galactic technology as somehow manifestly more egalitarian and advanced, even as the text juxtaposes its reproductive and military technologies. The central question returns to agency: who controls the mechanically-mediated processes of reproduction on Barrayar? Who owns the womb machine? On Cordelia's Barrayar, it is the woman who controls reproductive technology, and attempts to remove her reproductive control or dictate her subsequent action result

in the attempter's death. This notable circumstance seems to index the replicator's importance within the series' subversive projects.

12. Cetaganda provides an interesting, slightly terrifying alternate narrative, in which carefully-selected genetic keepers have invested all their speculative futurity in the creation and tending of the haut outcrossings. Their investment in genetic futurities include the asexual ba, sterile test-runs for new recombinants, who are *all* killable if they do not perform to adequate specifications. See both *Cetaganda* and especially *Diplomatic Immunity* for examples of ba responses to this deeply stigmatized state.

13. Admittedly, this freedom comes into being through the affective labor of the machine womb; however, the machines seem able to indifferently bear with it, pending any new messages from them.

14. See *Memory* 422–3, in which Miles's colonization of Piotr's old rooms is part of the immediate aftermath of Miles's own extensive personal refigurations. Cordelia takes the move in stride; without narrative access to her interiority, the reader has no way of knowing whether her humming has anything to do with Miles's decision to take Piotr's rooms and make them his own, or whether she's thinking of something else entirely.

Works Cited

Bujold, Lois McMaster. "Author's Afterword." In *Cordelia's Honor*. Riverdale, NY: Baen, 1996. 591–96.

_____. *Barrayar*. In *Cordelia's Honor*. Riverdale, NY: Baen, 1999. 257–590.

_____. *Memory*. Riverdale, NY: Baen, 1996.

_____. *Mirror Dance*. Riverdale, NY: Baen, 1994.

_____. *Shards of Honor*. In *Cordelia's Honor*. Riverdale, NY: Baen, 1999. 1–253.

Butler, Judith. *Precarious Life: The Powers of Mourning and Violence*. London: Verso, 2004.

Haraway, Donna J. "A Cyborg Manifesto: Science, Technology, and Socialist-Feminism in the Late Twentieth Century." *Simians, Cyborgs and Women: The Reinvention of Nature*. New York: Routledge, 1991. 149–181.

_____. *Modest_Witness@Second_Millenium.FemaleMan(c)_Meets_OncoMouse*™. New York: Routledge, 1997.

Irigaray, Luce. *An Ethics of Sexual Difference*. Trans. Carolyn Burke and Gillian C. Gill. Ithaca: Cornell University Press, 1993.

_____. *Sexes and Genealogies*. Trans. Gillian C. Gill. New York: Columbia University Press, 1993.

_____. *Thinking the Difference: For a Peaceful Revolution*. Trans. Karin Montin. London: Athlone, 1994.

Kermode, Frank. "King Lear." In *The Riverside Shakespeare*, 2d ed. New York: Houghton Mifflin, 1997. 1297–1302.

Shakespeare, William. *King Lear*. In *The Riverside Shakespeare*, 2d ed. New York: Houghton Mifflin, 1997. 1303–54.

Suvin, Darko. "On What Is and Is Not an SF Narration; With a List of 101 Victorian Books That Should Be Excluded From SF Bibliographies." 1978. *Science Fiction Studies* 14:5.1. 23 April 2012. http://www.depauw.edu/sfs/backissues/14/suvin14art.htm.

The Influence of Family and Moral Development in Bujold's Vorkosigan Series

SANDRA J. LINDOW

Nebula and Hugo winner Lois McMaster Bujold writes stories that are uniformly very good reads. Exciting and humorous, hers are books to take when you go on vacation (I have), books to read in bed when you have a very bad cold (that, too); but they are also serious studies in character development and, I believe, subtly subversive attacks on long accepted theories of moral development.

Historically the field of moral development has been male dominated. Theorists like Piaget, Erickson and Kohlberg described moral development from childhood through adulthood as a process of increasing separation, individuation, and autonomy. They saw moral decisions as existing in "a timeless world of abstract rules" (Gilligan, Prologue xii). Personal decisions, they suggested, could and should be made in the realm of universal principles divorced from their effect on any on-going human relationships. However, when female psychologists like Carol Gilligan began to study women's responses to moral dilemmas they found that women often balked at having their identity defined in isolation from others. In "Adolescent Development Reconsidered," the preface to her collaboration *Mapping the Moral Domain: A Contribution of Women's Thinking to Psychological Theory and Education* (1988), Gilligan writes,

> To see self-sufficiency as the hallmark of maturity conveys a view of adult life that is at odds with the human condition, a view that cannot sustain the kind of long-term commitments and involvements with other people that are necessary for raising and educating a child or for citizenship in a democratic society[...]. The equation of development with separation and of maturity with independence presumes a radical discontinuity of generations and encourages a view of human experience that is essentially divorced from history or time [Gilligan xii].

For the women in Gilligan's studies, the highest level of moral development was experienced through integrating the needs of self and others. The voices of self, family and society were all heard and considered whenever a

50

moral decision had to be made. In reading Bujold's Vorkosigan Series it eventually became apparent to me that the moral center of these novels often involves conflict between male-based and female-based theories of moral development. Like the archetypal hero, Bujold's viewpoint character, Miles Naismith Vorkosigan, leaves home to win glory and honor for himself, his family and his world; however, no matter how many light years he travels from his home world of Barrayar, he cannot escape the influence of his family, his history, his emotional connections, and, much to his immense chagrin, his own physical limitations. He is what Bujold calls an "anti-orphan" (Bujold, E-mail). When his schemes invariably begin to fall apart because he expects more of himself than is humanly possible, it is Miles's extended family that eventually saves him. Miles achieves leadership, not through good looks and strength, but through his uncanny ability to create emotional family. Miles attracts people willing to be totally loyal to him and his seemingly near-impossible plans. It is this persevering loyalty that gives him victory when all else points to humiliating defeat.

Like other authors as disparate as Jane Austen and Ursula K. Le Guin, Bujold consciously writes novels of character. In "Answers," an essay in her collection, *Dreamweaver's Dilemma* (1996), Bujold writes that her plotting involves putting a character into an extremely difficult situation that will test his character and require some kind of cognitive leap in order to solve the problem:

> It has to come out of his personality. What is the worst thing you can do to Character A will not be the worst thing you can do to Character B. They'll have some other set of personal horrors that will take the plot off in a different direction. So the plot becomes a kind of character scalpel, a living autopsy by which you lay them open and examine their guts and find out what they're made of. It's cold-blooded sometimes ["Answers" 215].

Thus, the action of her novels evolves from and revolves around character. Although the Vorkosigan Series books can be seen as thought experiments in moral development, it is important to recognize from the start that Bujold, though never didactic, does stack the deck in favor of the more feminist versions of that development. In a 1997 *Kaleidoscope* interview, Bujold recalls Australian academic Sylvia Kelso's description of Miles as "codedly feminine" ("Interview" 10). This descriptor originates in Robin Roberts's critical volume, *Gender and Science in Science Fiction*, and is used to describe a process where "an author [...] explores a singularly feminine dilemma using a male character as a stand-in, or cover" (16). Bujold might argue that Miles is himself and no stand-in. His personal characteristics fall somewhere on a continuum of male and female behaviors (as those of most educated persons do). In an exchange of letters with Kelso, Bujold writes that Miles's fans are divided approximately equally between men and women and adds, "My own personal view is that men and women aren't two different things, just slight variations on the one thing, a view rooted in genetics, embryology and my own experience" ("Letterspace" 388). Nevertheless, Miles is handicapped by his stature and health problems, much the way women are often handicapped by their gender. He grows up without the unconsciously easy access to the road to success that is given to men within his culture. Due to a terrorist attack before he was born, Miles, heir of a rich and politically powerful Barrayar family, was born a dwarf with brittle bone disease. Bujold goes on to say that "he's smarter than those around him, can't win a physical fight, is in a 'wrong' shaped body — has lots of medical problems — and has to beat the 'bastards' using only brains, wit and charm. The sense of being 'wrong' is deeply inculcated in females in our society" ("Interview" 10). Although he yearns to be capable of stereotypical heroics, Miles cannot be some ruggedly individualistic, space age Lone Ranger lightspeeding into town to defeat the bad guys in the black spacesuits. Time after time when he, or any other Bujold character, tries such a stunt, it is bound to end in ruin. However, Miles is not an anti-hero like Willie Loman. Even though Miles must, by authorial definition, be interdependent, in doing so he usually prevails and eventually achieves many of the masculine things he desires, without the loss of his compassion and sensitivity (Kelso 13).

Miles's early life is characterized by both considerable privilege and excruciating pain. Different, in a society horrified by mutation, where "infanticide was still practiced for defects as mild as a harelip" (*The Warrior's Apprentice* [*Warrior*] 4), Miles is nearly suffocated in his cradle by his paternal grandfather. This is only the first of many physically and emotionally painful experiences where Miles must struggle for his life. An "Inquisition's worth" of medical treatment makes him, in his own words, "a professional of pain" (*Warrior* 5). Miles could not have survived except through the heroic efforts of his family, his doctors, and his friends. When any small bump or fall can break his fragile bones, he learns that he must rely on others to be his legs. Young Miles, though brilliant, brave, and appealing, cannot be the traditional, archetypal hero. In *The Power of Myth*, an interview with Bill Moyers, mythologist Joseph Campbell describes the hero quest as one of separation, initiation and return (Campbell 123–4). Though Miles separates from his family home, and suffers to receive the boons of wisdom and reward, he never separates emotionally from the values he has learned from his parents. In Miles, Bujold creates an emotionally available hero at a crux, a morally-sensitive pivot point, who must constantly struggle between the male-dominated values of his father's feudally-based Barrayaran culture and his mother's feminist, humanistically-based Betan culture. By giving Miles genius accompanied by hyperactivity, ego-mania and extreme vulnerability, Bujold creates manifold possibilities for humor, heroism, and failure. Miles cannot succeed without suffering. Physically he pays an enormous price for anything that he gains. Yet, because he, as third in line to the throne of Barrayar, is living at the very center of his world's continuing cultural development, he is constantly thrust into situations where he must make moral choices that affect not only himself but his world as a whole. Over and over again in the series, when Miles must make a decision, it is the moral voices of his parents, Aral and Cordelia, that Miles hears.

Lord Aral Vorkosigan, Miles's father, and Cordelia Naismith, Miles's mother, first met in *Shards of Honor* as enemies in an interplanetary war and fell in love. At that time Aral's moral orientation can be described as what Gilligan calls in *In a Different Voice* a "justice perspective" (27). He is an officer, second in line to throne of Barrayar, and the representative of a militarist culture where honor is desired above all else. He has, in war, strangled one traitor with his own hands and executed another. He is a brilliant deep-thinker, a good man whose deep thinking reveals the imperfect nature of his culture's values and makes him, at first, prone to binge drinking and depression. After the grim necessities of war, Aral finds his personal code of honor broken in shards at his feet. Cordelia Naismith is a scientist and ship's captain. Brilliant, beautiful, and compassionate, she represents Gilligan's "care perspective" (*Voice* 30). When first introduced she is often confused by conflicting responsibilities, the expectations of her job, the needs of those in her care, and her own self-interest. Though she is drafted into the military service of her planet, she considers military codes of honor foolish and dangerous and sees soldiers as "hired killers" (*Warrior* 21). She consistently looks for the human, the face instead of the uniform. When Cordelia becomes a prisoner of war, she recognizes that Bothari, the soldier commanded to rape her, is haunted by personal demons, and forgives him. When the evil Admiral Vorrutyer asks if she has any last words,

> She stared at Bothari, shaken by a pity almost like love. He seemed nearly in a trance, lust without pleasure, anticipation without hope. Poor sod, she thought, what a mess they've made of you. [...] [S]he searched her heart for words not for Vorrutyer but for Bothari. Some healing words, I would not add to his madness[...].
>
> "I believe," she said slowly at last, "that the tormented are very close to God. I'm sorry, Sergeant" [*Shards of Honor* (*Shards*) 139].

Cordelia connects emotionally with Bothari and, in doing so, saves herself, for the soldier refuses to carry out the Admiral's order. Thus, she gains Bothari's lifelong, worshipful loyalty. Later, Bothari becomes Miles's manservant, protector, and bodyguard. Cordelia's acceptance of human weakness and her respect for human life so impress Aral that he begins to see her as representing not only the virtue of altruism but of honor as well. He tells her "you poured out honor like a fountain, all around you." When she responds, "I don't feel full of honor, or anything else, except maybe confusion," he replies, "Naturally not. Fountains keep nothing for themselves" (*Shards* 298). Both Cordelia and Aral can be considered to be living at the highest level of moral development for their cultures. That the two should meet and fall in love is indicative of the changing nature of both their worlds.

Because Aral has position and power in his world, their union speeds this process of change and Miles, their son, intimately experiences the conflicting ethics of care and justice. When Miles fails the physical competition for officers' candidacy in the Imperial Military Service, Aral tells him that he had some doubts about Miles's potential as an officer:

> To kill a man, it helps if you can first take away his face. A neat mental trick. Handy for a soldier. I'm not sure you have the narrowness of vision required. You can't help seeing all around. You're like your mother, you always have that clear view of the back of your own head [*Warrior* 22].

Miles, at seventeen, has already grown beyond the military justice code of his own culture. In the following thirteen years, he continues to mature in his grasp of complex moral issues. Eventually he embodies what may be the highest level of moral development when he achieves, in *Memory*, the status of Imperial Auditor (224). Acting as the "Emperor's Voice," he combines the duties of a Supreme Court Justice with those of a CIA agent.

One of the most pleasurable aspects of Bujold's work is that her characters are not static. Change, sometimes slow and subtle, sometimes sudden and obvious, occurs in all her significant characters. In *The Warrior's Apprentice*, Miles, a precocious, sex-obsessed (but woefully inexperienced) teenager, commandeers a space ship and creates a mercenary force through necessity and chutzpah. Bujold writes that "the idea of the plot is *The Sorcerer's Apprentice*: the young man who goes out and discovers he can start things bigger than he can finish" ("Answers" 217). Young Miles pushes himself to the point that, faced by his first battle combat, he passes out from a bleeding ulcer and wakes up in sickbay after the fighting is over. In the twelve books that follow Miles learns much from failing — falling on his face (sometimes literally) over and over again. Young Miles is, on the one hand, overflowing with romantic ideals and thoughts of dying heroically in the arms of the woman he loves. On the other hand, he sees himself as "an ugly twisted shrimp" and is bitterly cynical of his prospects:

Miles's eye fell on an antique mirror, clasped in a carven stand. "Capering dwarf," he growled.

He had a sudden urge to smash it with his naked fists, shattered glass and blood flying — but the sound would bring the hall guard, and packs of relatives, and demands for explanation. He jerked the mirror around to face the wall instead, and flopped onto the bed [*Warrior* 20].

By *A Civil Campaign,* Miles is still Miles but has matured considerably. He has stopped hating his own body (*Mirror Dance* 20), but he has not yet fully relinquished his tendency toward manipulation. When he badly botches a marriage proposal, his letter of apology, written to Ekaterin, the woman he loves, is indicative that he has gained wisdom and compassion through painful experience. He writes:

I tried to be the thief of you, to ambush and take prisoner what I thought I could never earn or be given. You were not a ship to be hijacked, but I couldn't think of any other plan but subterfuge and surprise. [...] I can't be sorry I asked you to marry me, because that was the one true part in all the smoke and rubble, but I'm sick as hell I asked you so badly. [...] I love you. But I lust after and covet so much more than your body. I wanted to possess the power of your eyes, the way they see form and beauty that isn't even there yet and draw it up out of nothing into the solid world. [...] I wanted your courage and your will, your caution and serenity. I wanted, I suppose, your soul, and that was too much to want [*Campaign* 213–4].

It is a love letter that would, in its naked honesty, most likely win the heart of any woman.

Another aspect of Miles's increasing maturity is that, at age 31, now fully aware of his own tendency to leap too high and fall on his face, he has begun to value, and ask for, his parents' advice. When he turns to his father for help after the botched proposal, Aral talks to him about honor and social position, saying,

Reputation is what other people know about you. Honor is what you know about yourself. [...] There is no more hollow feeling than to stand with your honor shattered at your feet while soaring public reputation wraps you with rewards. *That's* soul destroying. [...] Guard your honor. Let your reputation fall where it will. And outlive the bastards [*Campaign* 293–5].

Aral concludes by suggesting that personal honor is maintained through honesty and that this is particularly important in relationships: "Honesty is the only way with anyone, when you'll be so close as to be living inside each other's skins" (*Campaign* 297).

Throughout the novels, honesty has been a particularly hard lesson for Miles to learn. Not believing that he can achieve his goals by being himself, he becomes, in *The Warrior's Apprentice*, Miles Naismith, the little admiral of the Dendarii Mercenaries. Napoleonic in both his genius for battle strategy and in his charisma, Miles is able to win wars and save planets from destruction. But as Naismith, Miles habitually over extends, risking himself and flirting with death until, in *Mirror Dance*, he is actually killed in battle. Only medical progress and the selfless heroics and loyalty of his crew make it possible for him to be cryonically frozen, revived, and healed. Despite talented physicians, however, Miles is left with seizures that afflict him in times of stress. In *Memory* he is forced to take a medical discharge from the service. (Not for the seizures themselves but for lying about them.) He knows that Admiral Naismith is an addiction that has become too dangerous a drug for him. The awful loss of his alter ego gives him compassion for others' losses as well. By dying and losing his alter ego, Miles for the first time enters the realm of the archetypal hero. After Miles, like Christ, dies and is resurrected, his emotional relationships seem to have greater depth and seriousness. He has come face-to-face with his own mortality. Joseph Campbell writes that

> to evolve out of [a] position of psychological immaturity to the courage of self-responsibility and assurance requires a death and a resurrection. That's the basic motif of the universal hero's journey — leaving one condition and finding the source of life to bring you forth into a richer or [more] mature condition [124].

For Gilligan the highest level of moral development would transcend both the ethics of care and the ethics of justice in an integrated recognition of both. Moral theorists Mary Field Belenky, Blythe McVicker Clinchy, Nancy Rule Goldberger and Jill Mattuck Tarule call this a state of "Constructed Knowledge" and "Integrated Voices." In their book *Women's Ways of Knowing*, they write that "constructivists," their subjects with the highest level of moral development, integrated "knowledge that they felt intuitively was personally important with knowledge they had learned from others. They told of weaving together the strands of rational and emotive thought and of integrating objective and subjective knowing" (Belenky et al. 134). There is a certain amount of conflict inherent in this moral position and it necessitates living "with conflict rather than talking or acting it away." They do not "compartmentalize thought and feeling, home and work, self and other [but] try to deal with life [...] in all its complexity." They recognize that "*[a]ll knowledge is constructed and the knower is an intimate part of the known*" (137).

In *The Moral of the Story: An Introduction to Ethics and Human Nature*, Nina Rosenstand writes that in "ancient times the primary teachers of morals were the storytellers." A story is told to a particular audience at a particular time for a reason and "*the moral of the story* provides one of the most enduring ways of relating to the question of what's right and what's wrong" (15). She goes on to suggest that "the conflict between what we ought to do and what we want to do — between duty and inclination — is perhaps the most common form of a moral dilemma" (15). Inner conflicts in Bujold's novels often involve such dilemmas. Miles's sense of duty and his inclinations are often at odds. He often wastes considerable time and energy only to become more enmeshed in his problem. In *Memory* Miles becomes so depressed about his discharge from the service that he slips into a near catatonic state and his cousin Ivan must rescue him by dumping him clothed into an ice bath. Perhaps by creating an imperfect hero who must depend on others and work collectively to resolve conflicts, Bujold is quietly subverting her audience into becoming more accepting of their own interdependence.

In Bujold's more recent novels the adult Miles has, for the most part, come to terms with his physical limitations. He is able to live with the emotional ambiguity of his humiliating failures as well as his great successes. In *Komarr* Miles tries to impress the bright and beautiful Ekaterin and manages to fall headfirst into a pond (86). Despite this, he is also incredibly good at his job. He performs with brilliance and decisiveness in capturing a band of terrorists. Fully aware of his own mortality, Miles describes himself this way:

> I almost arrived at thirty in a coffin, a couple of times. An Auditorship was never an ambition of mine. [...] I wanted to be an admiral. [...] I've made a lot of grievous mistakes in my life, getting here, but ... I wouldn't trade my journey now. I'd be afraid of making myself smaller [*Komarr* 302].

In *Komarr* as well as her next novel *A Civil Campaign* and her novella "Winterfair Gifts" Bujold is effective in developing Ekaterin as a strong female protagonist who can hold her own both with Miles and in his dangerous, political intrigue fraught universe. Important here is Bujold's depiction of courtship and marriage and the committed relationship of equals who are able to work together to construct a solution to common problems. Although these stories are structured as romances, Bujold maps a love story that is believable in its interpersonal dynamics.

Miles is able to construct knowledge and solve problems through working with others. In *A Civil Campaign*, he becomes acting count, his father's voting proxy, and is embroiled in a constitutional crisis on Barrayar that could destroy the government if his attempts at coalition building prove ineffective. He expands the envelope of available solutions to his problem in constructivist ways "by making the unconscious conscious, by consulting and listening to the self, by voicing the unsaid, by listening to others and staying alert to all the currents and undercurrents of life" (Belenky et al. 141). As in "The Borders of Infinity" when Miles, naked, leads a successful mass escape from a supposedly inescapable Cetagandan prison, his political strategy depends in part on the efforts of strong women and on women's ways of knowing and solving problems. Once again he snatches victory from defeat in a way that would not have been possible had he not been willing to unite with unexpected others in unexpected ways.

In *Diplomatic Immunity* and *CryoBurn*, Miles continues to work as Imperial Auditor and intergalactic troubleshooter. In *Diplomatic Immunity*, Miles and Ekaterin are on a much delayed honeymoon and expecting their first children to be birthed from uterine replicators when Miles is called to handle a problem in Quaddiespace and Ekaterin accompanies him. As introduced in Bujold's earlier novel, *Falling Free*, Quaddies are four-armed genetically engineered humans who were developed to work in free fall, but here Bujold muses on the possibilities of bio-engineered gender and the potential for biochemical terrorism when Miles is suddenly immersed in the political intrigues of the gene-splicing haut-ladies of the Cetagandan Celestial Court and pushed once again to his limits. Structured like a murder mystery police procedural, the novel allows Miles to demonstrate effective problem-solving skills. Aware of the responsibilities of impending fatherhood, Miles earns the respect of others initially through his mature "task-oriented" approach (121), and later through his (classically Miles) intuitive "wild-assed empiricism" while saving the life of Bel Thorne, port master, hermaphrodite, and friend (211). Although Miles is able to solve a potentially dangerous political problem, he is infected with a highly lethal Cetagandan bio-weapon and nearly dies again.

In *CryoBurn,* Miles is sent to Kibou-daini, where large corporate cryo-facilities have managed to create a world obsessed with cheating death. Citizens sign contracts to be frozen at or shortly before death and then revived when science has advanced sufficiently to solve their medical problems. Although some of the facilities are morally focused, others are abusing their responsibilities. Since families pay to keep their loved ones frozen, there are corporate financial advantages in not revealing accidental damage to bodies. Furthermore, some very elderly individuals are reawakened when their contractual funding runs out only to find themselves as old and infirm as they were before. Darker than Bujold's previous novels, the novel elaborates on the morality of attempting to circumvent death, a theme also explored by Ursula K. Le Guin's novels such as *The Farthest Shore* and *The Other Wind*. Throughout the series, Bujold has allowed Miles to grow up in believable ways, not a cake walk but a moonwalk with almost as many backward steps as forward ones. In *CryoBurn*, Bujold reveals a married, responsible Miles who has a better handle on managing his disabilities. Like most mature, successful individuals, he is beginning to acknowledge his own hyperactive limits and because he now has a seizure disorder, he is learning to schedule planned seizures in safe places.

However, he continues to be physically fragile and politically at risk; when he escapes from kidnappers and is left naked and hallucinating in the Cryocombs beneath the city, he must be rescued by Jin, a street child who serendipitously holds the key to the possible corporate corruption that Miles was sent to troubleshoot.

Like the women in Gilligan's study, Miles has had to struggle to create his own identity. Bujold has suggested that, like other great men's sons, Miles's mania for achievement is based on the deeply held belief that he is worthless without it ("Interview" 19). This is another way that he is "codedly female" since, within our culture, women often see themselves as important only for what they do for others. Miles is a modern hero in that he does not fit comfortably into the world into which he was born. Perhaps in his struggle for identity he should be seen as a nontraditional Everyman. In her interview, Bujold concludes that

> one of the salient qualities of the modern age is the degree to which people no longer arrive with their identities and lives unalterably prearranged by culture, birth, gender, or class. We create ourselves, now. Some people find this very frightening. I find it exhilarating. But we have to take care to create ourselves human on the inside ["Interview" 19].

Traditionally the intergalactic space opera of the pulps was a masculine realm — big machines, big guns, big battles, big victories celebrated with big babes. Science fiction has come a long way from this not-so-humble beginning. Lois Bujold in her Vorkosigan Series returns us to these characters, scripts and locales but with light years of difference. Miles Vorkosigan is a small man with a great mind, a big heart, and a passion for big women (one, Taura, over seven feet tall!) but even more important to the considerable success of the series, is Miles's voice — witty, charming, and self-deprecating. As the viewpoint character of the tales, he first captures the interest then the hearts of his readers. Miles, constructivist that he is, "really talks." He bares his heart and soul on every page and thus creates an intimate, metafictional conversation with his readers that is cathartic. Good stories not only teach us but also uplift us. We, Bujold's readers, struggle with Miles through megalomania, humbling accident, pain, and indecision to insight and eventual success. We see it all. His adventures, though larger than life, make us feel better. Though each act of heroism is inevitably accompanied by some major embarrassment, Miles nevertheless succeeds despite it. Here is life in all its great ambiguity. On a very deep level, we are glad that friend Miles, like us, is imperfect. We identify with him, are pleased with his success, and are comforted. Imperfect is okay and that, dear readers, is the moral of the story.

WORKS CITED

Belenky, Mary Field, Blythe McVicker Clinchy, Nancy Rule Goldberger, and Jill Mattuck Tarule. *Women's Ways of Knowing: The Development of Self, Voice and Mind.* New York: Basic, 1986.

Bemis, Virginia T. "Barrayar's Ugliest Child: Miles Vorkosigan." *Kaleidoscope: International Magazine of Literature, Fine Arts and Disability* 34 (1997): 20—22.

Bujold, Lois McMaster. *Barrayar.* Bujold Riverdale, NY: Baen, 1991.

_____. *Borders of Infinity.* Riverdale, NY: Baen, 1989.

_____. *Brothers in Arms.* Riverdale, NY: Baen, 1989.

_____. *Cetaganda.* Riverdale, NY: Baen, 1996.

_____. *Civil Campaign.* Riverdale, NY: Baen, 1999.

_____. *CryoBurn.* Riverdale, NY: Baen, 2010.

_____. *Diplomatic Immunity.* Riverdale, NY: Baen, 2002.

_____. *Dreamweaver's Dilemma.* Framingham, MA: NESFA Press, 1995.

_____. E-mail correspondence, Feb. 26, 2000.

_____. "An Interview with Lois McMaster Bujold." Michael M. Levy, int.. *Kaleidoscope* 34 (Winter–Spring 1997): 6–19.

_____. *Komarr.* Riverdale, NY: Baen, 1998.

_____. *Memory.* Riverdale, NY: Baen, 1996.

_____. *Mirror Dance.* Riverdale, NY: Baen, 1994.

_____. *Shards of Honor.* Riverdale, NY: Baen, 1986.

_____. *The Warrior's Apprentice.* 1986. In *Young Miles.* Riverdale, NY: Baen, 1997. 1–372.

_____. "Winterfair Gifts." In *Irresistible Forces.* Catherine Asaro, ed. New York: Penguin, 2004. 1–71.

_____, and Sylvia Kelso. "Letterspace: In the Chinks Between Published Fiction and Published Criticism." In *Women of Other Worlds: Excursions Through Science Fiction and Feminism.* Helen Merrick & Tess Williams, eds. Melbourne: University of Western Australia Press, 1999. 385–409.

Campbell, Joseph. *The Power of Myth with Bill Moyers.* New York: Doubleday, 1988.

Gilligan, Carol. *In a Different Voice: Psychological Theory and Women's Development.* Cambridge: Harvard University Press, 1982, 1993.

_____. "Prologue: Adolescent Development Reconsidered." In *Mapping the Moral Domain: A Contribution of Women's Thinking to Psychological Theory and Education.* Carol Gilligan et al., eds. Cambridge: Harvard University Press, 1988. vii–xxxix.

Kelso, Sylvia. "Loud Achievements: Lois McMaster Bujold's Science Fiction." *The New York Review of Science Fiction,* October & November 1998, # 122, 123, Vol. II, No. 2, 3.

Le Guin, Ursula K. *The Farthest Shore.* New York: Bantam, 1975.

_____. *The Other Wind.* New York: Harcourt, 2001.

Roberts, Robin. *A New Species: Gender and Science in Science Fiction.* Urbana: University of Illinois Press, 1993.

Rosenstand, Nina. *The Moral of the Story: An Introduction to Questions of Ethics and Human Nature.* Mountain View, CA: Mayfield, 1994.

The Soldier and the Cipher

Miles, Mark, and the Naming Plots of Bujold's Vorkosiverse

JANET BRENNAN CROFT

A personal name is a nexus for many deeply important concepts and feelings about being a person and having a place in the world in relation to other people, and thus names and naming plots lie at the very core of storytelling. There is far more to a name than just what it *means*— that is, its etymological derivation. At a very basic level, a name has three essential components. First, there is the word itself— the name, along with whatever etymological or historical baggage it might carry with it. What does the name mean? Who has held it before? What hearers are likely to understand this background, and what will it mean to them? Then there is the person, entity, or thing being named, which becomes associated with that word — even somehow equivalent to it. Behind both of these stands the name-giver — the namer. This can mean either the entity that originally connected that particular name with that named person or object; or it can mean the entity that is using an already-given name to refer to that person or object. The name-giver, through giving or using a name, may assert a certain amount of power over the named, as is the case in the family plot — where "what is at stake in the [process of naming the child] is no less than an act of possession" (Ragussis 7). To complicate matters further, in many cases a person gives him or herself a name, thus asserting their own power over own their name and all it indicates; or an individual may answer to multiple names, diluting or multiplying their power. The name/power nexus is also complicated by the concepts of magic and taboo, which are ultimately based on the idea of the name being an essential and inseparable part of the named being.[1]

Michael Ragussis, in his *Acts of Naming: The Family Plot in Fiction,* shows that the deepest levels of plot can be revealed by acts that "bestow, find, reveal, or earn a name; [that] take away, hide, or prohibit a name; [or that] slander and stain or protect and serve a name" (Ragussis 3). And in the Miles Vorkosigan novels of Lois McMaster Bujold, we indeed find that these various acts drive her plots and motivate her characters. Names and naming are intricately woven into the parallel and intertwined patterns of family relationships and personal development of Miles and his clone-brother Mark. In their mirrored quests for names to call their own, for connection with and separation from their family and societal expectations, we see the central importance of the primal act of naming, and the way that the different names a character bears become shorthand for their life story (Ragussis 11).

Ragussis describes several different dualistic ways of classifying naming plots. One is the "American" versus the "Continental." In the American plot, one starts as a *tabula rasa* and earns one's name, while in the Continental plot one inherits a name; the plot may then turn on "the discovery of a noble name" (Ragussis 231) or attempts to live up to or live down the inherited name. Then there are the structural plots: seduction plots (losing a name, losing one's "good name") versus inheritance plots (finding a name, finding one's heritage) (Ragussis 233). And finally Ragussis divides plots by gender: the male plot of finding or making a name for oneself, and the female plot of losing one's name, having one's identity controlled or obscured in marriage or otherwise (233). Bujold's writing makes use of all of these structures, in combination or singly, often within the character arc of one individual.

The Vorkosiverse

The background for Bujold's Vorkosigan novels is a distant but all-human future in which planetary systems are connected by wormhole jumps; the number of wormholes within range is directly related to a system's economic and strategic importance. Shortly after the planet Barrayar was settled, its single wormhole collapsed, leaving it mired in a Time of Isolation for centuries. The surviving colonists developed a feudal government based on personal loyalties to district Counts and a planetary Emperor, and in defense against the unfriendly biology of their planet (later reinforced by the effects of nuclear attack), a ruthless intolerance for congenital defects and mutations.

Bujold has commented on her process of developing character names, saying she finds it is rather difficult to invent them:

> Names are such a pain. I work on them. I comb the telephone directory. I stare into my refrigerator at brand names and try to do permutations on them. I wander around the house mumbling, "What should I call these people?" They might be called "X" through half a scene until I come up with the right name. I'm really sorry about the Vor system, and the way I set it up, because if I want to write a story that's set on Barrayar, so many people have names that start with "Vor" that it is almost incomprehensible. I have to find ways of

limiting what we call these people so they aren't all Vorwhatever ["Answers" 207].

Yet in spite of having to work so hard to come up with names, Bujold is greatly skilled at manipulating names and name-stories. Names are vitally important as a foundation block for this system of personal loyalty: a Vor lord's oath on his name is the most binding oath he can make, and underlings who act in his name are said to speak with his breath. A terribly apt punishment for a woman who killed her grandchild is to be left with nothing *but* her name, which will die with her so no offerings can be burnt for her soul ("The Mountains of Mourning" [Mountains] 95).

In Miles's grandfather's time, a new wormhole opened and the expansionist Cetagandan Empire attacked. The Barrayarans quickly adapted and shifted their military strategy and tactics from cavalry to spaceships, and over the course of twenty bloody years defeated the invaders. Painfully aware of its dangerous place in the wormhole nexus, Barrayar then set about conquering its nearest neighbors, Komarr and Sergyar, to protect its jump routes. Miles's mother, Cordelia Naismith, is an astrocartographer from the advanced egalitarian planet of Beta who gets caught up in Barrayar's conquest of Sergyar and captured by the mission's commander, Aral Vorkosigan. She eventually joins and marries Aral on Barrayar. But when she is expecting their first child, the couple is attacked with soltoxin gas, which leaves them infertile and the treatment for which leaves their unborn son, though quickly transferred to a uterine replicator, with extensive teratogenic damage that will make him undersized and fragile until his bones are painfully replaced one by one. Aral becomes Regent for the young Emperor Gregor, and as part of a very long-term plot against Aral, a survivor of his conquest of Komarr begins raising a clone of Miles, who is later known as Mark.

But Miles should not have been Miles and Mark didn't know he could be Mark, and we shall see how these simple facts determine the patterns of their lives.

The naming system on Barrayar, at least among the nobility,[2] dictates that the oldest son shall bear the first names of his paternal and maternal grandfathers as his first and second names. The second son, similarly, bears the second names of his grandfathers. The Vor naming system is thus essentially "a way of placing the individual in a classificatory order" (Ragussis 8); the basic name plot of the ruling class of Barrayar is the Continental, the assigned name indicating a heritage and a position in society. Ragussis unpacks some of the significance of naming a child:

> [I]t is the family's system of naming that produces the immediate crisis to which fiction responds with what I will call naming plots. Precisely insofar as

the child is recognized as an individual, he or she arrives on the scene as a challenge to the family's attempt to fix the child's identity through naming. [...] [T]he family name functions to classify — and thereby nullify — the individual, while the proper name exerts the power of a magical wish that expresses the will of the family [Ragussis 6–7].

So both Miles and Mark, neatly classified, have to find a balance in their lives between the names and roles and expectations imposed on them by their society and family, and their consuming desires to freely make their own names for themselves — a tension between the American and Continental plots. Ragussis, speaking of contemporary children's fantasy, sees "the traditional *Bildungsroman* [...] refashioned as a coming of age through mastering a series of lessons in naming" (Ragussis 216), and in many ways that is what happens in this series. The brothers face a series of lessons connected to their names; given names worthy of living up to, they still face unusual complications and reverses in earning the full right to them or even deciding if they want them.

Bujold frequently, and especially in this series with its protagonists who are young adults in the early books, works with the themes of finding one's true identity and one's right work in the world, and then, with maturity, determining how much one's work should *be* one's identity — that is, what is left when the work is gone? Miles's deepest life crisis, as we shall see, comes when he loses both his work and his good name (along with his cherished alternate identity) through overreaching his abilities. Mark also goes through a similar crisis when he is no longer a chess piece in a plot, and must create a new life of his own, as something more than "not–Miles." For both, there is a deep ambivalence about using the position, wealth, and power of their mutual heritage to achieve their goals, which must be balanced against the purely pragmatic realization that refusing this heritage and society's expectations can only hurt themselves and those they are trying to help.

Miles and His Name-Story

The arc we are going to concentrate on here is that from *Barrayar* through *Memory*. Miles, up to arrival of Mark on the scene, is motivated primarily by making a name for himself — by succeeding with the hand of cards he's dealt, by showing all of Barrayar "what *only a mutie* can do" (Mountains 55), by proving that he can succeed on his own merits, crippled as he is, through sheer brilliance and perseverance. He desperately wants to surpass the achievements of his grandfather, the great hero of the Cetagandan invasion, the master of military adaptation and change, and his father, the strategic genius behind both the Komarran conquest and the retreat from Escobar, and canny survivor of political intrigue and assassination attempts at the highest level.

The first naming crisis of Miles's life occurs before he is even born. By rights, according to Barrayaran naming conventions, he should be called *Piotr Miles*; but when his grandfather learns that Cordelia and Aral refuse to abort the damaged fetus, that the child will be carried to term in a uterine replicator rather than in the womb, and that he will always be sickly and weak, he withholds his name, an act of "orphaning by unnaming" (Ragussis 12) and a variation of the "female" naming plot:

> "I don't want my name on that thing. I can deny you that, if nothing else."
> Aral's lips were pinched, nostrils flaring. [...] "Very well, sir."
> "Call him Miles Naismith Vorkosigan, then," said Cordelia[...]. "My father will not begrudge it" [*Barrayar* 189].

Piotr even attempts to kill the child himself, in the best Barrayaran tradition of culling mutations, but Miles lives. And fortunately, as Cordelia wryly notes, he tests out highly intelligent (not to mention hyperactive and egomaniacal [Lindow 28]) and eventually wins Piotr over. But as she muses at his birth — or should it be called decantation? —

> *Welcome to Barrayar, son.* Here you go: have a world of wealth and poverty, wrenching change and rooted history. [...] Have a name. Miles means "soldier," but don't let the power of suggestion overwhelm you. [...] Have a title, wealth, power, and all the hatred and envy they will draw. [...] Have a grandfather from hell. [...] [M]ake your own meaning, because the universe certainly isn't going to supply it. Always be a moving target. Live. Live. Live [*Barrayar* 377–8].[3]

Miles's next naming crisis comes when he fails to make it into Barrayar's military academy. Not trading on his name (even to biting his tongue when, according to policy, he is addressed without his Vor honorific), counting on his written test scores to counterbalance any physical deficiencies, he fails the first obstacle on the physical course and goes home in despair. Here he is talking with one of his oldest friends, Elena:

> "Did [your grandfather] ask you about changing your name [...] [t]o the usual patronymic[?]. He'd been talking about, when you — oh." She cut herself off, but Miles caught the full import of her half revelation.
> "Oh, ho — when I became an officer, was he finally planning to break down and allow me my heir's names? Sweet of him — seventeen years after the fact." He stifled a sick anger beneath an ironic grin. [...] "So he was thinking of swallowing his words, was he? Perhaps it's just as well I washed out. He might have choked" [*Warrior's Apprentice* (*Warrior*) 17].

But what is particularly wrenching is that Miles has no chance to work this out with old Count Piotr, whose death that night is announced with a great economy of words:

> Miles was awakened in a dim grey light by a servant apprehensively touching his shoulder.
> "Lord Vorkosigan? [...]" the man murmured.
> Miles peered through slitted eyes, feeling thick with sleep, as though moving under water. What hour — and why was the idiot miscalling him by his father's title? [*Warrior* 27].[4]

This dual disappointment — a denial of a rightful inheritance followed by the bitter, unwanted victory of the attainment of a title — is the impetus for what will come to define the next thirteen years of Miles's life: the head-long, reckless adventure that results in his cobbling-together of the "Dendarii Mercenaries" from "materials found ready to hand" (*Brothers in Arms* [*Brothers*] 260) and his masquerade, at first almost a fey game and soon deadly serious, as "Admiral Miles Naismith." At the end of *The Warrior's Apprentice*, when he faces death for the treason of having raised a private army, no matter how nearly-accidentally it happened, a solution is found: he is accepted into the Service Academy with the eventual goal of working in Imperial Security, or ImpSec, and his Dendarii Mercenaries, unbeknownst to themselves, become a covert arm of Barrayaran intelligence.

The act of choosing a new name like this can be a healthy act of resistance against being categorized, defined, or reduced to a single meaning by one's name (Ragussis 9–10). But "playing" Naismith becomes an "addiction" for Miles (Lindow 31), for all that he often speaks of the Admiral in the third person, as an entity separate from himself. Each time the Dendarii are called upon, he finds it more tempting to simply stay with them. To keep Naismith useful to ImpSec, his two lives must be kept tidily compartmentalized — the dashing Admiral, a man making his own name, a persona allowing him to exercise his strategic genius to its fullest, to be Miles "with no brakes. No constraints" (*The Vor Game* [*Game*] 193) (and to have a sex life), and the earnest, careful Lieutenant-slash-Lord Vorkosigan with "no love life at all" (Bartter 37) must never be connected in anyone's mind. At home, Miles must be just another young Vor lordling making his way through the military *cursus honorum* before inheriting his father's title and duties. As Naismith's lover Elli Quinn says, "Lord Vorkosigan is a dull and dutiful stick[...]. You're like half yourself [on Barrayar]. Damped down, muted somehow" (*Mirror Dance* [*Mirror*] 26).

There's a deep frustration here for Miles. Because of both his own drive to surpass his father and grandfather, and his awareness that he stands for the future of all disabled or handicapped Barrayarans, he needs to be *seen* to have achieved — he craves, even requires, recognition, both personally and as a political necessity. But working for the secret service means that he can't reveal most of his achievements, and certainly can't claim those of Admiral Naismith publicly in his own name. As he explains to his cousin Ivan in *Cetaganda*:

> I've thought about it, you know [...] What it's going to be like, ten or fifteen years from now, if I ever get out of covert ops and into a real line command. I'll have had more practical experience than any other Barrayaran soldier of my generation, and it's all going to be totally invisible to my brother officers. Classified. They'll all think I spent the last decade riding in jumpships and eating candy. How am I going to maintain authority over a bunch of over-grown backcountry goons[...]? They'll eat me alive [*Cetaganda* 300].

A physical representation of this naming dilemma is the Cetagandan Order of Merit he wins when, acting solely as Lieutenant Vorkosigan, he solves a murder and prevents a civil war on Cetaganda. A medal awarded by Barrayar's historical opponent would be too risky to display openly; as he describes it to the Cetagandan Emperor, it is "a lead weight, suitable for sinking small enemies" (*Cetaganda* 289).

In spite of the temptation to "repeatedly and voluntarily [...] revisit the 'adventure' of his alternate and opposite identity" (Bartter 31), he almost achieves some balance, albeit precarious, by the time of *Brothers in Arms*, the only adventure set on the ancient backwater of Earth. But Bujold rarely allows her characters to rest in a state of balance long. On Earth, a situation arises where both Admiral Naismith and Lieutenant Vorkosigan are known to be on the same planet at the same time, and people are starting to make some unwelcome connections. Miles has enough difficulty juggling his dual roles and keeping his stories straight — then Mark Pierre enters the picture.

Mark and His Name-Story

The two-book arc of *Brothers in Arms* and *Mirror Dance* deals with the unexpected introduction of Miles's clone-brother, Ser Galen's long plot against Aral Vorkosigan, and the effects of Mark's attempts to shut down the cloning industry of House Bharaputra on the planet Jackson's Whole.

Ser Galen was a survivor of the Barrayaran conquest of Komarr, which was practically bloodless except for a single tragic incident in which one of Aral Vorkosigan's subordinates massacred a gymnasium full of Komarrans, including Galen's sister. Though Aral summarily executed the officer on the spot, responsibility for the deed clung to his own name in many minds, and

Galen devoted his life to plotting revenge. Obtaining a sample of Miles's tissue, he commissioned a clone to be created as his exact physical duplicate; even to inflicting Miles's physical disabilities, injuries, and surgeries on what should have been the perfectly healthy, growing young boy. As Mark recalls:

> When the other clones went to the doctors for treatment they came back stronger, healthier, growing ever-faster. Every time he went, and he went often, their painful treatments seemed to make him sicklier, more stunted. The braces they put on his bones, neck, back, never seemed to help much. They had *made* him into this hunchbacked dwarfling as if molding him in a press, die-cut from a cast of his progenitor. *I could have been normal, if Miles Vorkosigan had not been crippled* [*Mirror* 46–7].

The child was brought up in the clone-crèches of Jackson's Whole, where the young clones thought "[t]hat they're all some kind of prince or princess, or rich man's heir, or military scion, and someday very soon their parents or their aunts or their ambassadors are going to come and take them away to some glamorous future..." (*Mirror* 52), not knowing that they were to be used as organ-banks or new bodies for the brains of their rich progenitors. What name he bore in the crèche is not revealed, but when he was claimed by Galen at the age of fourteen, he was called *Miles* and started on a program of training to *be* Miles. The name here is "the means by which [Galen] becomes the author of the text of [Mark-as-Miles]" (Ragussis 16). In this case, while it may look to a child brought up in this particular environment like a textbook example of the inheritance naming plot — the lost heir found and named — Galen's act of naming is a instead a limiting and defining of the child. It constrains him to his role the same way his body was "molded in a press," an explicit example of the division between "those who rule by naming and those who are ruled by being named" (Ragussis 13) — in other words, this is in reality the "female" naming plot of having one's name taken and replaced at will by another person.

Galen and his co-conspirators finally track Lieutenant Vorkosigan to Earth, but their plot is complicated by the discovery that Admiral Naismith is also Miles — as well as by the fact that Mark is beginning to guess that once he has achieved Galen's goal of replacing Miles and assassinating Aral, they have no further use for him and have lied to him about putting him on the Emperor's throne. The names and identities in the game are spinning out of their control.

The real Miles, once he discovers the clone and figures out the plot, faces a moral dilemma — he can't simply kill the young man like a clear-cut enemy, because by Betan law the six-years-younger clone would be considered his brother. And there is a definite element of brother-hunger in his makeup:

"I always knew," said Miles softly — the clone leaned closer — "why my parents never had another child. Besides the tissue damage from the soltoxin gas. But they could have had another child, with the technologies then available on Beta Colony." [...]

"The reason was me. These deformities. If a whole son had existed, there would have been horrendous social pressure put on them to disinherit me and put him in my place as heir. [...] [T]hey let me stifle my siblings before they could even be born. Lest I think, for one moment, that I wasn't good enough to please them..." [*Brothers* 201–2].

Once captured by the conspirators, Miles embarks on a program of seducing Mark towards his family — a reversal of the seduction naming plot, for in this case the seducee is to be *given* his proper name and a family rather than having them taken away or being taken away from them. Miles has an "uncanny ability to create emotional family" (Lindow 26); he attracts and retains people, builds connections, creates organizations of mutual support; again, an oddly effective form of seduction. The mirror view of this, though, is that he "has a dangerous tendency to try to turn the people around him into his annexes" ("Interview" 16), something that Mark instinctively resists. Miles doesn't really help by forcing his interpretation — by telling Mark he has no choice in the matter, that he has a name, a mother, father, brother, cousins, a position, whether he likes it or not (*Brothers* 197–8). Compare this to Miles giving a name to Nine, the genetically constructed female soldier he rescues from the basement of House Ryoval in "Labyrinth": by naming her *Taura*, he grants her uniqueness, gender, power over her future — an act of generosity rather than limitation. He redefines her as human, when she had previously been classified as a genderless monster (Haehl 232). It is an "inheritance" renaming rather than a "female" renaming, gifting her with a recognition of her place in the human race.

When the clone kills his false "father" Galen, he is in a way reborn as Mark. Like Taura's, this rebirth and re-naming is meant to be freeing, an opening up of possibilities; the name itself, *Mark* (a cipher, a symbol, an IOU) indicating a lack of definition, full of potential. But given his history Mark has difficulty accepting it this way — for him, a *Mark* is still something subject to being moved around on a game board by someone else, or worse, "Miles Mark Two" (*Brothers* 261), nothing original about him at all — a name forced on him, not welcomed as an inheritance.

Killing Galen isn't enough to free Mark from his "molding" and "casting." Three other progenitor figures must also die, or nearly so, for him to start over as himself. So in the next book, *Mirror Dance*, Mark kills his genetic sire Miles, or technically, gets him killed.

Shaking Up the Family Tree

Impersonating Miles and taking over a squad of the Dendarii Mercenaries in an attempt to rescue a group of clones from House Bharaputra's labs, Mark thoroughly botches the mission and it is on the verge of total disaster when Miles arrives with the rest of his troops to bail him out. But then Miles takes a direct hit to the chest and dies: "*I didn't think you could be hurt. Damn you, I didn't think you could be—*" Mark cries out (118). The medical team gets Miles into a cryo-chamber quickly enough, but the chamber is lost in the confusion of the retreat. Mark spends much of the rest of *Mirror Dance* frantically trying to locate him, often unwillingly forced to pretend to be Miles again in an attempt to keep up the fiction that he is still alive. Along the way he is ironically the sole witness to Count Aral's first heart attack, the one he was trained to cause as an assassin (*Mirror* 272). A third progenitor down — but fortunately Aral recovers.

Mark finds the fact of his acceptance by Aral and Cordelia unsettling in the extreme; he feels they should hate him for causing Miles's death, but here he looks "suddenly into the heart of an enemy and [sees] there love and understanding" (Tolkien II.7.347), and very importantly, instead finds an acceptance of himself as not "all we have left of Miles" but as "all we have left of *Mark*" (*Mirror* 255, emphasis in original). Eventually, Mark's search for Miles leads him into the hands of Baron Ryoval on Jackson's Whole, where he atones by first suffering the obscene tortures meant to be Ryoval's revenge on Miles (Mark's own fragile personality fracturing under the strain); then turning the tables and killing the Baron, who represents the corrupt cloning industry that both sired and tormented Mark. Fourth "father" down, Mark is finally free to begin again as himself.

Meanwhile Miles is being reborn, too. His cryo-chamber was sent to a private hospital on Jackson's Whole, where he is revived and slowly recovers physically. However, without his memory and with no identification, not knowing the secret key to the puzzle, the doctors of the Durona Group cannot help him figure out who he is — Vorkosigan, Naismith, Mark, even another unknown clone? A hall of mirrors indeed, each brother broken into pieces and desperately trying to become whole enough to save the other — and again, too many names and identities spinning out of control.

Memory deals with the aftermath — because in Bujold's writing, one simply doesn't jump off to the next adventure with no consequences. Mark, sensibly, gets help (off screen) in reintegrating the fragmented Black Gang he called up from the darkest depths of his psyche to deal with the horrific tortures Ryoval inflicted on him. He also quite simply ends any possibility he might be called upon to go by the name of Miles again by putting on a great deal of weight and staying as far from the military as possible. He will compete with Miles, as any little brother might, but never again on the same playing field, and certainly not for the prize of *being* Miles.

Miles, however, is not yet done with his latest birth. As an aftermath of his revival, he suffers periodic epileptic-like seizures, but hides them from his superiors, especially when given the chance to take the Dendarii on yet another mission. A seizure takes him in the midst of combat and he seriously injures the person he was meant to rescue; bad enough, but then he lies about it on the report he sends back to ImpSec. Seduced by the role of Admiral Naismith, unable to give it up even when he becomes a danger to those around him, he loses it all — Naismith and his military career both go down in disgrace as he is dismissed from the Service. It is necessary to his growth as a person, though; "the role [...] keeps him from completing his growth to fully individuated maturity" (Bartter 31). While writing *Memory*, Bujold said "Naismith as a personality has become so much more rewarding than Lord Vorkosigan that Miles has shifted more and more of himself into the secondary, or created, personality. [...] [N]ow he needs to reintegrate. [...] [H]e's trying to choose between two personalities: Admiral Naismith, who's got all the goodies, and Lord Vorkosigan, who won't surrender. [...] It's going to be fun working him through that one" ("SFC Interview" 40).

Work through it she does. "[N]ow that he can no longer be Naismith, who is Miles?" (Bemis 22). "Can he survive the amputation of more than half himself? [...] Once he loses his military status, he has no valid role on Barrayar" (Bartter 37). Put in charge of an investigation into corruption at the highest levels of ImpSec, the crisis comes to a resolution when his quarry offers him the chance to have it all back again — his job in ImpSec, command of the Dendarii, even a long-delayed promotion to captain in his own name. A chance to claim the name he has earned, American-plot fashion, as a reward for his own hard work. Wresting with temptation ("best two falls out of three" *Memory* 289), he finds himself thinking "*Who are you, boy? ... Who are you who asks? [...] I am who I choose to be. [...] I elect to be ... myself*" (289–90). Newly centered, appointed to the lifetime position of Imperial Auditor, he realizes finally that no one else really has power over his own identity, "to give or withhold" (345).

> He felt single and strange, not to be in pieces anymore. Not Lord Vorkosigan ascendant, not Naismith lost, but all of him, all at once, all the time. *Crowded in there?*
> *Not particularly* [*Memory* 345].

At this point, Miles and Mark have both reached a moment of equilibrium in their search for name, identity, and proper work, and instead, in the next several books, turn to another phase of maturation — finding love and suitable mates.

The Mother-Lode: Cordelia

While it may seem at first glance beyond the scope of this paper, it is not possible to truly explore the deepest layers of Miles's and Mark's name stories without examining their mother Cordelia Naismith Vorkosigan, her journey, and her influence on her sons.

As mentioned above, Cordelia was born and raised on Beta, one of the oldest and most socially advanced colonies of Earth. Naming conventions on Beta are not defined anywhere in the novels; while her mother and father have the same last name, which she also carries (*Warrior* 47), it's entirely possible, given Beta's aggressively egalitarian society, that the couple took her *mother's* name as the family name when they arranged their child-bearing contract. As Bujold points out, Cordelia comes from a culture where "people no longer arrive with their identities and lives unalterably prearranged by culture, birth, gender, or class" ("Interview" 19). Given this background, names have little power to define and limit Cordelia. To her, names and labels are fluid, change-able things, descriptors for the moment, not brands one must bear and never change for life, and thus she comes into unavoidable conflict with the far more rigid, classificatory mindset of Barrayar. Seen through the lens of her flexible, postmodern Betan sensibilities, Barrayaran name-labels are almost meaningless: Captain, Betan frill, Vor, Emperor, bisexual, mutie, rapist, butcher, damaged, disgraced, disowned, even dead, mean something else to her; a word for something one did or was or now is at a certain point in one's history, not what one unalterably *is* forever. This fluidity extends to her under-standing of her own life-path and its many phases, one which she passes on to others — for example Elena, Miles's childhood friend, who has managed to escape Barrayar's limitations in part due to Cordelia's example:

> [O]nce, reminiscing, she went into this sort of litany of all the things she'd ever been. Like astrocartographer, and explorer, and ship's captain, and POW, and wife, and mother, and politician ... the list went on and on. There was no telling, she said, what she would be next. And I thought ... I want to be like that. I want to be like her. Not just one thing, but a world of possibilities. I want to find out who *else* I can be [*Memory* 16].

With this sort of understanding, her bemusement at the importance attached to changes of her name on Barrayar — attempts to make her the sub-ject of a female naming plot — is understandable. She tries to take it seriously but still, at one level, it is a game to her. When first addressed as Lady Vorkosi-gan, she finds it "strange in her ear, ill-fitting" (*Barrayar* 3–4); her title "regent-consort" (5) and the thought of being expected to behave as fitting for a member of "House Vorkosigan" (158) are foreign to her experience. None of

Ragussis's name-plot variations would really make much sense to her; she views their working-out on Barrayar from the outside.

Yet before she even marries Aral, she sees that through this all too serious game, "Barrayar eats its children" (*Shards of Honor* 200) — and she makes it her work to try to protect them, by always keeping her attention on the person behind the name or label. It starts with her defense of the orphaned young Emperor Gregor, being hustled to safety before he can absorb what has happened to him:

> "He's [...] a little boy, Armsman. Emperor is ... a delusion you all have in your heads. Take care of the Emperor for Piotr, yes, but you take care of Gregor for me, eh?" [*Barrayar* 238].

For Miles, the conflict between his mother's approach to names and labels and Barrayar's rigid, conservative naming system is part of his psychological baggage. Without her Betan influence, he might not have had the ability to conceive of Admiral Naismith and smoothly (for the most part) switch between his roles, but without the Barrayaran obsession (as Cordelia might put it) with name, honor, house, and reputation, he would not be inevitably pulled back to his home and responsibilities there. In fact she thinks the lure of the Admiral might be too strong and tempt him away for good when he is discharged. But it is in part Cordelia's example of the integration of multiple serial roles and names, as well perhaps as her faith in the value of the process of wrestling with one's soul, that helps him in his deepest crisis to integrate the various aspects of his personality and become whole.

For her late-met other son — son-once-removed? — it is the revelation of the possibility of considering labels temporary, transitory things that helps Mark heal and accept himself as himself, as Mark-not-Miles, as not crazy, not doomed to be nothing but the killer he was trained to be, as a capable human being who simply has some temporary problems to understand and work through and a few extra people in his head to balance and manage. It is in part his exposure to Cordelia's fluidity, as much as her ability to see and accept the Mark behind all the labels and names, that helps Mark get out of his trap.

Bujold as Name-Giver

What does this all tell us about Lois McMaster Bujold as a writer and a person? By her own admission she works through long-standing personal issues in her writing, and has even called it "strip-mining my life" ("Interview" 15) — the "great man's son" syndrome evidenced by Miles in particular reflects her own relationship with her father ("SFC Interview" 37), and the quest for identity and right work certainly resonates with the way she discovered that writing was what she wanted to do ("Interview" 9, "My First Novel" 170). As a woman who changed her name at marriage and kept her married name when she divorced, one might also be tempted to deduce a heightened sensitivity to the female naming plot — the issues faced by someone whose name is dictated, bestowed, or given by someone else.[5]

In an interview while in the process of writing *Memory*, Bujold recognizes a split in her own personality — the "robot Lois" who interacts with people who don't know her books and don't know or understand the "*real*" Lois, the one who meets her readers as people who have already "internalized something" about her from her characters and themes ("SFC Interview" 40) — an echo of the damped-down Lord Vorkosigan and the exuberant Admiral Naismith, perhaps. About the recurrence of disabled characters in her fiction, Bujold has said, "I've sometimes wondered if this theme is not a personal metaphor for being born female" ("Interview" 10). Both damaged young men — Miles and Mark — can be viewed in some ways as "codedly feminine" (Kelso 9), not only through their physical disabilities, but Miles through his pattern of building family and his need for recognition and acceptance, and Mark through his lack of a sense of self-worth, difficulty with leadership roles (at least initially), and self-destructive body hatred, among many other markers. But there is also the structure of their name stories: name changes imposed by powerful older men, the seduction of Mark through the offer of a name, the self-seduction of Miles through the allure of the little Admiral, and for both, a loss and fragmenting of personality represented by juggling an overabundance of names and roles at once and an eventual collapse and reintegration.[6]

On the level of craft, the Miles–Mark split occurred because, as Bujold said,

> [T]here is too much inside my head for one character to carry. Miles can't be everything, so I've split him, and Mark carries a certain portion of the psychological baggage that is not appropriate to go into Miles's character. [...] [I]t allows me to do things with the character that I couldn't do with one character without making him completely insane ["SFC Interview" 38].

The name plots serve to keep visible on the surface of the story Bujold's exploration of the tension between one's imposed place in society and family versus one's desire to make it on one's own, and how these tensions can manifest in plot. A character just barely mentioned here so far — Emperor Gregor — might also be read as split off for the purpose of examining the desire for an independent self versus the demands of society. The young Emperor, only four years older than Miles and brought up as his playmate, is even more trapped by his name than either Miles or Mark. Of a more melancholy and private nature than either, at one point he is indeed tempted to escape, to become an ordinary person — and briefly does, simply by slipping off the balcony of his hotel room and drifting away under the name Greg Bleakman — "lighting out for the Territory," as it were (*Game* 145). Fortunately he encounters Miles and enough danger and adventure to last him a while, but his story shows the results of taking the avoidance option and simply attempting to leave behind an imposed name and position for good.

Bujold always emphasizes that this process of identity-seeking is not something done once and finished for life, though there may be long periods of stability and acceptance; there must always be a "continual process of maturation" (Bartter 39); "one keeps "growing up and growing up. [...] [I]t doesn't stop at 20" ("Starchild"). At the very end of *CryoBurn*, the most recent novel in the series, we see yet another reshuffling of names and titles that unbalances the worlds of our characters, Miles in particular, but rippling out to all his family and dependents and shaking their identities to the core — yet again announced with a terrible economy of words:

> Vorventa's steps slowed as he approached, [and he] offered Miles a very formal salute, though Miles was in no kind of uniform at all except his gray trousers and jacket.
>
> The messenger moistened his lips, and said, "Count Vorkosigan, sir?" [*Cryo-Burn* 334].

NOTES

This paper was originally presented at the Southwest-Texas Popular Culture Association Annual Conference, April 2011, and the Mythopoeic Society Annual Conference, July 2011, both in Albuquerque.

1. Much of this introductory paragraph is taken from my paper "Naming the Evil One."

2. Perhaps not among the lower born; when Miles has to invent a name for Armsman Bothari's father, he says, "Konstantine [...] same as his" (*Warrior* 34), and Bothari names his daughter Elena after her mother.

3. Interestingly, Bujold was not initially aware that "Miles" means "soldier" in Latin; Miles was named after a character in Mark Twain's *The Prince and the Pauper* ("Author's Afterword" 829).

4. Bujold explains the structure of aristocratic titles on Barrayar: "The heir of a count uses the last name: 'Lord' Vorkosigan if you were the heir of Count Vorkosigan. Everybody who is not themselves the heir of the count would be 'Lord' or 'Lady' firstname. The count's heir would be 'Lord' lastname and their wives would be 'Lady' lastname. I think by the third generation the title would be left off" ("Answers" 211).

Which does bring up the question — can a title be considered part of a name? I think it can, for the purposes of story — it can be earned, given, or taken away, and becomes part of the identity of the character.

5. Ekaterin keeps her late husband's name in *Komarr* and *A Civil Campaign*, even though she was on the verge of filing for divorce when he died and might have considered dropping

it. It had become part of her name-story — like the name of an Ent (Tolkien III.4.465), the length and phases of a woman's name can tell one part of her history.

6. Particularly useful for exploring these feminine naming issues are Ragussis's chapters on *Clarissa*, *Tess of the D'Urbervilles*, and *Lolita*.

WORKS CITED

Bartter, Martha A. "'Who am I, Really?' Myths of Maturation in Lois McMaster Bujold's Vorkosigan Series." *Journal of the Fantastic in the Arts* 10.1 (1999): 30–42.

Bemis, Virgina T. "Barrayar's Ugliest Child: Miles Vorkosigan." *Kaleidoscope* 34 (Winter–Spring 1997): 20–22.

Bujold, Lois McMaster. "Answers." In *Dreamweaver's Dilemma*. Framingham, MA: NESFA Press, 1995. 197–225.

_____. "Author's Afterword." In *Young Miles*. Riverdale, NY: Baen, 1997. 829–838.

_____. *Barrayar*. Riverdale, NY: Baen, 1991.

_____. *Brothers in Arms*. Riverdale, NY: Baen, 1989.

_____. *Cetaganda*. Riverdale, NY: Baen, 1996.

_____. *CryoBurn*. Riverdale, NY: Baen, 2010.

_____. "An Interview with Lois McMaster Bujold." Michael M. Levy, interviewer. *Kaleidoscope* 34 (Winter–Spring 1997): 6–19.

_____. "Labyrinth." In *Borders of Infinity*. Riverdale, NY: Baen, 1989. 103–211.

_____. *Memory*. Riverdale, NY: Baen, 1996.

_____. *Mirror Dance*. Riverdale, NY: Baen, 1994.

_____. "Mountains of Mourning." In *Borders of Infinity*. Riverdale, NY: Baen, 1989. 9–100.

_____. "My First Novel." In *Dreamweaver's Dilemma*. Framingham, MA: NESFA Press, 1995. 167–70.

_____. "SFC Interview: Talking with the *Real* Lois McMaster Bujold." Ken Rand, interviewer. *Science Fiction Chronicle*. October–November 1995: 7, 37–8, 40.

_____. *Shards of Honor*. Riverdale, NY: Baen, 1986.

_____. "Starchild." Terri Sutton, interviewer. *City Pages* 30 December 1998. 18 April 2011. http://www.citypages.com/1998-12-30/arts/starchild/.

_____. *The Vor Game*. Riverdale, NY: Baen, 1990.

_____. *The Warrior's Apprentice*. Riverdale, NY: Baen, 1986.

Croft, Janet Brennan. "Naming the Evil One: Onomastic Strategies in Tolkien and Rowling." *Mythlore* 28.1/2 (#107/108) (2009): 149–163.

Haehl, Annie L. "Miles Vorkosigan and the Power of Words: A Study of Lois McMaster Bujold's Unlikely Hero." *Extrapolation* 37.3 (1996): 224–33.

Kelso, Sylvia. "Loud Achievements: Lois McMaster Bujold's Science Fiction." 1999. (11 November 2002). Revised version, Dendarii.com; originally published *New York Review of Science Fiction*, October and November 1998. 14 April 2011. http://www.dendarii.com/reviews/kelso.html.

Lindow, Sandra J. "The Influence of Family and Moral Development in Lois McMaster Bujold's Vorkosigan Series." *Foundation* 30 (#83) (2001): 25–34.

Ragussis, Michael. *Acts of Naming: The Family Plot in Fiction*. Oxford: Oxford University Press, 1986.

Tolkien, J.R.R. *The Lord of the Rings*. Boston: Houghton Mifflin, 1994.

The Emperor's Shoe

Power, Home, and the Other
in the Vorkosigan Saga

ANDREW HALLAM

My study has two points of departure. The first is from Sandra J. Lindow's article (an expanded version of which is included in this volume) "The Influence of Family and Moral Development in Lois McMasters Bujold's Vorkosigan Series," in which Lindow identifies two distinct ways in which Bujold's characters react to moral dilemmas. Lindow defines the first as a "masculine" mode that insists matters of morality should be decided "in the realm of universal principles divorced from their effect on any on-going human relationships." The second is the "feminine" mode that rejects having "identity defined in isolation from others." Instead, the (female) individual achieves a high level of moral development "through integrating the needs of self and others" (Lindow 50).

My second point of departure arises from two related points in Janet Brennan Croft's essay (also included in this volume) "The Soldier and the Cipher: Miles, Mark, and the Naming Plots of Bujold's Vorkosiverse." First, Croft cogently observes that Michael Ragussis's "family" or "naming plots" as described in his book *Acts of Naming* are central elements of the Vorkosigan novels that "motivate [Bujold's] characters" (61). Second, in a move that allows for a connection with Lindow's argument, Croft also notes that "Ragussis divides plots by gender: the male plot of finding or making a name for oneself, and the female plot of losing one's name, having one's identity controlled or obscured in marriage or otherwise" (62). On Barrayar, the "male" naming plot invariably takes place within and in relation to the realm of universal (and, I would add, abstract) principles as Lindow defines them; the "female" plot takes place in obscurity, apart from and sometimes in quiet opposition to the "male" realm of universals that wants to control the female plot's outcome. My study below will concern itself with the ways in which these two kinds of naming plots generate and are generated by Barrayar's various social and political spaces.

Sigmund Freud's essay "The Uncanny" provides an opportunity to discuss further how Bujold explores this generative process in the Vorkosigan series. For in the English translation of Freud's essay, the word *uncanny* translates Freud's German *unheimlich*, the opposite of *heimlich*, "homely." *Heimlich*, Freud additionally notes, means "belonging to the house, not strange, familiar, tame, intimate, comfortable, homely, etc."; "[f]riendly, intimate, homelike; the enjoyment of quiet content, etc., arousing a sense of peaceful pleasure and security as in one within the four walls of his house"; "[o]f animals: tame, companionable to man"; a fourth, obsolete meaning denotes "belonging to the house or the family, or regarded as so belonging" (125–6). *Unheimlich*, or the uncanny, therefore signifies everything that is familiar-yet-strange. That is, the uncanny may at first seem familiar, of the home and family, when it is in fact strange or unfamiliar, denoting that which is not of the home or the family, everything *not* companionable to the human, that which causes unrest, a profound sense of unease or insecurity about things that lie outside the walls of one's house.

Since gender politics and Freud's theory of the uncanny both concern themselves with various dualities — masculine and feminine, the universal versus the specific, the public versus the private, the familiar versus the strange, safety versus danger — that are created aspects rather than givens of daily social reality, they point to the theories that biologist, historian, and feminist Donna Haraway describes in her famous essay "A Cyborg Manifesto." Gendered identity and naming schemas are cyborg entities *constructed* within, in relation to, and in support of a sense of socially embodied place (Haraway 149–81). If the "male" naming plot does indeed take place on Barrayar in relation to universal principles, it is something that unfolds in the often dangerous public and political sphere — outside of the home — where politicians and other public intellectuals formulate and debate about abstractions. Therefore a political, politicizing, and politicized process, "masculine" authority exerts pressure on the physical bodies and perceptions of men, women, and their proper place in the world. For a theorist like Haraway, such an authority wants to be a disembodied gaze; "all perspective gives way to infinitely mobile vision," Haraway writes, "which no longer seems just mythically about the god-trick of seeing everything from nowhere, but to have put the myth into ordinary practice" (189). Masculinized authority, in other words, wants to be a perceptual apparatus free of the physical limitations of the human body; it claims the transcendent realm of the spirit as its proper domain to conceal the fact of its constructed nature. As a reader of Jacques Derrida would surely add based on his essay "Before the Law," masculinized authority will want to place its viewpoint in a place of privilege with an origin outside of history — a mythic divine or semi-divine god-space — so that the moral purity of a man's authority cannot be questioned as merely human. Yet, of course, such a privilege must be questioned lest it lead to excess and injustice. Because this kind of masculinized authority is a social space that exists outside all other social spaces, it has difficulty integrating the needs of the self with the needs of the other. For its concerns are with the universal; it is not familiar with the individual self's social relations in specific, localized social spaces.

Barrayar's abstract political system has clothed itself in an at least semi-divine aura, inasmuch as it founds its claim to absolute power on ancestor worship that we will explore in the fourth section of this paper. Consequently, this aura also claims its origin is extra-historical, creating the impression that Barrayar's knowledge and power is unlimited, constrained by neither history nor the physical. Think of Negri's and then Ilyan's extremely effective, seemingly all-present, all-powerful, all-seeing intelligence network; yet it is a network built only on the intricate labors of well-trained *human* operatives who exist physically in time and space. Such political constructions allow Barrayar to hide and protect the actual limitations of its really very finite, physically and historically locatable vision. But these constructions do not represent, as both Lindow's and Haraway's studies arguably imply, an automatically lesser kind of morality or inferior naming plot, especially as such constructions appear in the Vorkosigan series. After all, because Barrayaran men are still situated bodily within the historico-cultural space of Barrayar as a *home*world, a necessary military ethic shapes the men on Barrayar at the most deeply physical level. That is, since Barrayar is a home-space set against the stranger and often perplexing dangers of galactic space that exists beyond the local wormhole junction, Barrayar's civilization must still be protected. Such an ethic turns Barrayar's men to face outward to the larger political realities beyond the home and homeworld to other worlds that threaten the needful desire for comfort and security. This ethic fulfills its protective function by convincing its members of the absolute authority of its all-pervasive, omnipotent gaze; only then can its male adherents have the confidence, fortitude, and moral certainty to fall into line on a united front against external threats. But, aside from disenfranchising and excluding women from power, that outward gaze has also prevented many of Barrayar's citizens from turning their gaze inward to scrutinize the foundations of their civilization and its potential moral failings.

The feminized naming plot on Barrayar presents the necessary contrast to and critique of this ethic. Taking place in the home, obscure and hidden from (the masculinized) view, it does not make nor can it make a pretense at infinitely mobile vision or moral purity. Its struggles are often secret, its visual capacity at once limited by the home's domestic walls and marked by the relational ties between individuals. For the feminized gaze must look inward, toward the intimate, familiar, and familial relations that belong to the human household — the domestic sphere that has historically informed so much of female identity and in which women have learned to integrate the needs of the self with the needs of the other. As Haraway would have it (183–201), women historically have been most obviously concerned with and develop from "situated knowledges"— epistemological constructs that encounter the world from the body's position in a specific socio-linguistic space, in this case that of the home. It is from this inward looking perspective that Barrayar's civilization and its ethical failings can be more closely scrutinized and criticized.[1]

The uncanny can consequently help to reveal the fact that gendered naming plots are not givens of Barrayar's culture. The division between inside and outside, public and private, political and domestic, constructs itself from and constructs the social, political, linguistic, semiotic, and technological elements of Barrayar's environment and perceptual apparatuses. Naming plots are a part and product of this process; they are constructed linguistic technologies that attach themselves to individuals as constructing, transformative narratives. Given such transformative power, I have taken pains to call naming plots not "male" and "female" but "masculinized" and "feminized" to recognize that they are arbitrarily gendered and engendering, politicized and politicizing, to suit the perceived needs of their culture. Men on Barrayar masculinize and are masculinized by the abstract universals of Barrayar's political space that was in turn constructed during the long Time of Isolation from the rest of the galaxy, however much they want to gloss over the fact of their rootedness in history; women feminize and are feminized by the relations found within the domestic sphere of the household, where neither the nature of the naming plot's transformative power nor the fact of its constructed origin can be easily ignored.

Precisely because Barrayar's heavily masculinized culture will not look inward and therefore chooses to gloss over the constructed nature of its masculinized naming plot to the point of excess, and because this excess too frequently leads to unnecessary and often horrific violence, I will argue that this masculinization of Barrayar's culture has become an ethical and social problem. Though it fulfills important defensive and political functions, and though it takes place in the public sphere where human connections would supposedly be easy to come by, the masculinized naming plot's tendency to found identity on universal principles has indeed ironically isolated its adherents from many important human connections, thus limiting many a Barrayaran's capacity for right moral action.

The Vorkosigan series presents the feminized naming plot as the solution to this problem. Concerned with the domestic sphere, with looking inward to the seemingly small and insignificant things that masculinized politics tends to ignore, the feminized naming plot serves as a critique of Barrayar's dated, masculinized traditions. Such a feminized viewpoint reveals that neither power nor morality are truly founded on universal principles. Such a viewpoint instead affirms that (moral) knowledge is indeed power produced by the act of naming, but only if that knowledge and its closely linked ethical system take the form of intimate, *situated* knowledge of individuals discovered in the relational dimensions of the home and Barrayar as a homeworld.

The Problem with Abstraction

Gendered, politicized knowledge and its connection to the uncanny occurs prominently as a significant force driving Bujold's plots after the attempted kidnapping of the four-year-old Emperor Gregor in *Barrayar*. Gregor relates to Cordelia Vorkosigan how he narrowly escaped capture by the would-be usurper Vordarian. A colonel and some soldiers loyal to Vordarian attempt to take Gregor from his mother Princess Kareen. The head of Imperial Security, Captain Negri, rushes in with his men, and the young Emperor becomes the center of a struggle between one of Vordarian's soldiers and his mother. Gregor loses his shoe when it comes off in his mother's hand. "I should have ... fastened it tighter, in the morning," the young Emperor tells Cordelia (*Barrayar* 448).

Cordelia keeps the shoe, imagining Kareen's "serene face, wrenched into screaming rage and terror as they tore the son she'd borne the Barrayaran hard way from her grip, leaving ... nothing but a shoe, of all their precarious life and illusory possessions" (*Barrayar* 449). She knows well how precious the other shoe must be to the Princess Kareen because she is herself a mother anxiously considering the fact that her son Miles gestates in a uterine replicator in one of the Barrayaran capital's military labs; like Gregor, he is also therefore vulnerable to Vordarian's malicious political designs. Though the shoe really is nothing but a tiny article of clothing — a thing that can only be possessed through illusory social convention — it acquires sudden emotional significance for Cordelia and Kareen. For these two women, the shoe is not merely a part of the technology humanity has developed to keep the body warm or even a semiotic object designed to signify universal social meanings within Barrayar's fashion codes. Situated in the more specific and emotional space of the home, the shoe becomes for Cordelia and Kareen a synecdoche — an intimate part of Gregor's technological, domestic, and familial world that serves to illustrate the whole of Gregor's precarious, illusory claim to life and the Emperor's power. When Cordelia presents Gregor's shoe to Kareen after finding her way into the occupied palace in her attempt to steal back Miles's uterine replicator, the sight of the shoe becomes a cause of struggle between Vordarian, Cordelia, and Kareen — a struggle for which these characters are equipped to differing degrees.

Kareen's and Cordelia's knowledge of the most minute aspects of domestic space and the concerns of motherhood prepare them the most for this struggle; Vordarian is the least prepared, since for him the shoe is familiar-yet-strange — an *uncanny* object. On the one hand, the shoe is a familiar object of the home's intimate comfort and safety, a familiar part of any child's or adult's life that should be inherently non-threatening and homely. To Kareen, the shoe is therefore an entirely familiar object she can recognize immediately as her son's. She stares at it "with passionate intensity" (*Barrayar* 549) because she knows it is a fixture and sign of the domestic space that had for so long constructed and maintained her identity. More importantly, its sudden presence declares to Kareen that Gregor is still alive, that a connection to that domestic space she thought she had lost along with Gregor still exists, and that a reunion with her beloved son is still possible. Similarly, Cordelia recognizes its significance because, as a mother-to-be, she shares a similar emotional and domestic perspective. On the other hand, the shoe's apparent familiarity as an ordinary object of clothing conceals an emotional significance that is strange, unfamiliar, inaccessible, and at least potentially threatening to those without the knowledge to identify it. The shoe's uncanniness arises from the fact that domestic space is an environment to which Vordarian has little access or connection, for his masculinized viewpoint does not equip him to look inward — in this case, to recognize and empathize with elements of the domestic scene, and much less to recognize and empathize with a mother's love and newly revived hope for her son. Consequently, he merely gives the shoe and Kareen a confused look. For him, the shoe remains uncanny — a familiar object with a significance that nevertheless possesses a strange and inexplicable meaning, foreign to his sense of what makes for a comfortable home and homeworld. It belongs to the concrete world of the domestic sphere which his abstract, intensely public and political, outward-looking principles cannot identify, and which cannot be integrated with the needs of another — especially if that other is more inwardly located as part of domestic space.

The moment becomes a cause of struggle for and a threat to Vordarian that leads to his death for exactly these reasons. Vordarian's Pretendership depends on isolating his Emperor from other political factions so that he can name Gregor within his conservative, masculinized political world; such is the reason behind his attempted kidnapping of Gregor. If he had been successful, he would have been able to control which side of Barrayar's political struggle Gregor could represent. At least two of Bujold's characters — Kly, one of Count Piotr's former but still loyal soldiers in the old Cetagandan war, and Aral Vorkosigan — know that Vordarian's coup will almost certainly fail without Gregor in possession (*Barrayar* 460, 467, 473). As is, Vordarian can only betroth himself to Kareen (whom he does hold prisoner) and name Aral Vorkosigan a traitor responsible for the "vile murder of the child-Emperor," a "would-be usurper," a "false Regent[,] faithless, outcast, stripped of powers and outlawed" (482–3). In other words, Vordarian must resort to writing a political narrative naming himself the stalwart defender of the legitimate Emperor and the Empire; he must label Aral Vorkosigan the true enemy of the state if he hopes to maintain control or the appearance of credibility. He cannot question the legitimacy of this narrative. For his masculinized perspective has conditioned him never to look inward, never to question his motivations, never to look into the emotional lives of others; he can only look upward and outward into the abstract space of his political narrative. To do otherwise would be to face the constructed nature of both his palace coup and his identity as Barrayar's new "Emperor."

Knowing Aral Vorkosigan to be a bisexual who once had a scandalous but doomed affair with the late and psychopathic Admiral Vorrutyer only reinforces this inclination toward abstract thought (*Barrayar* 330). From the viewpoint of Vordarian's masculinized politics, Aral is no doubt effeminate and therefore someone undeserving of the honor and power bestowed upon him by the late Emperor Ezar. As someone who thinks of himself as properly masculine, Vordarian must take that power back, never mind that he judges Aral's seeming effeminacy through the perceptual lens of Barrayar's abstract political notions that do not really apply to his actually rather manly enemy (bisexual or not). Aral's atypical masculinity challenges the usurper's narrow and overly abstract notions of manliness. But then, Vordarian's entire coup depends on the abstract. As Aral notes, "This is not, so far, a revolution, merely a palace coup. The population is inert, or rather, lying low, except for some informers. Vordarian is making his appeals to the elite conservatives, old Vor, and the military" (475). The narrative of legitimate revolution Vordarian attempts to construct and through which he hopes to transform Barrayar only exists within Barrayar's abstract political system, which signifies clearly only to the aristocratic (especially the conservative) Vor and their military underlings, who must deal with the Vor system as with daily realities. An actual revolution would have to include a majority of Barrayar's non–Vor populace.

The greater part of Barrayar prefers to stay out of it, however; the conflict Vordarian started can only seem confusing and abstract to the non–Vor, as if they were living through a war between gods who are too distant and far beyond their comprehension. Without Gregor and the support of the masses, Aral Vorkosigan therefore argues, Vordarian's dreams of having any real power must remain as tenuous, illusory, and abstract as the masculinized political system in which he lives daily. For the actual political reality will not be that he is in absolute control but that others not a part of his political designs will be able to challenge them.

Consequently, when Cordelia shows Kareen Gregor's shoe, she reveals Vordarian's lies for what they are — as an attempt to isolate Kareen, make her less "cyborg," less connected to and constructed by her familial relations and the technology of domestic objects, so that he can define her role in his failing revolution in the same way that he would like to isolate and define her son's role. "Vordarian's been controlling her access to information, surely," Cordelia muses at one point to her husband. "She may even be convinced he's winning. She's a survivor; she's survived Serg and Ezar, so far. Maybe she means to survive you and Vordarian both. Maybe the only revenge she thinks she'll ever get is to live long enough to spit on all your graves" (*Barrayar* 484). Later, when Cordelia spies Kareen sleeping in Vordarian's bed with "heavy arm flung possessively across" her, she is curled "in a tight, tiny ball in the upper corner of the bed, facing outward" (542). The shape of her body declares that she has turned inward, toward her pain; yet she wants to escape outward, away from the bed, away from Vordarian's sexually oppressive attempts to create a false domestic relation with her. Once Cordelia presents Gregor's shoe to her, she has the motivation and gains the momentum to escape. Seeing it, she is no longer isolated by Vordarian's abstract political narrative and the knowledge of events he chooses to provide for her. She finally has someone else's needs to consider, something more than survival and the possibility of some future revenge; she has a connection with and hope for her son, even hope for a life with him.

The knowledge that her son still lives transforms Kareen from a submissive, despairing, isolated, and inward looking prisoner into a woman finally seeking a world outside her palatial prison and willing to take action in the very immediate present; she tries to kill Vordarian. The attempt fails and Kareen dies instead, but in the ensuing struggle Cordelia and company manage to overcome Vordarian's soldiers; at the end of the conversation that follows, Bothari finally beheads the real usurper on Cordelia's orders. Gregor's shoe thus proves to be a danger indeed, something uncompanionable and hostile to the familiar but still abstract political system by which Vordarian lives and founds his hopes for a transformative revolution. The shoe causes the chain of events that lead to his death and his coup's failure because it reconnects Kareen to a world of intimate relations for which she felt passionately enough to risk her life.

As a synecdoche the shoe is therefore not only a part of Gregor's life that signifies the whole of his precarious, illusory life and role as Emperor. Accidentally caught in a network of power relations, the shoe is also a part of Barrayar's political machinery that signifies the whole of power's true nature in the Barrayaran Empire. If (gendered) politics and (politicized) knowledge are constructed perceptual apparatuses — cultural technologies that permit the human individual's interface with the world, as Haraway argues — then Vordarian's inability to recognize the shoe's significance likewise is a part of Barrayar's socio-political system that becomes an important key to understanding the whole of Barrayar's power relations and the way *not* to navigate moral complexity. For ultimately, Vordarian's Pretendership points to the fact that neither political power and knowledge nor the ability to resolve the ethical issues of political conflict reside in brute military force or abstract philosophical or political principles. Rather, power is situated in an intimate knowledge of transformative and always-changing relations between human beings (which is beyond Vordarian's abstractive visualizing tendencies), whether power is knowledge of the home and domestic relations, knowledge of the hearts and minds of the masses, knowledge of the masses' homely concerns and needs, or more intimate knowledge of actual strategic realities of a military coup that escape Vordarian's limited political imagination. The shoe also therefore points to Vordarian's obvious moral failings and the failure of his narcissistic brand of power to bring justice to those who need it: his politics blinds him to the needs and the pain of others, for his political agenda takes precedence over their suffering; they are, after all, only instruments in his designs, cogs to be manipulated for the convenience of his political machinery.

Cognition, Nominalism, and the Act of Naming

A return to Ragussis's naming plot is enlightening here, especially since *Acts of Naming* further illuminates both Gregor's precarious hold on power and the socio-political space into which Miles is born and with which he must struggle his entire life. Significantly, Ragussis writes,

> The child enters the naming system as the unpredictable, the unfixable, the power that threatens to resist our will or wish. The child is always potentially

deviant, the break in the chain, the hole in history, for the philosopher as well
as for the family. For this reason the family name functions to classify — and
thereby nullify — the individual, while the proper name exerts the power of a
magical wish which expresses the will of the family. [...] Both the family name
and the proper name form part of a system whose function is to determine
and fix the child's identity, to make the child serve the will of the family [7].[2]

As a child-Emperor, Gregor exists and is situated within a family whose members' identities are always determined by Barrayar's masculinized political realities. As the grandson of the Emperor Ezar, he was named Emperor-to-be
long before he could have any say in the matter. His desires could of course
pose a problem Barrayar's history and to his family's — especially his grandfather's — wishes on this matter. But as we have seen Gregor's potential desires
pose a political problem most immediately to Vordarian. His attempt to kid-
nap the child and, when that failed, to declare him murdered, were his ways
of attempting to classify, nullify, and isolate Gregor as a threat to his political
designs and place in history. Miles is born into the same social space; he is
also named by it but in his case — and because of his deformities and resulting
frailty — expected to fail to fulfill his culture's demands.[3] His grandfather's
attempt to kill him and then deny him a name is likewise an attempt to nullify
and isolate Miles, to name him as a creature without the protection of Barrayar's laws and unrecognized by Barrayar's socio-political space. We will
return to this second point later.

For now, though, we should understand that Ragussis's argument takes
its cue from the fact that the naming plot in the novelistic tradition is a
response to a shortcoming in the philosophical discourse of science. Enlightenment philosophy beginning with Locke, Ragussis writes, emphasized the
tenet of nominalistic thought that "we come to have general [universal] terms
when all things are particular" (4). Heavily influenced by the fourteenth-cen-
tury philosopher and logician William of Ockham, the science of the Enlightenment thus became a perceptual apparatus that attempted to order and
categorize all within its philosophico-scientific system of general (and abstract)
names, though first by attempting to identify a name that denotes the particular nature of each thing individually. Unfortunately, Ragussis says, Enlightenment philosophy took this project too far; it ignored the issue of proper
names because their connection to the particular over the general frustrated
science as a classificatory project (6). The novel addressed this shortcoming
with its naming plot by exploring the problems that arise from naming and
categorizing individuals.

This shortcoming of the Enlightenment's burgeoning scientific thought
comes from the fact that Enlightenment philosophers as Ragussis describes

them privileged one half of Ockham's theory of cognition over the other. It is a problem that Barrayar's less scientifically oriented culture shares. Ockham's nominalism (originally from the classical Latin *nominalis*, "of or belonging to nouns")[4] was concerned with the act of naming or "nominating" — that is, the process of designating a general name for objects. Within this process, he differentiated between intuitive and abstractive cognition (Ockham, *Philosophical Writings* [*PW*] 18–45; Boehner xxiii–xxix). Intuitive cognition is the way in which we encounter and know the world with our senses and intuit how the world's singulars (or individual objects) will interact with other objects in a space defined by contingency — that is, in a space defined by an object's contiguous proximity to other objects. We may infer that this contingent space makes for necessarily profound and intimate connections, especially if we know that *cognition*, according to the *Oxford English Dictionary*, comes from the Latin noun *cognitiō* which means "a getting to know, acquaintance, notion, knowledge, etc." We could thus understand cognition — especially intuitive cognition — as the process of *familiarizing* oneself with an object, of making it less *strange*, more a part of the *familiarity* we know within the *family*, so that it may be categorized within a system of familiar and normative cultural, scientific, or philosophical values.

Cordelia experiences this first kind of intimate cognition when, based on her own growing experience of motherhood, she muses to herself,

> *If I were Kareen* ... Was this a valid analogy? Could Cordelia reason from herself to another? Could anyone? They had likenesses, Kareen and herself, both women, near in age, mothers of endangered sons[...]. Maybe she should trust her own judgment. Maybe she knew exactly what Kareen was thinking [*Barrayar* 485].

Though she doubts her suppositions for lack of evidence, Cordelia is able to intuit the shoe's significance because as a mother-to-be she is situated similarly to Kareen: as a mother in an emotionally close proximal relation to her endangered son similar to Kareen's circumstance. She is able to understand Kareen so well in her absence only because she first can turn inward to examine her own powerfully maternal emotions. In any case, this kind of cognition is the first stage of naming, the one that begins with an intuitive — if in the beginning not entirely well founded — sense of a singular's significance within an always changing social space contiguous with Cordelia's person. Her intuition allows her to become more familiar with what Kareen might be thinking and feeling, as if Kareen was a part of Cordelia's own family or domestic environment; it permits her to develop and ultimately act on a hypothesis — the first stage of the scientific method — that proves to be true and leads to Vordarian's defeat. That same intuition also makes right moral action possible, as indicated by the fact that Cordelia's intuition leads to her campaign to rescue her own son, a mother's moral challenge to the malice of Vordarian's Pretendership.

By contrast, abstractive cognition is the intellect's ability to hold the idea of an object in the mind without the object being immediately present to the senses. In the absence of her son and his missing shoe, Kareen doubtlessly engaged in this kind of cognition by thinking of Gregor when he is absent and wondering what had become of him, even believing that he must be dead. Likewise, the shoe can abstractly represent Gregor in his absence and Cordelia can recall that her son is also in danger though he is far away. Cordelia's intuitive connection to the shoe also makes possible the abstractive reasoning about what the absent Kareen might be thinking and feeling. In this sense, abstractive cognition is an indispensable function of memory, of being human and remembering our connections to things, to one another, to the memory of home, and to other parts of the world not currently before us. Since abstractive cognition always moves toward absent things, it is an outward movement of the intellect that has become associated with the outward gaze of masculinized identity. Yet we cannot dismiss abstractive cognition based on such a premise, as I have already suggested. It is an indispensable function of language that allows the individual to summon to mind that which is elsewhere; language would be of little use without it, and the self's relation to the other would be severely limited.

The problem with abstraction in philosophical discourse and on Barrayar occurs when abstractive cognition makes possible the necessity of universal concepts when the intellect compares similar but absent objects to one another. The intellect can imagine an essential nature similar objects have in common that can be generalized, though this essential nature may really be absent, elusive, or non-existent. At this stage in abstractive cognition, universalizing is a cognitive process that can also make objects that are apparently strange in their singularity seem more familiar, closer to, and a part of the family; it makes the apparently different and foreign a part of the home. It allows us, for example, to speak of and construct a notion of home common to everyone, or to conceive of elusive concepts like love or justice that we want to assume are essential to our common nature as human beings. Indeed, it permits us to conceive of human nature, the human need for a home, and the human capacity for love and justice (or hate and injustice) as something common to the universal but elusive concept of the human being. It stitches together various different points of view into a working whole, so that people who grew to maturity in a different home may share similar ideas about morality and justice under the umbrella of a unifying cultural identity. It can even make the individual feel less isolated from others, more at home when they are distant from family — from the familiar — so that Kareen and Cordelia can feel less isolated from their sons.

Unfortunately, as we have seen, Vordarian's abstractive and universalizing tendencies have the opposite effect: they isolate him from his fellow human beings. For they construct and are constructed by a politically conservative viewpoint that limits his ability to accommodate difference, his ability to make that difference less foreign, and his ability to comprehend the actions and emotional lives of people like Kareen who do not fit into Vordarian's totalizing vision of Barrayar. Consequently, these tendencies define his concept of justice and his notions about whom or what he believes he should hate, whom or what he believes he should include within his too-abstract sense of what constitutes a homely, Barrayaran identity. In Vordarian's version of a just world, *he* is the privileged actor: *he* should be the hero; *Aral Vorkosigan* should be the villain, especially because of the effeminate perversions of his past; Kareen as an apparently submissive woman should be in the power of *his* more dominant masculinity; and Gregor's imperial name should be nullified under *his* power, the power of a political conservative who has the only right and good vision of Barrayar's future. Vordarian's abstract political principles insist on these points as uncontestable truths that describe a narrative his cognitive abstractions can find familiar and comforting; he relies on them to justify his actions and to address the moral dilemmas he perceives in the name of his perverted notion of justice and need for (a too-abstract) sense of home. That his political principles do not actually exist except as abstract space that nevertheless shape his perception of Barrayar's political narrative and predetermine the role he sees himself playing in it never occurs to him. Nor does he ever fully understand how his abstract political beliefs have failed him. He has succumbed to the "god-trick" of which Haraway writes; he therefore never looks inward to discover his willingness to be deceived by such an illusion.

His last words to Cordelia before Bothari beheads him, "What? [...] You're a Betan! You can't do —" (*Barrayar* 554), speak volumes about Vordarian's abstractive failings. His abstract conception of Betans as a people that apparently embody a certain kind of non-violent, soft, probably effeminate liberalism that cannot act — that cannot *do* — is clearly belied by the fact that Cordelia *can do*, and can do more with more passion in her heart than Vordarian can imagine. She is an individual, a *singular* person in every sense of the word, who transcends the generalized ideological system of her homeworld's culture and Vordarian's naïve assumptions about it; for in many ways Vordarian's idea of Beta Colony and its citizens does not exist except as an abstraction. In this sense, Vordarian dies not only because of the chain of events set in motion by the appearance of Gregor's shoe. He dies also because as one who always looks and sees what is outward, he can only read surfaces through the lens of his abstract political perceptions; he cannot see the emotional depth of which the shoe is a part, and he cannot recognize that Cordelia is more than she appears to be. Both have depth that he cannot see. For the shoe and Cordelia have the ability to be other than the apparent limitations her Betan background would suggest to a Barrayaran like Vordarian. Through Bothari, knowing that Vordarian's cruelty will not end until he dies, she *can* and *does* kill from a sense of right moral action based on the needs of others. One of the many things Vordarian therefore fatally fails to understand is that Cordelia's notions of love and justice — though still necessarily abstract — come from more emotionally intimate social relations than he can imagine or perceive. He cannot understand her ability to integrate the needs of the self with the needs of the other. His mind's cognitive abilities — that should be able to make her actions more familiar, more comprehensible — ironically cannot accommodate her singularity within his abstract system. Because Cordelia severs along with his head his ability to speak and define her, she in her turn defines him on a physical, political, moral, and linguistic level. Her ability to resolve moral dilemmas so decisively (like how to end Vordarian as a threat to her family and her new home by ending his life) as a result remains a puzzle to him right up to the end.

This Barrayaran penchant for excessively abstract reasoning explains Cordelia's critique of Barrayar's government that is in keeping with Ockham's philosophy. She wonders at one point how Barrayar's government could exist "with all its unwritten customs [...] And yet it seemed to work for them somehow. Pretending a government into existence" (*Barrayar* 297); later, in *The Warrior's Apprentice*, Miles therefore unsurprisingly recalls how his mother "had never come to regard the Vor system [of government and culture] as anything other than a planet-wide hallucination" (*Warrior* 28). Cordelia's critique of Barrayar and Vordarian's politics prove something that Ockham insisted on: *Quod universal non est res extra*, which translates "A universal is not a thing outside the mind" (*PW* 35). It is no less true for Barrayar's political system; it is a product — the god-trick — of the intellect and abstractive cognition, however much it may subsequently affect the physical world. All governments depend on such illusory pretenses to greater and lesser degrees; they necessarily also depend on their constituents' belief that the pretense is not an abstract illusion but an inexorable fact of life. For a government's laws, if we remember Derrida's argument in "Before the Law," will then seem to have their autonomy from history and historical processes, to be above and outside of the banality of the everyday and the merely human. Barrayar's abstractive tendencies in government practice and more broadly throughout its entire culture become a problem not because abstractive cognition is inherently bad (it is not) but because the universals that abstractive cognition can conjure into being have become more real and familiar — more perceivable, tangible, and important — to many Barrayarans than physical objects and people. Abstractive cognition on Barrayar has attempted to shed its long history and its complex connections with the material world and the human beings that generate that history. Its status as an absolute, totalizing power on Barrayar therefore serves to isolate its adherents from the more real and concrete human relations that inhabit Barrayar's social space. In this context, and as we have seen in the person of Vordarian, abstraction becomes a moral problem that makes empathy and compassion for others difficult. His political abstractions isolate him from the emotional realities of others, including those whom he would rule. The fact of his early demise reveals the actual impotency of his pure abstractions in the face of a simple shoe's emotionally situated significance as the sign of an entire world's plea for right moral action against an unjust, cold, and calculating usurper.

This tendency toward pure abstraction defines the political system into which Miles is born. Yet it began on Barrayar centuries before during the Time of Isolation, when the people of Barrayar had an intuitive cognition of mutants in the contingent physical space of their newly colonized but alien world. This cognition made the at-first strange phenomenon of mutation that occurred even inside their own homes something increasingly more famil- iar, if only so that the early Barrayarans could begin to intuit the increasingly and apparently dangerous consequences of letting a mutant live. Barrayarans therefore felt that, especially given limited resources, killing mutant infants seemed like a reasonable solution to the problem of protecting one's civiliza- tion; it was their way of excising from the home what clearly seemed to be alien, and a threat. Over time, an abstract category of mutants evolved in which mutants equaled "bad." Unfortunately, as a culture that had in its isolation and desperate fight for survival lost the scientific institutions that could have made finer distinctions, its collective intuitive practices were not so complex and subtle as to allow for the difference between those defects caused by genetic mutation and those caused by birth defects. As becomes clear in "The Mountains of Mourning," infants with the birth defect of harelip or "cat's mouth" were lumped together under the universalizing category of mutants, as creatures actually foreign to (despite actually being born within) the home and family. But once the Time of Isolation ended, the contingencies of Barrayar's situation changed; they could finally look outward beyond the bounded space of their homeworld. Because they had new connections to the wider human community they had more material resources and access to a wider range of perspectives (especially the scientific); consequently, the threat mutations posed to Barrayar's survival diminished. Barrayarans could now, at least potentially, explore new ways to understand and relate to genetic anomalies and other kinds of deformity without feeling so strongly that their sense of home and family was being threatened. They could be freer to consider ways of integrating their needs with those of the formerly dangerous other.

Nevertheless, such abstractive tendencies still saturate all levels of Barrayaran society. Small rural communities like that of Silvy Vale in "The Mountains of Mourning" still cling to the universalized concept of mutations as a familiar threat to the human community and home; nor have they stopped conflating the category of mutations with other seemingly similar phenomena. They still remain curled protectively around their fears and anxieties about what are really incidental and trivial differences because they still believe that their actions against "mutants" do actually defend the home. Their fear of mutation is so deeply imbedded that they use the diminutive "mutie lord" to speak or refer to Miles and his deformities when he comes to investigate the murder of a deformed infant with harelip. Though surely used with the naïve innocence of the ignorant, "mutie" is still a slur that diminishes the social and moral stature of those to whom it is applied.

Furthermore, while Barrayar's more educated and cosmopolitan urban culture may be on occasion somewhat more enlightened, even its upper echelons still struggle to maintain their abstract notions of mutation. General Metzov also frequently uses the term "mutie" as a pejorative in *The Vor Game*, for example (679, 681, 689); and Captain Ungari, Miles's commanding officer for a brief time, uses it in his frustration at Miles's apparent insubordination (784). The abstractive tendencies of Barrayar's culture prevent peasants and others like Metzov and Ungari from fully perceiving Miles in the singularity of his humanity and the depth of his emotional being; they prefer the more familiar universals that place the strangeness of his deformities in a comprehensible social and ideological context. Those tendencies also reinforce the idea that the outward reality of their socio-political space is absolute, immune to the critique of an inward-looking emotional space and the changing needs of Barrayar's citizens. It claims to stand alone as an unofficial and unspoken law that can judge Miles's existence independent of history, regardless of the fact that such a law is not separate from and was produced by Barrayar's historical space no longer compatible with present realities.

Ancient Rome, Doubling, and
Barrayar's Cult of the Dead

Otto Rank, a former friend and colleague of Freud's, presents an opportunity to frame this systemic problem of abstractive excess in terms of the psychological, cultural, and religious desire for the double. In his study *Der Doppelgänger* (*The Double* [D]), Rank argues that this desire is a result of narcissism (69–89), for the narcissist "cannot free himself from a certain phase of his narcissistically loved ego-development" (80); the psychology of the individual's self thus becomes obsessed with his or her image and a desperate wish to double that image outwardly, to place its narcissism above reproach in a doubled abstract space without history. The desire for the double achieves a metaphysical dimension when the human subject "does not want to admit that death is everlasting annihilation" (84); to assuage the narcissistic desire for the individual to transcend his or her mortal limitations, the idea of the soul thus assumed the form of an immaterial and immortal double of the material and mortal body. The soul could occupy a place outside of the space-time continuum free of death's critique of the body's actual mortal limits. In his later work *Beyond Psychology*, Rank argues further that religious *cults* as the central and generative element of human *culture* became the means by which to construct and perpetuate both the idea of such a supernatural possibility and the reality of a continuing civilization (62–101).

In other words, while the culture of civilization became a means to further the cult of— the desire for — the doubling of immortality, it is also therefore a means to perpetuate familiar brands of political power and an attempt to elevate that power to a place beyond the reach of criticism. For the cult of civilization could at least seem to double a political structure and its normative values in the next generation, and the next, and the next, which seems to prove that its power to propagate itself has no actual limit, that the death of the individual and the individual's comfortably familiar cultural identity is no impediment to that culture's power in space and time. Immortality could be achieved if not through an actual soul then through the duplication of one's genetic, cultural, and political identity. Such a line of reasoning helps us understand Ragussis's argument that the family or naming plot is a struggle between the rights of the family to name the individual (to make the individual a double of the family's genetic and cultural identity) and the individual's desire for a proper name (for unduplicated singularity). The family or naming plot is a struggle to maintain a communal continuity in which the notion of and hope for (an at least cultural) immortality may thrive outwardly in public space despite human mortality and the individual's inner, private desires.

Such plots are struggles to maintain a lasting, familiar, and *civilized* sense of home against both the internal and external threats that would destroy it. Consequently, this desire is another way to explain Vordarian's actions. Vordarian wants to double his conservative politics in the next generation so that he will not have to face and address the needs of the other, for the other disturbs him and would not exist in the world that he would prefer. Given Barrayar's political context, he could only achieve such a doubling by naming Gregor a double of his political will, which would have nullified the possibility of the young Emperor's independent agency. Gregor's shoe indicates without ambiguity that his narcissism does not exist in a vacuum; it is not above reproach. That Cordelia beheads him through Bothari is the final critique of that power — the response that declares Vordarian's power severely limited in its ability to double itself.

Unfortunately, problems arising from such an excessive desire to double oneself are not restricted to the more public space of Vorish political games; they also invade the private sphere of the Vorkosigan household when Evon Vorhalas attempts to assassinate Aral Vorkosigan for having ordered Evon's brother Carl executed. The attempt does not succeed because Aral and Cordelia receive in time the antidote to the lethal soltoxin gas Evon used. When captured and confronted with his crime, the young Vorhalas at first feels nothing but contempt for the man responsible for his brother's death and spits in Aral's face. He justifies his hate with much the same abstract good/evil duality that rules Vordarian's actions, for Evon has difficulty seeing the deep singularity of Aral's identity or the complex political realities that influenced his decision to execute his brother; he sees only appearances — namely the politically visible executive decision Aral made to execute his brother. A naïve double of Barrayar's abstract socio-political system, Evon understands the new Regent as the villain without depth in a more familiar feudalistic revenge narrative. Also like Vordarian, he does not want to believe that his vengeance can be criticized — for then he would have to accept his own moral lapse and the reality of his guilt.

At this point, Cordelia's and Aral Vorkosigan's problem with Barrayar's need to double itself becomes far more personal and internal to the family, and in ways that only incidentally have anything to do with the angry Evon Vorhalas. Because the soltoxin gas Evon used is a teratogen that attacks a fetus's ability to generate bone tissue, the risk to the unborn Miles is very great. He must be transferred to a uterine replicator so that Barrayar's military scientists may try an experimental biochemical therapy that would save him but would be dangerous to his mother. But this transfer has unforeseen consequences. Once Miles as a fetus has been removed from the Vorkosigan household and the private, inner space of the womb (a kind of comfortable "home" that protects the vulnerability of the unborn), he becomes vulnerable to the public space of Barrayar's abstract ideology. Not only does he become vulnerable to Vordarian's political machinations, but latent familial, cultural, and political anxieties about mutation common to Barrayar come to the fore. While Aral supports Cordelia in her decision to have Miles moved to the replicator and he accepts that his son will likely be born deformed, his father Count Piotr has considerably more difficulty on the grounds that Vorkosigans have "never been *mutants*" (*Barrayar* 393, Bujold's emphasis). When Cordelia points out that the soltoxin is teratogenic, not genetic, and that it therefore does not produce mutants (an issue that really matters not at all to her Betan values), Piotr counters with, "But people will think it's a mutant." He thus announces his perspective situated in abstract socio-political concerns that preclude a scrutiny of his moral certainty. For in one sense he is more concerned with how his deformed grandson's existence will reflect on his personal honor and the honor of his family name than with his grandson's well-being. The cognitive processes that should allow his grandson to become more familiar to him short-circuits; he becomes far less willing to become familiar and intimate with his grandson as a person, a human rather than mutant other, with legitimate needs that should be integrated with Piotr's needs and the needs of his community. Indeed, he is so unprepared for a challenge to the limits of his selfhood that he later attempts (but fails) to kill the unborn Miles while his grandson is still in the replicator.

The Count's struggle is of course with the uncanny. When Count Piotr suggests that Miles will be perceived as a mutant, he is affirming his culture's belief that Miles's deformities represent such an extreme deviation from "normal" human genetics as to be no longer actually identifiable with his human parents and grandparents. He will be something wholly other than the home or the family; he will be an alien, something (certainly not a some*one*) that will make the enjoyment of quiet content or peaceful pleasure inside the Vorkosigan home impossible for the aging Piotr; others will assume something horribly aberrant is hidden in the Vorkosigan DNA. Count Piotr imagines Miles's presence in his family tree will be so intolerable that, realizing his specious arguments have no leverage with his son or with Cordelia, he spitefully refuses to be Miles's namesake as Barrayaran tradition would normally dictate. "I don't want my name on that thing," he declares, as if Miles does not rank high enough in the hierarchy of beings to be named either a Vorkosigan or a person (*Barrayar* 419). Yet, to be fair, Piotr may not be solely concerned with the honor of his name and family; as a Count, he may also be worried that his grandson will have needs alien and antithetical to the human community's security, and worse, that Miles will not be able to serve the will of the Vorkosigan family or the needs of Barrayaran civilization. He thus also feels honor-bound to protect the integrity of Barrayar's civilization by first excluding Miles from the continuity and doubling of his genetic line and cultural identity as a Vorkosigan.

Nowhere is Piotr's concern for social and political stability more evident and identifiable (if subtle) than in the moment when Cordelia observes her husband's ecstasy at knowing he will have a boy; Aral Vorkosigan responds with, "Yes, but you haven't seen anything until you've seen an old-fashioned Barrayaran *paterfamilias* in a trance over the growth of his family tree" (*Barrayar* 283; my emphasis). In the Latin of ancient Rome, *paterfamilias* literally meant "father of the family"; it is the word the Romans used to indicate the (always male) head of the household, extended family, or clan. Such an allusion to Roman culture and family is important here because the *paterfamilias* held the *patria potestas*, the "paternal power," that decided matters of life and death for the members of this community (Severy 9–10).[5] Table IV of the Twelve Tables that founded Roman law even granted the *paterfamilias* the right to kill a deformed child (Adams) — a right that Count Piotr accepts as his. That his son takes from him the paternal power to decide the fate of his family members — to decide the matter of his grandson's survival and the contingent security and integrity of his family line — radically undermines his paternal authority and the normative social structure that supports and is supported by it. From such a point of view, denying Piotr the rights given him by Barrayar's equivalent to *patria potestas* also undercuts the Emperor's power. For (we may infer from Piotr's anxiety) that power ostensibly depends on the seemingly incontestable authority of its counts and heads of household, who may then ensure unquestioned obedience to even Barrayar's more grisly traditions to maintain Barrayar's socio-political stability. In other words, Count Piotr may understand his rights as *paterfamilias* as a synecdoche, a part that signifies the whole of the Empire's power. Take those rights away, his anxieties imply, and the Emperor's powers fail. The good that he and his Counts protect would double itself in the next generation only with great difficulty, if at all; it would be for Piotr and many others the beginning of the end of Barrayaran civilization. Yet, since Count Piotr's conception of mutation is still informed and constructed by abstract assumptions, his perception and politics are still akin to Vordarian's, though he finds himself on the opposing side of Vordarian's civil war. Piotr's anxieties are as illusory as the abstractive thought processes that produce them, however much that process may have once been founded on real fears for the human community.

This concern for the future, however, exists because Barrayar's native religion — a form of ancestor worship that resembles the ancient Roman cult of the dead — is a product of abstractive cognition that perpetuates the desire for genetic and cultural immortality. In the Roman world, as a part of his function as head of the household, the *paterfamilias* also presided over the rites for the family's ancestor worship. Because the dead could be quick to anger and would seek revenge for wrongs done to them — especially for the wrong of failing to give them their due — their spirits literally demanded shelter and food in the afterlife. To provide for such supernatural needs, the wealthy Roman family provided their dead ancestors with lavish tombs in the shape of sheltering houses and offered sacrifices of food and drink to slake the hunger and thirst that the dead would otherwise endure in the afterlife. By extending the home's protection to the afterlife and one's ancestors, the *paterfamilias* ensured the happiness of his ancestors in the afterlife; at the same time, he could avoid their wrath and incur their favor so that his household could enjoy their protection. We may infer that by making sure his family honored its ancestors the *paterfamilias* could insure in his household a greater fidelity to himself, the honor of his ancestors, and the continuing honor of his family.[6] We could add that he would also thereby hope to guarantee the cultural and genetic immortality of his family line in Roman political space, thereby ensuring that his ancestors (and himself, when he died) would continue to be honored and continue to receive sacrifices and shelter while otherwise isolated from the living in the unending immortality of the afterlife. Infanticide, though infrequently practiced in later Roman centuries, would have been understood as the means to continue this tradition of immortality; killing the weak and deformed would have been a means to guarantee that the Roman family and culture had the strength to continue from generation to generation, to continue to honor and make sacrifices for the family's ancestors, and therefore to guarantee Rome's future despite the mortality of the family's individual members.

In a comparable manner, Barrayar's strikingly similar ancestor worship — most prominently represented by Miles's occasional sacrifices of burnt offerings to the dead — attempts to exert this kind of control over its practitioners. For example, in "The Mountains of Mourning" at his grandfather's grave Miles burns the cloth insignia of his cadet's rank, a copy of his newly minted officer's commission, and a copy of his transcript from Barrayar's military academy (complete with commendations and demerits) at which he had just graduated (383). Clearly, no offering here has anything to do with satisfying the literal hunger and thirst of spirits, as in Roman ancestor worship; nor do we find any reason to believe the Vorkosigans' ancestors protect and shelter their descendants. Instead, Miles at first glance seems to offer his grandfather's spirit emotional and psychological comforts, since even in the afterlife his grand-father presumably suffers anxieties about his grandson's disconcerting strange-ness and his doubtful ability to continue and honor the impressive potency of his family name in military service to the Emperor. But the reality is more complicated. Miles's outburst at his grandfather's grave, "Well, old man [...] ARE YOU SATISFIED YET?" (383), emphasizes the conflict between Piotr's hopes and expectations that have survived his death and Miles's desire at once to integrate the desires of his grandfather by fulfilling their culture's expectations and to achieve an independent selfhood free of the burden his ancestors' legacy.[7] His grandfather, after all, expected fidelity to his personal, familial, and ancestral honor, as Piotr's father and grandfather no doubt expected of him. Miles desires, almost paradoxically, both to give his proper name a place of honor within his family's history — a means to please his grandfather's imagined spirit — and to establish that proper name separate from the Vorkosi-gans' ancestral legacy and a generational imperative to double the vitality of the Vorkosigan line. To do either would validate his personhood in regard to his familial relations and the culture that has tried to deny it to him; to do both would secure it beyond reproach.

The point of the scene, though, is only partially that Miles feels the inex-orable pressure of Barrayar's history demanding that he honor his family name as a loyal and adept servant to the Emperor, like his father and grandfather before him. The more subtle point is that Miles can only feel the pressure of history as a product of abstractive cognition that seems to reach out from the supernatural outside of history. Neither his grandfather's ghost nor the spirits of his ancestors ever manifest themselves in the physical world to excoriate Miles for his failings or praise him for his successes; the Vorkosigan series remains science fiction, not fantasy, so they truly remain as silent as the grave. Only Miles's ability to produce the idea of his grandfather and his other ances-tors in their absence gives them a kind of afterlife in the intellect's abstractive tendencies. When he shouts, "ARE YOU SATISFIED YET?" he questions only the apparition of an abstraction, the memory of a person who is not there.

Instead of invalidating religion, this moment points to the indispensable role the cult of the dead plays in maintaining Barrayar's civilized culture and honoring the sacrifices its ancestors have made to preserve human life and civilization. It removes the history of Barrayar's ancestors from the concrete, physical world to place it in the abstract space of the afterlife, where it would exist outside space-time. Through religion, Barrayar's history thus attempts to escape critique by isolating itself from any spatio-temporally located per-spective. It is a part of Barrayar's god-trick, the means by which Barrayar seeks to transform its history into an incontestable mythic system. But in trying to do so, Barrayar motivates its citizens. The spirits of Barrayar's ancestors may not actually protect Barrayar as the ancient Romans believed their ancestors protected them; but the memory of Barrayar's now dead and absent ancestors, kept alive and vibrant by abstractive cognition and religious ritual, certainly inspires their descendants to do so. Living Barrayarans will strive to make themselves doubles of their ancestors to honor those sacrifices, and possibly to sacrifice their own lives, thereby continuing and preserving their civilization as more than simply an illusion or elusive wish; yet, delusive as such a desire may prove to be, it will nevertheless continue as real social space doubled in the next generation, seeming to prove that the non-space of the ancestor's abstract afterlife continues to have great potency. Miles and his fellow Barrayarans will experience this non-space as situated knowledge, a seemingly intimate and personal (but probably delusional) knowledge of their ancestors that seems to make Barrayar a comfortable home still inhabited by the beloved dead. Miles's question at his grandfather's grave is directed at just such an abstraction; Barrayar's religion as a product and partial cause of abstractive cognition is his impetus for externalizing, giving the semblance of reality to, and facing the memory of his ancestors so that he can remember to honor them in his every action. Miles can thereby be a part of protecting his home-world even as he wants to be free of the heavy burden of its expectations.

Conclusion

Yet ending here, with the conflict between Miles and his deceased grandfather, leads to no final conclusion — not to the Vorkosigan series and not to any discussion of Bujold's masterful storytelling. At best, a conclusion is an opportunity to think on a moral to the story — to consider how we might situate such literary texts in the socio-political space that their readers occupy and the moral dilemmas that such readers inevitably face.

Darko Suvin's theory of estrangement in the reading of science fiction points the way to the realization of such an opportunity, inconclusive though it finally is. The effect of estrangement, Suvin writes, "is one of confronting a set normative system [...] with a point of view or look implying a new set of norms" (6). Many of Bujold's characters experience just this effect. Whether we read of Cordelia confronting Vordarian with Gregor's shoe, of Piotr with the idea of a deformed grandson, or of Miles crying his questioning protest at Piotr's gravesite, we witness Bujold's characters enduring the disorientation of estrangement. Confronted with the uncanny, the familiar-yet-strange, the likes of Vordarian and Piotr — who act as doubles of their culture's normative system — suddenly feel *estranged* from their sense of home; they know them-selves to be living in a strange universe hostile to and threatening their much-loved security.

Lest we as readers think that we are more secure in our reality than Bujold's characters are in theirs, Suvin also implies that reading a series like that of the *Vorkosigan* novels becomes an exercise in estrangement; by situating otherwise familiar gender and identity politics within Barrayar's foreign (for the reader) social space, Bujold challenges our abstractive excesses. For science fiction is "a reflecting *of* but also *on* reality" (Suvin 10; Suvin's emphasis). Just as the Emperor's shoe, the thought of deformity, and the revelation of strange new technologies like the replicators provoke Bujold's characters to ask what kind of strange universe they inhabit, the Vorkosigan series is always a mirror that can provoke us as readers to consider the same question. We cannot but face this fact because Bujold has written a series of novels that confront the reader's set normative system with a literary construct that seems strangely familiar. When Cordelia confronts Vordarian by extending Gregor's shoe to Kareen and as Miles burns his offerings before his grandfather's grave, we see them as figures in a dark glass; only after much thought — much cognitive processing — might we begin to see more clearly the truth of such figures. Bujold's characters are allegorical figures that can cause us to reconsider the nature of the social space in which we live, the place we occupy in it, and the name with which it furnishes us. They force us to face an important fact: that the universal and the abstract do not "belong" to the masculine, that the sit-uated and the intuitive do not "belong" to the feminine. Such categories and the gendered identities to which they have been connected have been assigned their places within gendered socio-political space as a part of their constructed nature; we have mistaken such an arrangement for reality because we have forgotten that it could be otherwise. The Vorkosigan series recovers this knowledge for us, thereby opening an opportunity to construct identity dif-ferently.

What we see in the dark glass of the Vorkosigan series therefore situates us in relation to apparently universal abstractions, an experience that at once seems comforting yet profoundly uncompanionable to our sense of self and our homely place in the world. One of Derrida's conclusions in "Before the Law" frames this apparent contradiction when he writes, "there is no literature without a work, without an absolutely singular performance, and this nec-essary irreplaceability again recalls what the man [who stands before the law] asks when the singular crosses the universal, when the categorical engages the idiomatic, as a literature always must" (213). Reading of Bujold's characters as they play out the implications of the moral dilemmas they discover in relation to one another, we discover that there is no literature — no grand science-fictional drama — without the small works of its characters to drive the narrative and produce its themes. We discover that when Cordelia extends the shoe to Kareen to challenge Vordarian's power, when Miles cries his outraged plea before his grandfather's grave, they are granting us a singular performance with a universal appeal that transcends arbitrary gender distinctions or the difference between the reader and the read. Since we also may suddenly know ourselves to be living in a strange universe hostile and uncompanionable to our sense of self and home, we may realize that Bujold's characters are strangely doubled (therefore also strangely familiar) figures of ourselves. For we too extend ourselves and cry out to the abstract universals that strangely seem to lie outside of history; we too challenge the seemingly immense and implacable authority of those abstractions that would name us. We demand that the depth of our singular identities not be nullified, that they instead should be seen, acknowledged, and allowed the proper names that are their due.

Along with literary scholars and philosophers like Ragussis, Haraway, Derrida, and Ockham, Cordelia and Miles in their strangely familiar singularity as constructs of science fiction consequently remind us of two of the few, apparently universal certainties that situate us in the realm of abstract ideas and the social space defined by the other's existence. The first certainty is that our desire for a proper name will always be at odds with and a constant companion of the drive toward abstraction, an outward movement to remember what is absent, and the impetus to name — to situate — ourselves in relation to that absence, historical or otherwise. The second is a certainty that this desire must always be tempered by a movement inward, a seeking for the situated knowledge hidden behind the walls of homes and within the seemingly most insignificant objects and people. The need for and protection of civilization and justice find their genesis in such moments. For all power proceeds from this intimate encounter with the strangely familiar other, even when power proceeds from the simple presentation of a child's shoe.

NOTES

I would like to thank my friend Daniel Fusch for providing feedback on and helping me to find the right structure for this paper. More specific contributions will be footnoted as necessary below.

1. My distinction here between an outward (masculinized) gaze and the inward (feminized) gaze has been influenced by reading the French sociologist Pierre Bourdieu's study *Masculine Domination*, in which he outlines his theory of *habitus* as it relates to gendered identity. In brief, his study of Kabylia culture in the mountains of Algeria preserves in isolation traditions that European culture has weakened. As a consequence, he is able to

isolate and describe the means by which men establish their dominant role over women that applies to a wide number of cultures, including the European. Men are taught on a bodily level that they can look upward and outward to the public and political sphere because their supposedly guiltless nature will not cause harm. Women are taught that they must look inward and downward into the domestic and private domain where their allegedly sinful natures will do less damage. Because an analysis of the Vorkosigan series in light of Bourdieu's theory and the long history of *habitus* beginning with Aristotle is too lengthy and complex to include here, it will have to wait until a later date to be published.

2. Janet Brennan Croft first pointed out the significance of this passage in relation to Miles Vorkosigan and his clone Mark, whom we meet later in *Brothers in Arms*. See Croft 63–64.

3. Due to my reliance on Ragussis and Janet Brennan Croft, the logic of this comment follows the logic of Croft's observation, "So both Miles and Mark [Miles's cloned twin], neatly classified, have to find a balance in their lives between the names and roles and expectations imposed on them by their society and family, and their consuming desires to freely make their own names for themselves" (64).

4. For this etymology, see the adj. and n. *nominal*, not *nominalism*, in the *Oxford English Dictionary*.

5. For other authoritative definitions of *paterfamilias*, see the entry in *The Oxford Classical Dictionary*; for extensive discussions of the *paterfamilias*, see Lacey and Rawson. For an extensive discussion of *patria potestas*, see Lacey.

6. Little recent discussion of the Roman cult of the dead and the Romans' view of the afterlife exists, perhaps because Franz Cumont's analysis in 1922 still stands as the authoritative text on the topic. Thus, for a comprehensive view of Rome's cult of the dead, see Cumont 44–69. For a more recent perspective, see Warrior 27–40.

7. I am indebted to my friend Daniel Fusch for pointing out the full significance of this passage.

WORKS CITED

Adams, John Paul. *The Twelve Tables*. 10 June 2009. California State University at Northridge. 24 Sept. 2011. http://www.csun.edu/~hcfll004/12tables.html.

Boehner, Philotheus. Introduction. *Philosophical Writings: A Selection*. Philotheus Boehner, ed. Indianapolis: Hackett, 1990.

Bujold, Lois McMaster. *Barrayar*. In *Cordelia's Honor*. Riverdale, NY: Baen, 1986. 255–590.

_____. "The Mountains of Mourning." In *Young Miles*. Riverdale, NY: Baen, 1997. 373–464.

_____. *The Vor Game*. In *Young Miles*. Riverdale, NY: Baen, 1997. 465–827.

_____. *The Warrior's Apprentice*. In *Young Miles*. Riverdale, NY: Baen, 1997. 1–372.

Bourdieu, Pierre. *Masculine Domination*. Trans. Richard Nice. Stanford: Stanford University Press, 2001.

Croft, Janet. "The Soldier and the Cipher: Miles, Mark, and the Naming Plots of Bujold's Vorkosiverse." In *Lois McMaster Bujold: Essays on a Modern Master of Science Fiction and Fantasy*. Ed. Janet Brennan Croft. Jefferson, NC: McFarland, 2013. 61–76.

Cumont, Franz. *After Life in Roman Paganism*. New Haven: Yale University Press, 1922.

Derrida, Jacques. "Before the Law." Trans. Avital Ronell. In *Acts of Literature*. Ed. Derek Attridge. New York: Routledge, 1992. 181–220.

Freud, Sigmund. "The 'Uncanny.'" 1958. Trans. Alix Strachey. In *On Creativity and the Unconscious*. Benjamin Nelson, ed. New York: Harper & Row, 1986. 122–63.

Haraway, Donna J. "Situated Knowledges: The Science Question in Feminism and the Privilege of Partial Perspective." In *Simians, Cyborgs, and Women: The Reinvention of Nature*. New York: Routledge, 1991. 183–201.

Lacey, W.K. *"Patria Potestas."* In *The Family in Ancient Rome: New Perspectives.* Ed. Beryl Rawson, ed. Ithaca: Cornell University Press, 1986. 121–144.

Lindow, Sandra J. "The Influence of Family and Moral Development in Lois McMaster Bujold's Vorkosigan Series." In *Lois McMaster Bujold: Essays on a Modern Master of Science Fiction and Fantasy.* Ed. Janet Brennan Croft. Jefferson, NC: McFarland, 2013. 50–60.

The Oxford Classical Dictionary, 3d ed. Simon Hornblower and Anthony Spawforth, eds. Oxford: Oxford University Press, 2003.

Rank, Otto. *The Double.* Harry Tucker, Jr., ed. and trans. Chapel Hill: University of North Carolina Press, 1971.

_____. *Beyond Psychology.* 1941. New York: Dover, 1958.

Ragussis, Michael. *Acts of Naming: The Family Plot in Fiction.* New York: Oxford University Press, 1986.

Rawson, Beryl. "The Roman Family." In *The Family in Ancient Rome: New Perspectives.* Beryl Rawson, ed. Ithaca: Cornell University Press, 1986. 1–57.

Severy, Beth. *Augustus and the Family at the Birth of the Roman Empire.* New York: Routledge, 2003.

Suvin, Darko. *Metamorphoses of Science Fiction: On the Poetics and History of a Literary Genre.* New Haven: Yale University Press, 1979.

Warrior, Valerie M. *Roman Religion.* Cambridge: Cambridge University Press, 2006.

William, of Ockham. *Ockham's Theory of Terms: Part I of the Summa Logicae.* Trans. Michael J. Loux. Notre Dame: University of Notre Dame Press, 1974.

_____. *Philosophical Writings: A Selection,* rev. ed. Philotheus Boehner, ed. and trans. Indianapolis: Hackett, 1990.

Chaos and Quest
Miles Vorkosigan's Disability Narrative
VIRGINIA BEMIS

Miles Vorkosigan, a.k.a. Lord Miles a.k.a. Lord Auditor Vorkosigan, a.k.a. Admiral Naismith, a.k.a. "the hyperactive little git," is probably the best known, and certainly the most realistic, disabled character in science fiction. Lois McMaster Bujold's work is unusual in the realm of fiction of any genre, since it is so rare to find a disabled protagonist. Disabled characters tend to be either minor characters, often used to arouse pity, or villains, for whom disability is both cause and sign of villainy. In creating a well-developed character, growing over a series of books, and one for whom disability is a central fact, Bujold has made Miles a very authentic person with a disability. Miles is so authentic, in fact, that one can apply techniques from the field of Disability Studies to his story with success. In making Miles genuine, Bujold has created a fully-realized disability narrative that can be analyzed using the critical methods used to study actual disability narratives.

An author may use illness or disability as a phase, or find that the narrative "explores the full existential implications of an illness or disability" (Couser 14). Bujold explores every possible aspect of Miles's lived-with disability, and the implications it has for his life and future. It is quite usual for an author or a character to identify the self with the body, and Miles certainly does. His body, and its shape, shape his life. If his body were different, his life would be different in a great many ways. An able-bodied Miles would be a more typical Vor lord, probably far more like his cousin Ivan Vorpatril. There would still be interesting stories, since this other person would still be the son of Aral Vorkosigan and Cordelia Naismith, with all that implies in the way of brains and character, but the central conflict of all the narratives is grounded in Miles's disability. Without it, he would not take the path in life he does. He pits himself against Barrayar, and sometimes against himself, in proving himself not only worthy but more than worthy. Through the series of novels and short stories, Bujold explores all the implications of disability in a technologically advanced culture which still clings to pre–Time of Isolation thought patterns. From his infancy, indeed before he is born, Miles's existence requires people to think and act in new ways, or to keep the fear of the new and unknown they have been raised with.

Early in *Barrayar,* Aral Vorkosigan remarks to Cordelia, "As for injuries like Koudelka's, or worse ... the social stigma is very great. Watch him in a larger group sometime, not his close friends. It's no accident that the suicide rate among medically discharged soldiers is high" (29). Barrayar's cultural script operates to marginalize and stigmatize even the wounded soldier. In a military-centered society, one would expect wounded warriors to be honored, with their wounds seen as proof of success in combat, but not so on Barrayar. Wounds are equated with mutations, and Barrayar has always been very mutation-conscious, dating back to the first settlers. Infanticide was the usual response to a perceived mutation. Guarding the genome was women's work, and it was often seen as their duty to kill defective babies.

Miles isn't a mutant, but people assume he is, because he is different. In fact, his own grandfather tries to kill him before birth and during infancy. His disabilities, however, stem from a teratogenic antidote to a poison gas his mother was exposed to, but he is still perceived as weak, defective, or even cursed. He becomes so used to people making warding signs against evil when they see him that he is surprised when they do not, or when a salesclerk remarks, "Ah. Bachelor?" instead of "*Ah, mutant?*" (*Memory* 41).

Miles's life in the profoundly ableist Barrayaran society is partly a struggle for acceptance, and partly a determination to prove that society wrong. He wants to be a soldier, because that is the most valued status on Barrayar. He wants to be worthy of his name and do great deeds. And eventually, he wants to improve society for those who come after him. Miles is one of the stigmatized, and one who has a unique power to effect change because of his status and abilities. Miles grows to understand what his father was hinting at: that the problem is with those who stigmatize, rather than with those, like Koudelka and Miles, who are the targets of that stigma.

The main form of disability literature up to this point has been the autobiographical narrative. In such a narrative, we are told of someone's lived experience of disability and how, for the reader, this narrative functions "by heightening one's awareness of one's mortality, threatening one's sense of identity and disrupting the apparent plot of one's life" (Couser 5). Miles's story is largely told from his own viewpoint, thus making it almost an autobiography. While reading, we come to share in Miles's experience of disability at various key stages of his life. We certainly see Miles being aware of his mortality, especially in *Diplomatic Immunity,* when he faces death from a Cetagandan bioweapon, having his sense of identity threatened when he wakes from cryofreeze not knowing who he is, and having the plot of his life disrupted so often that it becomes an expected part of each book. As readers we share these experiences with Miles and come away changed in some degree. In fact, Bujold has said that her starting point is to think of the worst thing that can happen to Miles, let that happen, and grow the story, an apt description for plot disruption.

Disability studies scholar G. Thomas Couser points out, "It may be, then, that prolonged, serious or chronic illnesses and disabilities may ultimately yield more complex and multidimensional narratives than acute illnesses; because lasting dysfunction has to be lived with for some time, rather than survived as a mere episode" (12). This is certainly true for Miles, whose disabilities encompass his entire life and inform the narrative in complex ways. Miles grows as a character not only through his adventures but through his lived experience of disability in an ableist society. As Arthur Frank, another leading scholar in the field, remarks, "the teller's diseased body shapes the illness story" (2). If Miles's body were different, his life, and hence his life story, would be equally different. In the Miles Vorkosigan narrative, we see what Couser has termed "the developing discourses of the conditions represented — the negotiation between the narrator, on the one hand, and the cultural scripts of bodily dysfunction, on the other" (15). The cultural script is the way in which a culture gives meaning to disability and locates it within the culture. Disability may be seen, for instance, as a result of divine vengeance, or as a gift from the gods. It may be seen in any number of ways. The fact of a body dysfunction is assigned meaning by the cultural script, and from this is determined how the disabled person will be seen and treated by the society. For Miles, the script he must engage with is the Barrayaran cultural script. This script places great importance on military prowess, and sees physical difference as the greatest danger. The predominant fear is of mutation, a legacy of the Time of Isolation and the lasting effects of radiation on the first settlers. Miles, with his crippled body, is assumed to be a mutant, and as such is situated as an object of fear and hatred within his cultural script.

Body deformity or dysfunction is the sign of the evil other, the mutant, and to be avoided at all costs. At the beginning of the series, infant euthanasia is still a common practice on Barrayar, and disability of any sort is stigmatized. One of Miles's goals is to combat that stigma, to force his society to accept him on his terms, fighting for "the destigmatization of illness and disability, which such narratives at once reflect and advance" (Couser 8). Narratives of disability, particularly those like Miles's stories that are read and re-read, that claim our attention, engage in what Couser calls the "negotiation between the narrator" and "the cultural scripts of bodily dysfunction" (15). Miles's story is a process of devictimizing, destigmatizing, and subverting dominant cultural tropes (Couser 291) with the disabled person moving from passive subject to active (or in Miles's case hyperactive) object.

The Taxonomy of Disability Narratives

Frank recognizes three basic categories of disability (or illness) narrative: restitution, chaos and quest. Each has its own characteristics, and each appears at various times in the Vorkosigan cycle.

The restitution narrative is the story of restoring good health, and reflects not only a desire to get well and stay well, but a construction of illness and disability that focuses on cure, on returning control of the body to the occupant. The body returns to predictability, to its default condition, and nothing less is acceptable. Any disabling condition is only temporary, and always followed by a triumphant return to health.

Bujold, however, knows that there are many times when restitution is not possible, and even if possible, comes at too high a cost. The restitution story is of being well and whole again. In this story, one can get well and stay well. It is possible to get the body's former predictability back again (Frank 85). This slice of the future provides an interesting ethical challenge to the restitution narrative. In the Vorkosiverse, cloning of organs is so widespread that transplant rejection is a thing of the past. The rich and disabled can go further still. On Jackson's Whole, where law is optional and only the Deal is sacred, it is possible to have one's entire body cloned. The rich person can then have his or her brain transplanted into the new body, thus gaining renewed youth and a disability-free life, but at a cost. To do this involves murdering the cloned body's original occupant, one's clone-twin. Miles would not do so, but enough do to make it profitable for the Jacksonian Houses involved.

Where illness is an intimation of mortality, one can push that off by getting well. On Jackson's Whole, this is literally possible in a horrifying new way. Miles and Mark are equally sickened by the transplant idea. Mark's quest to end this arrangement results in encouraging the Durona Group to research life-extension treatments for the original body. Keeping the original body in reasonably good condition with fewer risks and lower cost than a brain transplant seems far more likely to prove useful, and is the closest thing to restitution available.

When restitution is closed off, one must look at the narrative possibilities of the body that will not be well again. This leads to Frank's other two types of disability narrative: the chaos narrative and the quest narrative. Bujold employs both, and they recur where the plotline makes them logical, just as they would in mundane life.

We first see Miles taking on adult responsibilities when he acts as his father's Voice in "The Mountains of Mourning." He is sent to investigate the death of Harra Csurik's baby daughter in the mountain community of Silvy Vale. Harra first sees Miles with his "[t]oo-large head, too-short neck, back thickened with its crooked spine, crooked legs with their brittle bones too-often broken, drawing the eye in their gleaming chromium braces" ("Mountains of Mourning" [Mountains] 377). The villager's half-fascinated, half-fearful stares make Miles realize he is more accepting of the facts of his life than he had been. "Time was, such openly repelled fascination with the peculiarities of his body had driven Miles to grind his teeth; now he could take it with a serene amusement only slightly tinged with acid. They would learn, all of them. They would learn" (Mountains 379). Acceptance does not require him to believe that what is, is good, but to acknowledge that what is, is. He is disabled, and that has become his starting point for forcing both Silvy Vale and Barrayar to acknowledge his worth. In doing so, he hopes to make society question some of its basic assumptions about physical condition and individual worth.

Paradoxically, his *dis*ability makes him *more* able to find out the truth and punish the child's murderer. He notices things others have been unwilling or unable to face, and finds that the murderer is Ma Mattulich, the child's grandmother, carrying on the tradition of killing deformed babies even as her own had been killed. Under fast-penta, she discloses everything she had kept hidden, and the ramblings of a truth-drugged old mountain woman reveal what underlies the fear and hatred that upper-class Barrayarans express in more sophisticated ways. Her attitude toward baby Raina is eerily like Count Piotr's attitude toward the infant Miles. "The cat's mouth, the dirty mutation. Monsters in us. Cut them out. [...] Muties make more muties, they breed faster, overrun. [...] You want to make mutie babies on clean women, poison us all" (Mountains 450). Like Count Piotr's insistence that *that* could not possibly be a future Count Vorkosigan, her statements come from a visceral loathing of disability and deformity.

Ma Mattulich reaches another insight that is unlike Count Piotr's. Whereas he eventually comes to see his grandson as an exception to the rule, she predicts and fears the social and cultural change that is beginning thanks to Miles's presence: "A mutie made lord over us all, and all the rules changed, betrayed at the end by an off-worlder woman's weakness. You make it all for *nothing*. Hate you. Dirty mutie..." (Mountains 453). Changing all the rules is precisely the result Miles is aiming for, not just for himself, but for others. He is the embodiment of everything those resistant to change on Barrayar fear, and an old hill woman is the first to articulate it.

Speaker Karal sums it up for Miles: "Ordinary people need extraordinary examples. So they can say to themselves, well, if he can do *that*, I can surely do *this*. No excuses." Miles replies: "No quarter, yes, I know that game. Been playing it all my life" (Mountains 456). This is our first indication in Miles's story of what Frank terms the *ethic of inspiration*. The game, as Miles puts it, is the game of forcing Barrayar to recognize him as something other than an oddity. Doing so will make life better for those who come after, as well as inspiring others to face and surmount their own difficulties.

It is in *Memory* that he comes to realize that the ImpSec section of the game is over, and another part is beginning. After handing in his report, Miles walks home from ImpSec Headquarters. "No long stares, no rude gestures or comments, not even one covert old hex sign against mutation. Had getting rid of his uneven limp, leg braces, and most of the crookedness in his back made that much difference? Or was the difference in the Barrayarans?" (*Memory* 36).

This is the beginning of the chaos story for Miles, the story of total loss of integration and meaning. The chaos story, in its ultimate form, is a worst-case scenario in which nothing can be repaired or ameliorated. There is no understanding, no control, no possibility of doing anything other than being swept along with the current until it is possible to emerge from chaos, and only when this emergence starts can the story really be told. As Frank defines it, "Chaos is the opposite of restitution: its plot imagines life never getting better. Stories are chaotic in their absence of narrative order. Events are told as the storyteller experiences life: without sequence or discernable causality" (97). Chaos stories mean that the teller is not living a "proper" life. One event doesn't lead to another. "Chaos stories are as anxiety provoking as restitution stories are preferred" (97). We see Miles's life fragmenting, breaking apart, and his future disappearing entirely.

Miles's chaos story takes place in *Memory*. The aftereffects of his cryorevival include a seizure disorder that he had hoped would be temporary. As he explains to his cousin Ivan and Duv Galeni, his medical status has changed, and not for the better.

> After my cryo-revival last year ... I had a problem. I started getting these seizures. Convulsions, lasting two to five minutes. They seemed to be triggered by moments of extreme stress. My surgeon stated that, like the memory loss, they might right themselves. They were rare, and seemed to be tailing off as promised. So I ... didn't mention it to my ImpSec doctors, when I came home [*Memory* 74].

Naturally, stress as a trigger means that seizures seem to happen at the worst times, culminating in his slicing through Lieutenant Vorberg's legs with a plasma arc during a hostage rescue.

Even after the seizure disorder turns out to be permanent, he continues in his denial, to the point of falsifying a report and getting thrown out of ImpSec. The chaos of his life, having lost both ImpSec and the Dendarii Fleet, is paralleled by the chaotic seizures, described as his world breaking up into colored confetti. The confetti, splintering and dissolving, is an apt symbol for his life. His life is broken, as is his identity and his self-concept. He no longer knows who he is, or what kind of life he will live.

This is the opposite of the restitution story. The chaos story "imagines life never getting better"; in the typical chaos story, the surface "cracks to reveal vulnerability, futility, and impotence" (Frank 97). A chaos story tells how easily any of us could be sucked under. This teller is the true wounded storyteller. If one is living the chaos, one can't put it into words. Some perspective is necessary for the story to be told. Living in the midst of chaos means that things can't make sense. This part of the story really can't be told, just lived. That explains why Miles isn't thinking clearly in *Memory*. His thought process is as beyond his control as his body now is. "Chaos feeds on the sense that *no one* is in control" (Frank 100, emphasis in original). Miles thought his life was under control, only to find his body betraying him, and holding only chaos; as Frank observes, this is "the most embodied form of story," the one "beyond speech," "told on the edges of a wound, [...] the edges of speech" (101). The body is swept along, without control; relationships are damaged or destroyed, there is no way out; "consciousness has given up the struggle for sovereignty over its own experience" (104). When it can be told, it is because some distance has been achieved; some part of the teller is out of the chaos.

Only when Miles begins to emerge from the chaos can he start to create his new normal. Becoming an Imperial Auditor allows him to use all of himself; Admiral Naismith was only a part. The little Admiral allowed him freedom of movement, but left him rootless, and required him to deny the Barrayaran aspects of his self. Lord Vorkosigan he hardly even knew, yet it is Lord Vorkosigan who links him to Barrayar, his home and the place of his loyalties. Miles realizes that nobody knows Lord Vorkosigan, not even Miles.

> *I just met the man myself.* He'd known a boy by that name, long ago, confused and passionate and army-mad. Properly, that boy had been left behind by Admiral Naismith, striking out for his larger identity, his wider world. But this new Lord Vorkosigan was someone else altogether, and Miles scarcely dared guess his future [*Memory* 289].

Getting to know himself as Lord Vorkosigan turns out to be productive. Once he knows that aspect of himself, he can integrate the parts of Admiral Naismith that are valuable, and become a whole person. The chaos story turns into a quest story, with his first quest being self-discovery. He goes to Silvy Vale, the site of his first actions as Count's Voice, to burn an offering for the infant girl whose murder he investigated. He finds the area much changed. The village has a school, named for baby Raina, whose grave is lost under the lake that will soon provide hydroelectric power for the area. He finds himself a celebrity, a beloved public figure whose acts have brought not only truth but improvement to the village.

The only one he can share his questions with is Harra Csurik, mother of the dead baby. She shares with him the insight she has gained from dealing with loss and pain.

> "You go on. You just go on. There's nothing more to it, and there's no trick to make it easier. You just go on."
> "What do you find on the other side? When you go on?"
> [...] "Your life again. What else?" [*Memory* 117].

The goal of the quest is encapsulated in this dialogue. Miles has been looking for his life for a long time, and has finally found it. Harra has been on the quest before him, and thus is qualified to act as his guide.

Miles not only goes on, but finds he has somewhere to go. His post as acting Lord Auditor becomes permanent, and allows him to use his talents for Barrayar as he had always wanted. He is also able to bring himself to deal with his seizures and learn to live with them, rather than hoping they will go away. He comes to realize the truth of Elli Quinn's insistence that "You can't just ... ignore them out of existence, though apparently that's exactly what you've been attempting" (*Memory* 18). Miles later has an important insight: "I'm no longer of the secret opinion that death will somehow overlook me if I don't do something personally about it. And given life ... it seems stupid not to make the most of what I do have. Not to mention deucedly ungrateful" (222). Quest stories meet suffering head on; they accept illness and seek to *use* it.

Memory ends with Miles realizing he isn't in pieces anymore. Not Lord Vorkosigan, not Admiral Naismith, but "all of him, all at once, all the time" (345). His body-self has been both unmade and remade, with a new integrity and completeness. This new self is a communicating body, being *for* the other as well as for the self (Frank 126), desiring for itself in relation to others. This is how Miles is able to develop true and lasting relationships. In the quest narrative, the meeting with Ekaterin must of necessity come after the trip to Silvy Vale in *Memory*. The self is connected to its own memory, and further changes in self and in character occur: the product is not just a self story but a dyadic self/other story (Frank 131). Now the time is ripe for Miles to be part of a pair, rather than the lonely figure he has been.

The three issues of voice, memory, and responsibility merge. Finding a voice becomes the problem of "taking responsibility for memory" (Frank 132). One's past actions can't be disowned, but can be disapproved — by taking responsibility for what one has done. Miles takes full responsibility for his past, and becomes fully the hero of his own story, not split between Admiral Naismith and Lord Vorkosigan.

Here we are seeing Miles moving beyond the chaos story to Frank's third category, the quest. Here, the search is for new meaning, new identity, the "new normal." Getting to know Lord Vorkosigan is but a part of this process: "The quest hero accepts *contingency* because the paradox learned on the quest is that surrendering the superficial control of health yields control of a higher order" (Frank 126).

The control Miles gains is the control of his self and his story. In sharing his story, he shares himself, and is open to intimacy in a new way. This makes it possible not only for Miles to find a new life-path, but to find love. His journey has been one of self-discovery, and his new unity makes it possible to go forward in life: "Harra Csurik had been almost right. It wasn't your life again you found, going on. It was your life anew. And it wasn't at all what he'd been expecting. [...] He was beginning to be very curious about his future" (*Memory* 345).

Miles's chaos story is paralleled by Simon Illyan's. Illyan's life is fragmenting too, as his memory chip breaks down. His memory is sporadic as the chip randomly discharges items from the past. Disoriented and without the eidetic memory he has relied on for so many years, he faces a frightening and uncertain future. Bujold shows just how quickly something one has depended on can vanish, leaving instability and uncertainty behind. Illyan will never be the man he once was, can no longer function as head of ImpSec, and at first has little idea how to be anything else. There is no restitution, no possibility of getting his old life back, since that life depended on the no longer functioning biochip. With the aid of the audiofiler he describes as "nearly a prosthetic memory" (*Memory* 314), he embarks on what Reynolds Price described as "a whole new life" (Price vii). Both Miles and Illyan have to relinquish what they most want, the life they lived before, and the identity that went with it. As Price says, "you're not that person now. Who'll you be tomorrow? And who do you propose to be from here to the grave, which may be hours or decades down the road?" (Price 182). For Illyan, as for Miles, chaos must be accepted as a fact before that new life can be lived. They may grieve for the past, but it is time to begin the quest for the new self and new life.

Illyan too has lost a past but gained a future. In all his years as an ImpSec officer, and later as head of ImpSec, he has never had time for a life of his own. Now that he has been as suddenly retired as Miles, he begins to develop the personal side he had long repressed in favor of duty. He gets to know Simon, the civilian, just as Miles gets to know Lord Vorkosigan. He even develops a romantic relationship with Lady Alys Vorpatril.

The Ethical Results of the Quest Narrative

Miles's love life has always been complicated, to say the least. All of his relationships were with part of him — not all of him, all the time. Now that he is always present, and coming to know himself, it becomes possible for him to find a true complement, someone with whom he can build a life. He has always secretly hoped for a marriage of the quality of his parents', but never found a relationship that could compare with theirs. When Ekaterin meets Miles, she notices at once that he is comfortable in and with his body. While no taller than nine year old Nikki Vorsiosson, he has a commanding presence that is effortless without being superior, and not at all defensive. He projects a message: here I am, this is how I look, you deal with it.

Here we see in action one of the three ethical results Frank believes stems from the quest story: *inspiration, solidarity and commitment, and recollection.* By acting as he does both then and when helping Ekaterin deal with Tien's death and the need to tell Nikki about Vorzohn's Dystrophy, Miles demonstrates what can be possible, in the face of the impossible, as he has done so often before.

Ekaterin's first view of Miles is of "A mutie, a mutie *Vor*, yet he carried on as if nothing were the least out of the ordinary" (*Komarr* 11). As she looks further, she sees

> a presence which, by ignoring his elusive physical peculiarities himself, defied the observer to dare comment. But the little lord had had all his life to adjust to his condition. Not like the hideous surprise Tien had found among his late brother's papers, and subsequently confirmed for himself and Nikolai through carefully secret testing [14].

It is clear that Tien feels the stigma acutely, and wishes to hide it at all costs, even the cost of potential harm to himself and his son. He fears rejection, fears being called a mutant, and fears being treated where there is the least possibility that anyone on Barrayar might find out. He hopes to pass as abled and not have to fear the reaction of an ableist society. Miles, of course, has never had such a choice. His disability cannot be hidden, so he must confront it and dare others to do likewise.

What Frank terms an *ethic of solidarity and commitment* is found "when the storyteller offers his voice to others, not to speak for them, but to speak *with* them as a fellow-sufferer" (Frank 132). Miles's first opportunity to do this is in *Komarr*, when he calmly talks Nikki Vorsoisson through the discovery of Vorzohn's dystrophy. Miles not only tells Nikki the truth about what the soltoxin and its antidote did to him, he shows Nikki the scars from later surgeries. Rather than trying to make Nikki "feel better," he treats the boy as a compatriot, an agent in his own story.

In *A Civil Campaign*, Nikki asks if being called *the mutie lord* bothers Miles. "When I was your age, it bothered me a lot. It doesn't seem very relevant anymore" (*A Civil Campaign* [*Campaign*] 260) is his answer. Once again, Miles takes Nikki's concerns seriously, and meets them with honesty. Nikki says regarding one of his mother's suitors,

> "Lieutenant Vormoncrief wouldn't want us ... wouldn't want Mama if he knew I was a mutie, I bet."
> "In that case, I urge you to tell him right away," Vorkosigan shot back, deadpan [*Campaign* 260].

This response acknowledges the importance of Nikki's question, while not treating it as some awful hidden truth. As Ekaterin thinks:

> Secrets so dire as to be unspeakable, thoughts so frightening as to make clear young voices mute, kicked out into the open with blunt ironic humor. And suddenly the dire didn't loom so darkly any more, and fear shrank, and anyone could say anything. And the unbearable seemed a little easier to lift [260].

Ekaterin's thoughts illustrate one aspect of Frank's typology of communication. The story Miles shares with Nikki, and by implication with the reader, forms a bond, not to make the truth vanish, but to make one able to live with the truth, and embark on one's own quest story. Later, when discussing honor with Ekaterin, Miles recalls Harra Csurik's advice: "A very wise woman once told me — you just go on. I've never encountered any good advice that didn't boil down to that, in the end. Not even my father's" (327). This is one of several examples of Frank's *ethic of recollection*, in which the speaker shares memories of past actions as a guide to present living.

The events of *Memory* and his experience with his new and unified life seem to have made Miles better at coping with chaos when it presents itself again in *Diplomatic Immunity*. Where the previous disruptions came courtesy of a needle-grenade, his new chaos arises from a Cetagandan bioweapon. Once again, he has to adjust to a new normal, one in which he can add a greater likelihood of cardiovascular problems to the effects of past wounds. And then, of course, there are the seizures. What, he wonders, will happen when the bioweapon's effects and his seizure disorder combine? "He was going to be a damned research project, again" (288). By now, he is grudgingly accepting of the reality, as one more thing to deal with, though he is pleased to graduate from the floatchair he despises a cane he despises less.

The cane reappears in *CryoBurn*, as a fixture in his life. By this time, he treats it as a tool to make his life easier rather than as something to be despised. He is seen selecting a cane to replace one that has been stolen, and using a cane on numerous occasions, though he does use it not just as a walking aid but to substitute for a foot in the door. *CryoBurn*'s main narrative ends with Miles and Mark discussing recent events and the financial and political results they expect. Miles is pleased with his success at foiling an entirely new kind of coup d'etat, while Mark is equally satisfied with having found an excellent startup situation for the Durona Group's longevity treatments. They are interrupted by the uniformed Colonel Vorventa, who addresses Miles as "Count Vorkosigan, sir" (334). This is the end of Lord Vorkosigan's chapter. Miles's world is once again thrown into chaos, reassembled, and he must embark on a new quest. "The Count-my-father" is dead, I am now the Count, who am I and what shall I be?

The only thing the reader can be sure of is that any further narratives of Miles Vorkosigan, now Count Vorkosigan, will be disability narratives. His disability is part of his existence, along with his clever mind. Miles has not surrendered to the invisibility expected of the disabled on Barrayar. He is assertively, sometimes aggressively visible. Bujold has given us a disabled character who fits neither traditional category: suffering saint or triumphant over tragedy. Miles is more interesting for being neither, and more realistic. Seen through the lens of disability studies, Bujold's work gives us a valuable and authentic portrayal of disability as it is lived.

WORKS CITED

Bujold, Lois McMaster. *Barrayar*. Riverdale, NY: Baen, 1991.
_____. *A Civil Campaign*. Riverdale, NY: Baen, 1999.
_____. *CryoBurn*. Riverdale, NY: Baen, 2010.
_____. *Diplomatic Immunity*. Riverdale, NY: Baen, 2002.
_____. *Komarr*. Riverdale, NY: Baen, 1998.
_____. *Memory*. Riverdale, NY: Baen, 1996.
_____. "The Mountains of Mourning." 1989. In *Young Miles*. Riverdale, NY: Baen, 2003. 373–464.
Couser, G. Thomas. *Recovering Bodies: Illness, Disability and Life Writing*. Madison: University of Wisconsin Press, 1997.
Davis, Lennard J., ed. *The Disability Studies Reader*, 1st ed. New York: Routledge, 1997.
Frank, Arthur. *The Wounded Storyteller: Body, Illness and Ethics*. Chicago: University of Chicago Press, 1995.
Mitchell, David T., and Sharon Snyder, eds. *The Body and Physical Difference: Discourses of Disability*. Ann Arbor: University of Michigan Press, 1997.
Price, Reynolds. *A Whole New Life: An Illness and a Healing*. New York: Atheneum, 1994.

Broken Brothers in Arms
Acting the Man in The Warrior's Apprentice
LINDA WIGHT

Miles Vorkosigan, the seventeen-year-old protagonist of Lois McMaster Bujold's *The Warrior's Apprentice*, has spent his young life aspiring to the Barrayaran military ideal of masculinity. His family belongs to Barrayar's elite warrior class, and his father and grandfather are both renowned war heroes. Miles is highly intelligent, but his bone development was impaired by a poison gas attack on his father, Lord Aral Vorkosigan, and pregnant mother, Cordelia, almost eighteen years earlier. Miles's parents insist that his unusual appearance and weak bones do not make him less of a man, but Miles is aware that their attitude is not typical on Barrayar, where the able-bodied warrior is valorized and those who are perceived to be physically deformed face extreme hostility, prejudice, and even death. Miles nevertheless attempts to live up to his patriarchal heritage by closely observing his father and grandfather and performing masculinity as best he can.

Queer theorist Judith Butler argues, however, that awareness of masculinity as a performance can open up the space for alternative performances: the reformulation or even rejection of seemingly natural gender roles. Miles's opportunity to reformulate the warrior identity comes when he travels off-planet and creates the Dendarii mercenary force. Empathy forms the basis of his reformulated warrior persona. As Dendarii Admiral Miles Naismith, he empathizes with other men and women who have been deemed lacking, and inspires them to exceed through performance the roles imposed upon them by rigid social structures. Miles's capacity for empathy transforms hierarchical and competitive relationships between men into queerly-inflected interdependent bonds, reformulating both the Barrayaran military ideal, and a stock masculine icon of the science fiction genre: the heroic space opera warrior.

Going Down Fighting for the Warrior Identity

The Warrior's Apprentice opens, however, with Miles still on Barrayar, preparing to tackle an obstacle course designed to test whether he is physically fit to be admitted into the Imperial Service. At this point in his life, Miles is less than five feet in height with a twisted spine, oversized head, and weak bones; repeated fractures have left his left leg four centimeters shorter than his right. At the time of the attack on his parents, the chemical used to neutralize the gas and save his pregnant mother's life destroyed the normal bone development of the fetus. Controversially, his parents placed the damaged fetus into a uterine replicator in an effort to save Miles's life and rectify the bone damage. However his treatment was interrupted by the civil war between Aral's forces —fighting to protect the regency of child-Emperor Gregor — and the usurper who stole Miles's replicator in an effort to devastate his father. Miles was saved, but was born undersized with a severely deformed spine and fused hip sockets. Years of painful surgical operations, along with Miles's own fierce determination and resilience, were needed so that Miles could merely walk, let alone attempt the physical tests for entry into the Imperial Service, the career appropriate to a Barrayaran man of his class.

Aral and Cordelia's decision to save Miles's life by placing him in a replicator was controversial in the context of Barrayar's extreme intolerance of any form of perceived physical abnormality. The early colonists of Barrayar developed a "survival of the fittest" philosophy when a collapsed wormhole cut them off from Earth and the rest of the colonized galaxy. Their prejudice was reinforced when the planet was rediscovered by the hostile Cetagandans who attacked with mutation-producing weapons. Even in Miles's lifetime deformed infants are still killed at birth or soon after in the backcountry, despite periodic official attempts to stamp the practice out. Although Miles is no mutant — "Look, no gills [...] no antlers" (*Warrior's Apprentice* [*Warrior*] 229)— he suffers from this tradition of prejudice. An old woman makes hex signs at him, and a fellow candidate for the Imperial Service Academy looks at his leg brace with suspicion and edges away as if fearing Miles has a contagious disease, "Unclean, unclean, thought Miles wildly" (3). Soon after the poison gas attack, Miles's own grandfather had argued that he should be aborted.

Miles's grandfather, Count Piotr Vorkosigan, is a Barrayaran military hero. At twenty-two he led the fierce guerrilla war against the Cetagandans, earning the rank of General in the Imperial Service. Twenty years later he played a pivotal role in the civil war that brought down Mad Emperor Yuri and installed Ezar Vorbarra — Gregor's grandfather — in his place. His daughter-in-law, Cordelia, an outsider from Beta colony who married into the Vorkosigan family, observes that Barrayar is "Army-mad" (*Barrayar* 21). Military success particularly defines the Vorkosigans, as it does all Vor, the warrior caste which rules Barrayar. Despite increasing off-world influence, Barrayar remains a highly patriarchal militarized society, and the Vor place enormous pressure on their sons to carry on their military legacy. Cordelia observes that, "A man without a son is a walking ghost there, with no part in their future" (*Shards of Honor* [*Shards*] 168), and Piotr is therefore passionately interested in his future grandson when Cordelia becomes pregnant in *Barrayar* (preceding *The Warrior's Apprentice* in the Vorkosigan Saga chronology, though not published until 1991). He is equally horrified by the prospect of a "mutie" diluting the family gene pool and destroying the honor of nine generations of Vorkosigan warriors: "We cannot afford to have a deformed *Count Vorkosigan*" (*Barrayar* 158). Thwarted in his efforts to order or bribe the doctors to abort the damaged fetus, Piotr emphatically signals his disapproval by refusing to allow the child to be named after him.

Despite the pressure from his father, Aral Vorkosigan supports his wife, Cordelia, when she insists on Miles's right to life. Unlike Piotr, he accepts that change to Barrayaran customs is inevitable and necessary. When he first meets Cordelia in *Shards of Honor* he admits, "Today we are betwixt and between. The old customs are dead, and we keep trying on new ones, like badly fitting clothes. It's hard to know what's right, anymore" (47). Piotr beseeches Aral to think of the example he will be setting, "We cannot carry the deadweight of millions of dysfunctionals!" (*Barrayar* 188), but Aral sees it as his opportunity to influence positive change, "Where a Vorkosigan goes, maybe others might not find it so impossible to follow" (188). Nonetheless, Aral knows that change to traditions deeply ingrained during the Time of Isolation will be gradual; Miles is conceived only eighty years after Barrayar re-established contact with other galactic civilizations. Aral himself once took his society's attitudes to physical limitations for granted, yet his commitment to change is galvanized by Cordelia's demand that he "Remake this world into one Miles can survive in" (359).

Aral and Cordelia encourage Miles to believe that his physical problems do not make him less of a man. Miles, however, constantly grapples with his felt need to prove himself worthy of the Vorkosigan name. He particularly seeks to model his performance of masculinity on his father. Aral's military legend is as impressive as his own father's had been; his name known throughout the galaxy, Aral is variously praised as a brilliant military tactician and (unfairly) condemned as the "Butcher of Komarr." For his loyalty to Emperor Ezar Vorbarra, Aral was appointed Gregor's regent upon Ezar's death. Therefore, when Miles fails the Imperial Service test, breaking both legs in the process, he is devastated that he has failed to live up to his patriarchal legacy. His guilt is compounded by the death of his grandfather the day after he hears of Miles's failure. Piotr had warmed to Miles over the years, impressed by his fearlessness and hopeful that he might carry on the family's military tradition despite his physical disadvantages. Notwithstanding Piotr's age, frailty, and ill-health, Miles fears he died of disappointment.

Miles does not think at this stage to question his society's idealization of the warrior. He perceives the problem to be located in his own inability to overcome or properly manage his physical limitations, rather than within the social structure that defines him as lacking (Gerschick and Miller 203). In "Coming to Terms: Masculinity and Physical Disability," Thomas Gerschick and Adam Miller observe that men who experience marginalization or stigmatization as a result of physical impairment often react by internalizing the ideals of hegemonic masculinity and exerting themselves to meet its demands, particularly its demands for physical toughness, strength, and ability (183; 191). This *reliance* pattern is characterized by a hypersensitive adoption of predominant attitudes to masculinity as a way to gain acceptance from others (192). Men who favor the reliance strategy, however, are continually reminded in their interactions with other men, such as the physically-impressive cadets competing with Miles for admission to the Imperial Service, that they are "incomplete" (192). Gerschick and Miller identify more constructive alternatives: *reformulation* and *rejection*.

Reformulation involves men redefining hegemonic ideals of masculinity on their own terms, "shaping it along the lines of their own abilities, perceptions, and strengths" (187). Class-based resources play an important role, making it easier for some men than others to reformulate masculine ideals in order to emphasize certain hegemonic traits, such as intelligence and leadership, while downplaying the importance of the physical (203). Gerschick and Miller claim that reformulating masculinity presents little real challenge to the gender order (203). However as the following section will show, Miles's method of reformulation goes beyond affirming his hegemonic strengths; his empathy for other men and women who have been defined as somehow damaged or lacking is central to his reformulated warrior identity, and far from typical of the Barrayaran masculine ideal.

Miles, however, stops short of *rejection*, which moves further towards completely renouncing hegemonic standards of masculinity. This pattern is characterized by the creation of an alternative social identity, or by the denial of the importance of masculinity in one's life (187). Gerschick and Miller recount their interviews with men who describe "letting go" of society's behavioral expectations. After endless hours of exercise and training which reaffirmed the body as the central foundation of how men defined themselves, these men recognized that it was societal conceptions of masculinity, rather than their own physical limitations, that were problematic (183; 202).

Until he leaves Barrayar, Miles lacks the space and opportunity needed even to reformulate the warrior ideal. Despite the influence of his Betan mother, who is highly critical of the demands that Barrayar makes of Vor men, Miles has been raised as a member of the warrior caste, and therefore tends towards reliance on the Barrayaran masculine ideal. He was determined to get into the Imperial Service, no matter the physical cost to himself. Failure was so unthinkable that he refused to consider alternatives. Devastated and depressed when he does fail the physical test, Miles briefly considers suicide but instead decides to take his grandfather's advice and "go down [...] fighting" (*Warrior* 26). Hyper-aware of how his performance of masculinity is perceived, he presents himself as resilient and jovial when the surgeon sets his broken legs, though he longs to "get off stage and collapse" (9). According to Douglas Kleiber and Susan Hutchinson, men like Miles who favor the reliance strategy are attracted by the promise that transcending the limitations of the impaired body will bestow an even more dramatic masculinity, that of the archetypal hero (136). The "super crip" (Longmore 10) is a familiar figure in literary and filmic narratives: "This model [...] teaches men to override their needs and limitations and learn instead to [...] push onward relentlessly in spite of fatigue, hardship, illness, or desire" (J. Robinson qtd. Kleiber and Hutchinson 138). In line with the reliance model, Miles draws on the warrior rhetoric to define his legs as his enemies, "Rebellious provinces — mutinous troops — quisling saboteurs" (*Warrior* 21), suppresses his physical and psychological pain, and re-commits himself to overcoming his physical limitations.

Yet his exclusion from the Imperial Service makes it difficult for Miles to operate according to complete reliance on the normative Barrayaran military ideal. Though still aspiring to a heroic identity, he gives the first indication of his willingness to reformulate hegemonic notions of masculinity by embarking, not on a warrior's quest, but on a romantic off-planet quest to find the mother of Elena, the woman he loves, in the hope of winning Elena's gratitude and hand in marriage. Soon after arriving on Beta colony, however, this quest is superseded by Miles's impulsive crusade to save spaceship pilot Arde Mayhew, whose outdated neural implants are about to render him obsolete. Suddenly free of the constant scrutiny that he endured on Barrayar, but retaining the wealth and privilege of his class, Miles allows himself to act on his empathetic impulse. Empathy, rather than ambition to create a mercenary army, motivates him to purchase Mayhew's spaceship and, accompanied by Miles's bodyguard, Konstantin Bothari; Bothari's daughter and Miles's love interest, Elena; and Baz Jesek, a Barrayaran serviceman whose life is forfeit for deserting in the heat of battle, commit himself and his crew to smuggling weapons for use in a battle between galactic forces for the planet of Tau Verde IV. Nonetheless, Miles soon finds himself performing the role of military leader that his own society denied him. Encountering a blockade run by Oseran mercenaries on behalf of the enemy force, Miles and his companions seize the Oseran spaceship. Faced with the impossibility of keeping the captured mercenaries under constant guard and unwilling to execute them, Miles invents a new mercenary force called the Dendarii mercenaries, presents himself as its captain, Miles Naismith (adopting his Betan mother's family name), and invites his captives to join. Though he intends this as a temporary measure, the ranks of the Dendarii swell after each successful military action until Miles finds himself Admiral of three thousand troops and nineteen ships of war.

Gender Performance: Queering the Warrior

As leader of the Dendarii, Miles continues to associate masculinity with military command; however, his acute awareness of masculinity as a performance, along with his physical distance from Barrayar, opens up a space in which he can reformulate this ideal. Furthermore, Miles inspires others who have been deemed lacking by society to exceed through performance the roles imposed upon them by rigid social structures and their own psychological limitations. Though Miles's actions are carefully calculated to ensure his followers' loyalty, his genuine interest in helping others to excel through performance differentiates *The Warrior's Apprentice* from the tradition of literary narratives which imagine physically-impaired individuals being motivated solely by a desire for revenge on the able-bodied world.

Miles's positive strategy of using performance to reformulate identity draws attention to gender as a construction arising from culturally coded behaviors, rather than an innate or natural quality. Specifically, his hyperaware performance of the warrior identity can be understood in terms of queer theorist Judith Butler's claim that gender is a doing, a repeated performance of certain acts and gestures which create the illusion of a naturally gendered subject: "Gender is the repeated stylization of the body, a set of repeated acts within a highly rigid regulatory frame that congeal over time to produce the appearance of substance, of a natural sort of being" (*Gender* 33). Taking gender as natural and inevitable discourages critique, while drawing attention to gender as a performance opens up the possibility of performing in a way that is not constrained by hegemonic ideology. As science fiction theorist Veronica Hollinger observes, it is only when gender is recognized as performative that a radical critique into essentialist categories may be initiated (307). In a phallocentric society, however, the male body is generally rendered invisible, discouraging recognition of the "stylization of the body." As the neutral body, the universal body, it is beyond scrutiny and critique (Cranny-Francis 150).

By contrast, Miles's unique physical appearance and limitations draw attention to the male body and the way that it is manipulated in order to convey an impression of an innate, essential masculinity. As a result of his perceived distance from the Barrayaran masculine ideal, Miles is more aware than most able-bodied men that his masculinity is the "stylized repetition of acts through time" (Butler, *Gender* 141). His awareness contributes to his success as Admiral Naismith. Taking center stage in the Dendarii briefing room, Miles repeats gestures that he has observed his father and grandfather using to convey an air of authority and icy competence: "Miles glanced up from lowered brows, shooting her his best imitation General Count Piotr Vorkosigan military glare" (*Warrior* 57). Acts and gestures produce the effect of an inner core or substance on the surface of the body (Butler, *Gender* 136), and Miles's performance is so convincing that eventually even the Oseran Admiral submits to his authority. Appropriate props are also crucial to Miles's success. He carefully positions Bothari, Mayhew, and Jesek around the negotiation room so that their physical presence can supply the menace that his own body lacks. Bothari remarks, "You're not a commander, you're a bloody holovid director" (*Warrior* 141). One of the most crucial things that Miles does in his role as "director" is convincing his "actors" that they can also deliver an inspiring and believable performance. For instance, Miles teaches Jesek to imitate one of his former engineering commanders: "You're rough and tough and you eat slovenly engineering technicians for breakfast" (135). Jesek's transformation from desperate outcast incapacitated by fear to Commander Baz Jesek of the Dendarii mercenaries reveals that hegemonic masculinity is an impersonation that can be learned by all men.

Miles's commitment to impersonating a successful military commander may suggest uncritical valorization of Barrayar's hegemonic masculine ideal. Indeed, reliance on, rather than reformulation of, this ideal is suggested by his romanticization of traditional hierarchical relationships. Susan Smith observes that Miles imagines himself a sword-wielding nobleman who uses his power to help other men less fortunate than himself (243). To Mayhew, he says, "What you need is a liege lord, to take sword in hand and slice through all the red tape. Just like Vorthalia the Bold and the Thicket of Thorns" (*Warrior* 63). In an interview with Michael Levy, Bujold acknowledges Miles's "dangerous tendency to try to turn the people around him into his annexes" (16).

Nevertheless, Miles's actions are inspired by empathy, and it is his empathy with men like Mayhew, Jesek, and Bothari, who bear emotional, physical, and psychological burdens, which implies a distance from the conventional Barrayaran construction of the hero. Terry O'Neill and Myra J. Hird argue that for marginalized men, the distance between hegemonic description and their own lived experience may provide the reflective space in which counter-subjectivities are formulated (207). Miles's mother, Cordelia, hints at this possibility by defining Miles's physical impairment as his great gift. Moreover, Butler points out that although gender acquires its naturalized effect as a result of the kind of ritual practice that Miles employs in his dealings with his liege men, the apparently essential identity is destabilized by that which escapes or exceeds the norm (*Bodies* 10). Although constructed within a traditional hierarchical framework, the interdependency, vulnerability, and deep affection that characterize Miles's bonds with other men far exceed the norm. All military leaders depend on their followers' support, but Miles's dependence on others is overt and highly embodied. Bothari becomes an extension of Miles's own body, his physical ability and menace compensating for Miles's lack: "Seeing his bodyguard and the non-com together, the non-com suddenly bothered Miles less. The proctor looked shorter, somehow, and younger; even a little soft. Bothari was taller, leaner, much older, a lot uglier, and considerably meaner-looking" (*Warrior* 6). By swearing to be Miles's Armsman, Mayhew legally becomes another part of Miles's body.

Just as Miles depends on his followers to support his performance as mercenary leader, Mayhew, Jesek, and Bothari depend on Miles to enable their own successful performance of masculinity. Although Mayhew and Jesek are much closer than Miles to the physical ideal, their bodies are similarly threatened with destruction and marginalization. Until Miles bought Mayhew's spaceship it was destined for the scrap heap, and without this particular ship Mayhew would have been unable to fly through the wormholes due to his obsolete neural implants; his reflections on the limitations of this prospective existence resemble a disability narrative. Jesek's problem is psychological rather than physical, but his immobilizing fear renders him less physically capable than Miles in a fight. Furthermore, without Miles to give him a figurative "heart transplant" (*Warrior* 112) and a position of authority within the Dendarii, Jesek faces being sent back to Barrayar to be sentenced and executed.

Literary narratives often overlook the possibility of such bonds. Disability theorist Paul Longmore complains that some writers use physical impairment as a marker of difference, rather than being interested in exploring the actual experience of disability; the function of disability as a literary device in these narratives makes social integration impossible (5). David Mitchell and Sharon Snyder agree that in an effort to make a character stand out, writers often ascribe absolute singularity to disability, but this exceptionality denies him or her a shared social identity (55). For instance, Melville's Ahab is the sole physically impaired person on the *Pequod*, making him unusual among the able-bodied population (135). By contrast, disability scholars point out that all bodies, at some stage, are constituted by disability (Crutchfield 145): "Our bodies need care; we all need assistance to live. Every life evolves into disability, making it perhaps the essential characteristic of being human" (Garland-Thomson 524). Bujold similarly suggests that all men are disabled, in the sense that none can live up to the impossible masculine ideal. Yet she reveals the positive benefits for men who acknowledge this state of existence; awareness of physical and psychological limitations can encourage intimacy between men who rely on each other in order to achieve a convincing performance of masculinity. Miles, for instance, constructs a community of individuals who have been denied opportunities due to either a rigid social structure or perceived personal limitations. Elena says, "You make anything seem possible" (*Warrior* 145). Miles allows his followers to be more than tradition decrees and then challenges them to perform their way to a new identity.

Miles must reciprocate by performing for his followers. A cipher, he becomes whoever each one needs him to be. For Jesek, for instance, Miles plays the disinherited son of a Vor Lord who wanted his deformed son out of sight. Miles does not invent this story, but he does not correct it either, aware that these kinds of tales fill the gaps in his own performance and cement his followers' loyalty. Yet, although Miles's performance allows inaccurate assumptions — Jesek believes they share a bond based on mutual shame and exile — the empathy on which the bonds are based is real. Miles's capacity for empathy significantly reformulates the military ideal which insists a warrior should be indifferent to another person's pain. Miles knows instinctively that this is wrong and much of his military success stems from his ability to empathize, not only with his friends and followers, but also with his enemies, to imagine himself not only in their place but also in their bodies, as when he thinks himself into the skin of the fleeing Pelian captain.

Without question, Miles's most intimate relationship is with the psychologically-damaged Bothari. Before Miles was born, Bothari depended on Miles's parents to help him keep his psychological problems in check. *Shards of Honor* reveals the extent of his psychosis. "A real bona fide, paranoid schizophrenic" (101) who hears demons' voices, suffers visual hallucinations, and takes sadistic pleasure from inflicting pain, Bothari is almost ruined during the Escobaran War by the equally sadistic Admiral Ges Vorrutyer, who drugs Bothari and uses him as his personal torturer and rapist. Cordelia is an intended victim, but her empathy for Bothari as a mutual victim of Vorrutyer's depravity — empathy which also provides a model for Miles's reformulated warrior persona — inspires Bothari to kill Vorrutyer instead. In gratitude, Aral asks Count Piotr to employ Bothari in his personal guard. Aral was Bothari's commanding officer before Bothari served as Vorrutyer's batman, and he therefore knows that performing the role of a soldier — with uniforms and strict regulations to follow — will give Bothari the mental anchor he needs. Bothari, however, continues to struggle with his demons. In *Barrayar* he mutters to himself and cannot get out of bed for days at a time, his long-term psychosis now exacerbated by Barrayaran mind-therapy treatment designed to block his memory of killing Vorrutyer. This treatment involves psychoengineering his body so that it will punish any forbidden thoughts with crippling pain. Cordelia again provides a sympathetic and non-judgmental ear, so when she and Piotr clash over Miles's right to life, Bothari switches his allegiance to Cordelia and helps her rescue Miles in his uterine replicator from the enemy's stronghold. When Miles is born, Bothari is assigned to be his personal bodyguard.

Throughout his life, Bothari's psychological issues have been compounded by the shame of this birth: "Don't know who my father was. Being a bastard here is damn near as bad as being a mutant" (*Barrayar* 313). The son of a whore who sold him to her customers until he was twelve and big enough to beat them up and run away, Bothari is determined to secure a better life for his daughter, Elena. Therefore, as Miles's bodyguard, he strives daily to impersonate the noble and honorable Barrayaran ideal. Lacking the ability to judge appropriate behavior for himself, he relies on those around him to guide his performance. Aral observes, "He's a chameleon. A mirror. He becomes whatever is required of him" (358). Despite his sadistic impulses, Bothari wants to be a good and honorable man, so he clings to those — first Cordelia and then Miles — whose empathy allows them to look beyond his sadistic traits to require him to perform that role. As Aral explains to Cordelia in *Barrayar*, "[Y]ou are the only person I know who looks at Bothari and sees a hero. So he becomes one for you. He clings to you because you create him a greater man than he ever dreamed of being" (358).

In *The Warrior's Apprentice*, however, Bothari's world falls apart when Elena discovers that her mother, Elena Visconti, was another of Ges Vorrutyer's victims who was impregnated when Bothari raped her. Bothari had told Elena that he and her mother had been happily married. Bothari created this fantasy when he first met Elena Visconti and was desperate for redemption from the role of monster that Vorrutyer required him to play. Keeping the catatonic Elena in his cabin, he play-acted the role of loving husband, nursing and "making love" to her, and conducting whispered conversations in which he supplied both voices. The younger Elena discovers the truth when her mother, a new Dendarii recruit, confronts her tormenter from whom she has been estranged for almost two decades, kills him, and rejects her daughter. Devastated, the younger Elena condemns her father's performance as an honorable Barrayaran soldier: "[I]t was all *lies*. Faking glory, while all the time underneath was this — cesspit" (*Warrior* 228). Miles, however, understands it as Bothari's attempt to forge a new truth.

Acutely aware of his own self-conscious performance of the masculine military ideal, Miles empathizes with Bothari's efforts to recreate himself through performance. He also understands that as much as Bothari depended on Miles and his parents to direct and support his performance of the role of the loyal and upright Barrayaran soldier, Miles equally depended on Bothari; for instance, when Miles was fifteen Bothari stopped him from committing suicide. This interdependency carried over to the Dendarii context, where Bothari continued to compensate for Miles's tendency to treat his body as his enemy. Aware that his own performance as a loyal retainer depended on Miles remaining well enough to play the part of military leader and Vor Lord, Bothari insisted that Miles eat, drink, and sleep, when Miles would have continued to ignore his body's needs and limitations and run himself into the ground. Mutual awareness of the vulnerabilities that threaten each man's performance of masculinity signal an interdependency that can be compared to that of Vincent and Jerome in the science fiction film, *Gattaca* (1997). Jackie Stacey argues that Vincent and Jerome's interdependency required the improvisation of an intermasculine kinship with a distinctly queer feel (1855), and the same argument can be made for Miles and Bothari. Miles and Bothari's secret — that the Dendarii mercenaries were Miles's invention — depended on their mutual loyalty and devotion (1855). Stacey points out that sharing a space full of secrets that would put them at odds with society if discovered and which required their utter loyalty to each other in the project of passing evokes relations of the closet (1869). Although Miles and Bothari did not exchange bodily substances in the same way as Vincent and Jerome, Miles knew every minute variation of Bothari's voice.

A queer reading of this relationship is made more interesting by the fact that Miles's father, Aral Vorkosigan, is bisexual, though there is no indication that the intimacy between Miles and Bothari was of a sexual nature; furthermore, it is unlikely that Miles was aware of his father's sexual history. In *Barrayar*, a political rival tries to destroy Aral's marriage by telling Cordelia that Aral was once the lover of her torturer, Ges Vorrutyer. Cordelia already knew this from Vorrutyer, and in any case, as a Betan — a planet famed for its celebration of sexual variation — she is unperturbed. Barrayar is a much more conservative society and Aral's choice of the sadistic Vorrutyer as sexual partner heightens the sense of perversion. Aral has a self-destructive streak, and this seems to have at least partially motivated his relationship with Vorrutyer which began when Aral's first wife — Vorrutyer's sister — committed suicide after Aral killed her two lovers. Bujold hints, however, at Aral's genuine attraction to, and feeling for, Vorrutyer, and thus at the possibility of a more positive queer relationship, in the sketches Aral made of him as a young man.

Nonetheless, Barrayar remains a deeply conservative society in Miles's lifetime. In heteronormative societies, expressions of love and affection between men are usually muted in response to the demand for behavior which signals close friendship without sexual involvement (Buchbinder 38), and the potential for homoerotic intimacy is often disrupted by a third female term: "[M]ale-male desire [becomes] widely intelligible primarily by being routed through triangular relations involving a woman" (Eve Kosofsky Sedgwick qtd. Stacey 1870). Thus, Miles falls in love with Bothari's daughter; however his marriage proposal to Elena, coming soon after Bothari's death, encourages a queer interpretation: "I love you, I don't know what the Sergeant was but I loved him too, and whatever of him is in you I honor with all my heart [...] I can't live without my Bothari, marry me!" (*Warrior* 229). Kath Weston claims that "death becomes the terminus that marks the forever in a relationship" (qtd. Stacey 1869), and although Miles is upset by Elena's rejection of his proposal, his devotion to Bothari's memory is unwavering. When he places the seized Oseran payroll on Bothari's coffin which he keeps in his room, Miles's behavior far exceeds the norm for a Barrayaran military leader. Butler claims that awareness that gender is constructed opens up possibilities of agency that are foreclosed when gender is taken as foundational and fixed (*Gender* 147). Thus, Miles's awareness of masculinity as a performance frees him to reformulate the military leader ideal to encompass both empathy and such deeply intimate bonds between men.

Body Trouble

Miles's success in the role of Admiral Naismith is due both to these close empathetic bonds with his followers and to his own intellect, energy, determination, and belief in his ability to talk himself out of most situations. The successful conclusion of the battle for Tau Verde confirms Miles's performance as military leader, as does the reluctant admiration of a number of experienced mercenary leaders, many of whom are defeated by Miles before committing to serve under him in the Dendarii. Most of Miles's recruits are unaware of his Vorkosigan heritage. Chanting "Naismith," they celebrate Miles's constructed identity. Miles, however, is despondent: "My name isn't Naismith" (*Warrior* 278). He reflects, "Being Vor is [...] like wearing an invisible uniform you can never take off" (84); although he enjoys playing the part of Dendarii leader, he remains obsessed with proving to his father and late grandfather that he can successfully perform the role of *Barrayaran* military leader.

Bujold observes that Miles has "the worst case of Great Man's Son Syndrome you ever saw" ("Interview" 9). When he is sedated, suffering a bleeding ulcer, Miles hallucinates that his grandfather smothers him with a pillow and hides him under the bed. In his delirious state, he waits eagerly for his father to appear on the Dendarii ship so that he can impress him with his cleverness, and weeps bitterly when Aral fails to materialize. Smith notes the significance of Miles's dagger as a symbol of his Vorkosigan heritage. Dating back several generations and passed on to Miles by his grandfather, the dagger promises to masculinize Miles (258). When Miles wears the dagger he feels "warmed, as by an old man's handclasp" (*Warrior* 197), and when he finally returns to Barrayar and is admitted to the Imperial Service, another cadet's admiration of this obviously phallic symbol — the same cadet who previously expressed discomfort about the potential contagion of Miles's "disease" — signifies Miles's achievement: "That, ah, — blade of yours came in pretty handy after all" (*Warrior* 311; see also Smith 259).

Bujold, however, problematizes Miles's unwavering dedication to the Barrayaran ideal of military masculinity by exposing its costs. This ideal requires men to ignore or deny their bodily limitations, and Miles transfers this demand to the Dendarii context. He hides the fact that he is throwing up blood, afraid that it will jeopardize his performance as Admiral Naismith, which he believes is already tenuous as a result of his other physical limitations. His silence almost costs him his life. Nor is Miles the only male victim of the Barrayar system. In *Shards of Honor* Cordelia is highly critical: "Barrayar eats its children" (145). She observes that Aral is nearly psychologically and emotionally destroyed by the role the Emperor requires him to play in the Escobaran War, a role that transforms him from a man of honor into an accomplice to political assassination of the Emperor's son. This plot also results in the collateral deaths of five thousand innocent people. By the time the war ends, Cordelia has stopped looking at the Barrayarans as enemies, seeing them rather as "assorted victims, variously blind" (*Barrayar* 18). Stacey argues that *Gattaca* positions its audience to recognize the problems of the system that Vincent aspires to be part of (1861); Bujold similarly positions her readers to be dubious about Miles's desire to achieve hegemonic masculinity as defined by a social system that inflicts such significant physical and psychological costs.

Although Miles fails to critique this system, his recalcitrant body refuses hegemonic Barrayaran masculinity's unrealistic demands. Butler points out that "bodies never quite comply with the norms by which their materialization is impelled" (*Bodies* 2), and Bernice Hausman agrees on the importance of acknowledging the body as more than a passive surface upon which culture is written: "we [...] need to recognize the body as a system that asserts a certain resistance to (or constraint upon) the ideology system regulating it" (qtd. Hird and Germon 174). Stable gender identity is predicated on the stability of the body (Hendershot 373), but Miles's body is constantly breaking down. It disrupts his performance of the warrior just as he is about to lead an attack on the spaceship carrying the Oseran payroll. Doubled over in pain and throwing up blood before passing out completely, Miles has no choice but to acknowledge his body and abandon — at least temporarily — his impossible quest for the Barrayaran military identity.

Miles's body further disrupts the Barrayaran definition of hegemonic masculinity by its indeterminate status. Neither clearly representative of the Barrayaran ideal, nor definitively other — courtesy of his social standing as a Vor Lord — Miles troubles the binaries upon which his social system is based. His successful performance as Dendarii Admiral destabilizes the able/disabled body dichotomy which insists that physically-impaired bodies are unproductive and incapable of commanding power or respect (Smith 253). This prejudice is not limited to Barrayarans, and Captain Auson — an Oseran mercenary captain — pays for underestimating Miles by losing his ship and (temporarily) his command. By contrast, the officer who initially contracts Miles and his companions to smuggle arms, comes to believe that Miles is in fact very old, that his body has been damaged in the course of battle, and that he is on his way to Beta colony for rejuvenation treatment. Once again, Miles allows this story, inspired by his unusual appearance and indeterminate age, to fill the gaps in his performance as an experienced mercenary commander.

Miles's indeterminate status has encouraged some critics to read him as codedly feminine. Although Miles is physically male, Bujold reflects on how her own experiences as a woman may have inflected his characterization: "[H]e's smarter than those around him, can't win a physical fight, is in a 'wrong' shaped body — has lots of medical problems — and has to beat the 'bastards' using only brains, wit, and charm" ("Interview" 10). Although he holds to the old-fashioned opinion that women should not fight on the front line, Miles empathizes with Elena, who has been oppressed by the patriarchal Barrayaran system, and assigns her a position of high authority with the Dendarii. Miles's affinity with women is made evident when he dons a woman's space suit, the only one small enough to fit his slight frame. Though space suits are largely unisex, Miles comments on the suit's female "plumbing" (*Warrior* 194).

As a figure who exhibits affinities with both women and damaged men, Miles also reformulates the classic science fiction stereotype of the space opera hero (Smith 260). Joanna Russ describes the space opera "He Man" as invulnerable. He has no weaknesses, is sexually super-potent, self-sufficient, and does what he pleases when he pleases. He is protective, possessive, and patronizing to women; he gives orders to men. He is never frightened or indecisive and he always wins (136–37). As Virginia Bemis notes, Miles is clever, nobly born, friend of Emperors and saver of planets, a daring leader of space armies (20). In *The Warrior's Apprentice*, Miles repeatedly wins against all odds and he takes advantage of his status as Vor Lord to do what he wants when he wants, such as boarding and then buying Mayhew's spaceship and expecting Bothari and the rest of his inner circle to follow him, even when he leads them into mortal danger. Miles's physical weaknesses, however, are obvious and many, and Elena not only rejects his offer of marriage, but also outmachos him by leading the attack on the Pelians when Miles is incapacitated (Smith 257–58). Furthermore, it is Miles's interdependent bonds, particularly with other "damaged" men, and his insight into others' emotions and motivations, rather than an idealized self-sufficiency, which allow him to play the space opera hero.

These bonds spare Miles some of the costs that Russ sees endured by the traditional space opera warrior. She argues that the traditional hero is a lonely man; although he can be fond of people, no one can be tender to him as that would signal dependence (140–41). Miles never completely shakes the feeling that he has failed as a hero; however, Bujold shows that he has the potential to construct an alternative heroism. Miles's ability to reformulate the warrior role is significant given that disability narratives generally imagine either that agency is precluded by physical impairment, or that it motivates revenge on the able-bodied world (Mitchell and Snyder 127; Shakespeare 287; Longmore 3). Miles's positive action to "create his own identity in a world set on supplying him with a lesser one" ("Interview" 9) rejects this "mutilated-avenger motif" (Mitchell and Snyder 97).

Conclusion

In comparison to the reliance pattern, Gerschick and Miller see reformulation of hegemonic masculinity as a more constructive and empowering strategy for physically-impaired men. They observe, however, that reformulation tends to be an independent project which is heavily dependent on class-based resources (203). Indeed, in *The Warrior's Apprentice*, Miles is uniquely positioned, in that his privilege and wealth opens up in the space wherein he can test out and reformulate both the meaning and significance of his physical limitations and the parameters of the military leader ideal. Other men lack the resources needed to create similar opportunities, as evidenced by Mayhew's state of drunken despair when he believes his spaceship is destined for the scrap heap. Miles's action to save Mayhew demonstrates, however, that empathy may motivate socially-privileged men to use their resources to empower others, creating a community of "broken" men (and women) bonded together by mutual awareness of vulnerability, and supporting each other to exceed through performance the limitations imposed both by society and by their own fears and assumptions.

Gerschick and Miller express further concern that reformulation of the hegemonic ideal by individual men presents little real challenge to the gender order (203). Miles's personal transformation is enacted off-planet. While this allows him the space in which to undertake his reformulated performance of the military leader role, it ultimately has little impact on his own society, as he acknowledges on his return to Barrayar when he observes a guard's fingers twitching into a sign intended to ward off mutants. Nonetheless, by asserting his right to be admitted into the Barrayaran Imperial Service by virtue of his military performance with the Dendarii, Miles forces his society to reassess both its narrow definition of the military leader ideal which excludes the physically impaired, and its understanding of disability and mutation.

Miles does not consider the rejection strategy. He understands that he has to reformulate the warrior ideal in order to approximate a hegemonic performance, but accepts as natural the Barrayaran valorization of this identity. Nevertheless, Miles's acute awareness of masculinity as a performance allows him to reformulate the warrior persona to encompass traits and behaviors that exceed the Barrayaran military norm. Although Miles was raised to aspire to the Barrayaran ideal, his Betan mother, supported and protected by his open-minded Barrayaran father, critiqued the system and offered an alternative model for Miles to draw upon. The impact of his mother's influence is most evident in his capacity for empathy, which forms the basis of the intimate interdependent bonds which contribute to Miles's success as Admiral Naismith. Miles's successful, self-aware performance requires readers to reformulate their understanding of the space opera hero, just as it challenges his own society to reassess its assumptions.

Miles's effort to overcome Barrayaran prejudice becomes a life-long project. In "The Mountains of Mourning," next in the chronology of the *Vorkosigan Saga*, Aral challenges Miles, recently graduated from the Imperial Service Academy, to continue his project of challenging hegemonic attitudes to disability and mutation, by sending him to Silvy Vale, a remote Barrayaran mountain village, to investigate the murder of a "mutie" baby who was born with a severe harelip and cleft palate. The baby's grieving father insists that Barrayar needs Miles to go on fighting such injustice and to continue to show others that physical impairment is no bar to a productive life. Inspired once again by empathy and drawing on his experiences in *The Warrior's Apprentice*, Miles pledges himself as a reformulated hero for the weak and vulnerable of Barrayar: "*You've won a twisted poor modern knight*[...]. *But it's a twisted poor world* [...] *that rejects us without mercy and ejects us without consultation.* [...] He knew who he served now. And why he could not quit. And why he must not fail" (464).

WORKS CITED

Bemis, Virginia T. "Barrayar's Ugliest Child: Miles Vorkosigan." *Kaleidoscope* 34 (1997): 20–22.

Buchbinder, David. *Masculinities and Identities*. Carlton, Victoria: Melbourne University Press, 1994.

Bujold, Lois McMaster. *Barrayar*. Riverdale, NY: Baen, 1991.

———. "An Interview with Lois McMaster Bujold." Michael M. Levy, interviewer. *Kaleidoscope* 34 (1997): 6–19.

———. "The Mountains of Mourning." 1989. In *Young Miles*. Riverdale, NY: Baen, 2003. 373–464.

———. *Shards of Honor*. 1986. Framingham, MA: The NESFA Press, 2003.

———. *The Warrior's Apprentice*. Riverdale, NY: Baen, 1986.

Butler, Judith P. *Bodies That Matter: On the Discursive Limits of "Sex."* New York: Routledge, 1993.

———. *Gender Trouble: Feminism and the Subversion of Identity*. New York: Routledge, 1990.

Cranny-Francis, Anne. "The Erotics of the (Cy)Borg: Authority and Gender in the Sociocultural Imaginary." *Future Females, the Next Generation: New Voices and Velocities in Feminist Science Fiction Criticism*. Marleen S. Barr, ed. Lanham, MD: Rowman & Littlefield, 2000. 145–63.

Crutchfield, Susan. "The Noble Ruined Body: Blindness and Visual Prosthetics in Three Science Fiction Films." *Screening Disability: Essays on Cinema and Disability*. Christopher R. Smit and Anthony Enns, eds. Lanham, MD: University Press of America, 2001. 135–50.

Garland-Thomson, Rosemarie. "Disability and Representation." *PMLA* 120.2 (March 2005): 522–27.

Gattaca. Dir. and Writ. Andrew Niccol. Perf. Ethan Hawke, Uma Thurman and Jude Law. Colombia Pictures, 1997.

Gerschick, Thomas J., and Adam S. Miller. "Coming to Terms: Masculinity and Physical Disability." *Men's Health and Illness: Gender, Power, and the Body*. Donald Sabo and David Frederick Gordon, eds. Thousand Oaks: Sage, 1995. 183–204.

Hendershot, Cyndy. "Vampire and Replicant: The One-Sex Body in a Two-Sex World." *Science-Fiction Studies* 22 (1995): 373–98.

Hird, Myra J., and Jenz Germon. "The Intersexual Body and the Medical Regulation of Gender." *Constructing Gendered Bodies*. Kathryn Backett-Milburn and Linda McKie, eds. Basingstoke: Palgrave, 2001. 162–78.

Hollinger, Veronica. "(Re)reading Queerly: Science Fiction, Feminism, and the Defamiliarization of Gender." *Reload: Rethinking Women and Cyberculture.* Mary Flanagan and Austin Booth, eds. Cambridge: Massachusetts Institute of Technology, 2002. 301–20.

Kleiber, Douglas A., and Susan M. Hutchinson. "Heroic Masculinity in the Recovery from Spinal Cord Injury." *Talking Bodies.* Andrew C. Sparkes and Martti Silvennoinen, eds. Jyväskylä: SoPhi, University of Jyväskylä, 1999. 135–55.

Longmore, Paul K. "Screening Stereotypes: Images of Disabled People." *Screening Disability: Essays on Cinema and Disability.* Christopher R. Smit and Anthony Enns, eds. Lanham, MD: University Press of America, 2001. 1–17.

Mitchell, David T., and Sharon L. Snyder. *Narrative Prosthesis: Disability and the Dependencies of Discourse.* Ann Arbor: University of Michigan Press, 2000.

O'Neill, Terry, and Myra J. Hird. "Double Damnation: Gay Disabled Men and the Negotiation of Masculinity." *Constructing Gendered Bodies.* Kathryn Backett-Milburn and Linda McKie, eds. Basingstoke: Palgrave, 2001. 204–23.

Russ, Joanna. "Alien Monsters." *Turning Points: Essays on the Art of Science Fiction.* 1969. Damon Knight, ed. New York: Harper and Row, 1977. 132–43.

Shakespeare, Tom. "Cultural Representations of Disabled People: Dustbins for Disavowal?" *Disability and Society* 9.3 (1994): 283–99.

Smith, Susan Ursula Anne. "Shifting (A)Genders: Gender, Disability and the Cyborg in American Women's Science Fiction." Ph.D. Thesis. University of Leicester, 2010.

Stacey, Jackie. "Masculinity, Masquerade, and Genetic Impersonation: *Gattaca's* Queer Visions." *Signs: Journal of Women in Culture and Society* 30.3 (2005): 1851–77.

Difference and Ability

Conceptualizing Bodily Variation in the Vorkosigan Series

SHANNAN PALMA

Rosemarie Garland-Thomson defines one of the central premises of feminist disability theory as re-conceptualizing disability as "a cultural interpretation of human variation rather than an inherent inferiority, a pathology to cure, or an undesirable trait to eliminate. In other words, it finds disability's significance in interactions between bodies and their social and material environments" ("Feminist" 1557). Lois McMaster Bujold's Vorkosigan series explores a range of the bodily and mental variations commonly labeled disability or illness. The number and variety of differently-abled characters appearing throughout the Vorkosigan books allows the portrayal of individuals to remain idiosyncratic rather than to become symbolic of disability in general. As the affected characters travel throughout their universe, the cultural interpretations of their variations shift dramatically. Using Garland-Thomson's concept of *misfitting* as a liberatory epistemic position, I perform close readings of several differently-abled characters, including Bothari, Miles and Mark Vorkosigan, and Taura, and their relationship to place.

The Vorkosigan books are a science fiction series primarily centered on Miles Naismith Vorkosigan, a complex man determined to live up to a family legacy of military and political service to his emperor. Two books in the series revolve around his parents' romance and his own birth; a third addresses the creation and subsequent flight of the Quaddies, a genetically-engineered people whose descendants cross path with Miles centuries later; and a fourth chronicles an early side-adventure of Miles's friend and sometime-lover Elli Quinn. The rest of the series centers on Miles, with occasional diversions to follow his friends and family. Cultural background and context are extremely important within the series, as characters are constantly coming into contact with others whose assumed values and prejudices are different from their own. This interaction between bodies, minds, and places further unsettles literary stereotypes of mental and physical disabilities by emphasizing the breadth and possibility of human variation.

134

Miles grows up on the planet Barrayar surrounded by people who are somewhat larger than life. His father Aral is a military strategist par excellence. Before Miles's birth, Aral successfully defeats an imperial coup and agrees to take on the position of Lord Regent until the child heir reaches majority. Aral's most shocking political maneuver occurs when he steps down and lets the boy-emperor take over when it's time. Aral's father Piotr similarly had a long history of service to Barrayar. The Vorkosigans are of the Vor class, warrior-aristocrats who owe protection to their subordinates and allegiance to their emperor, and they take this legacy very seriously. Miles's mother, on the other hand, is an off-worlder who believes Barrayar's Vor system is a dangerous planetwide delusion (*The Vor Game* [*Game*] 818). Cordelia Naismith's Betan sensibilities are more cosmopolitan. She prefers a state that ensures the basic needs of its people are met without regard to their status, a system of morality that proffers no judgments as long as all parties are consenting, and a culture of respect for science and rationality over tradition. When Cordelia and Barrayar come into conflict, it is Barrayar that changes (*Brothers in Arms* [*Brothers*] 117).

While pregnant with Miles, Cordelia is exposed to a toxic gas. Barrayar spent many centuries cut off from the rest of the galaxy, and its traditions regarding "mutants"—children born with any kind of physical abnormality—are deadly. The damage to the fetus's bones and tissues is such that everyone expects Cordelia to abort, but she chooses treatment instead. Barrayaran prejudice against mutation is so strong that Piotr attempts to murder his grandson twice.[1] From birth onward, Miles has a bodyguard, his fourth larger-than-life role model, his father's armsman, Sergeant Konstantine Bothari.

Bothari appears in only three of the Vorkosigan books,[2] but his presence is felt in all of them. Aral Vorkosigan first mentions Bothari by name while trying to figure out the logistics of (yet another) failed assassination attempt. He realizes that his enemies must have assumed his armsman would be on their side and not counted him their opponent in the coup. Bothari hates him, Aral tells Cordelia, but would never stab him in the back. His subsequent summary of Bothari's character is both utterly accurate and ridiculously oversimplified: "I can't pretend he's a moral or intellectual giant. He's a very complex man with a very limited range of expression, who's had some very bad experiences. But in his own twisty way, he's honorable" (*Shards of Honor* [*Shards*] 46). A paranoid schizophrenic, Bothari's psychosis is alternately exacerbated and moderated by his environment. Initially terrified of the man, Cordelia comes to view him as her double—they are "two personalities separately but equally crippled by an overdose of Barrayar" (*Barrayar* 497). Ironically, Bothari's madness later becomes Miles's genius and Mark's salvation, as a similar sort of mental splitting occurs within each man as he copes with the ways he misfits.

Bothari's known crimes include rape, and possibly murder. He suffers from auditory and visual hallucinations (*Shards* 112). In *Shards of Honor*, the book where Cordelia and Aral meet and fall in love despite being on opposite sides of a war, Bothari is initially stable, if still dangerous. However, politics transfer Bothari into the service of the sadist Vorrutyer. When Cordelia becomes Vorrutyer's prisoner of war, she finds Bothari much changed.

> His body — it was all wrong, somehow, hunched in his black uniform, not like the straight figure she had last seen demanding pride of place from Vorkosigan. Wrong, wrong, terribly wrong. A head taller than Vorrutyer, yet he seemed almost to creep before his master. His spine was coiled with tension as he glowered down at his — torturer? What, she wondered, might a mind molester like Vorrutyer do with the material presented by Bothari? [...] Her thoughts kept time with her racing pulse. There are two victims in this room. There are two victims in this room. There are two ... [*Shards* 113].

Cordelia's perception of Bothari as her fellow victim as opposed to her enemy allows her to reach him. Instead of raping her, he slits Vorrutyer's throat, an act of treason that could get him executed. In the aftermath, Aral and Cordelia protect him, and in order to protect the secret and to restore him to some measure of sanity, Imperial Security erases his memories of the event.

Bothari knows something is wrong with his memory and fights the conditioning despite extreme pain. His piecemeal memories horrify him. He knows he made at least one positive moral choice when he saved Cordelia's life, but he doesn't remember how he made that choice and so doesn't trust his ability to repeat it. He asks Cordelia to be his conscience, to let him know when his desire for violence is safely contained under the rubric of acceptable service. Though extremely reluctant to take on that kind of responsibility for another, Cordelia realizes Bothari's need for an external control on his actions: "That's why your uniform is so important to you, isn't it? It tells you when it's all right. When you can't tell yourself. All those rigid routines you keep to, they're to tell you you're all right, on track" (*Barrayar* 354). After his experiences with Vorrutyer, Bothari worries that the uniform is no longer enough.

David Mitchell and Sharon Snyder contend that representation of disability in literature generally falls into two categories of narrative prosthesis — first, as "a stock feature of characterization," a common way to differentiate or motivate a character — so common as to be cliché; second, as a "metaphorical signifier of social and individual collapse" (205). The difficulty with both trends, they argue, is that "while stories rely upon the potency of disability as a symbolic figure, they rarely take up disability as an experience of social or political dimensions" (205). Bothari could so easily have been written as the embodiment of Barrayar's toxic infighting, the narrative prosthesis through which Bujold manifested her world-building; however, his portrayal is never so simple. His relationship to Barrayar is as much literal as metaphorical, and it is one that he chooses to purposefully upset. When Barrayaran politics manipulate his illness and steal his only memories of making good choices, he acknowledges his own mutability and chooses his own off-world container for it. He removes control of his psychosis from Barrayar's grip.

Aral later observes,

> Bothari ... does not have a good sense of self. No strong center. When I first met him, at his most ill, his personality was close to separating into multiples. If he were better educated, not so damaged, he would have made an ideal spy, a deep-penetration mole. He's a chameleon. A mirror. He becomes whatever is required of him. Not a conscious process, I don't think. Piotr expects a loyal retainer, and Bothari plays the part, deadpan as you please. Vorrutyer wanted a monster, and Bothari became his torturer. And victim. I demanded a good soldier, and he became one for me. You [...] you are the only person I know who looks at Bothari and sees a hero. So he becomes one for you. He clings to you because you create him a greater man than he ever dreamed of being [*Barrayar* 566].

Years later, Bothari is killed by an Escobaran woman he raped while in Vorrutyer's service. As Barrayaran sensibilities encourage his violence and Betan ones acknowledge his victimhood, so Escobar's demand his accountability. His intervening years of loyal service to the Vorkosigans, his decision to save Cordelia and give his conscience over to her keeping, none of these override the fact of his past violation of another. His impairments do not make his crimes acceptable. Miles grieves his bodyguard's death without confusing the geography of his relationship to Bothari with that of Bothari's executioner.

> "Admiral Naismith, I apologize for inconveniencing you. But this was no murder. It was the just execution of a war criminal. It was just," she insisted, her voice edged with passion. "It was." Her voice fell away.
> It was no murder, it was a suicide, Miles thought. He could have shot you where you stood at any time, he was that fast. "No..."
> Her lips thinned in despair. "You call me a liar too? Or are you going to tell me I enjoyed it?"
> "No..." He looked up at her across a vast gulf, one meter wide. "I don't mock you. But — until I was four, almost five years old, I couldn't walk, only crawl. I spent a lot of time looking at people's knees. But if there was ever a parade, or something to see, I had the best view of anybody because I watched it from on top the Sergeant's shoulder" [*The Warrior's Apprentice* (*Warrior*) 265–6].

In Bujold's universe, the social and political relationships among bodies change according to each character's contextual relationship to society and politics. The location of events, the cultural and personal baggage each individual brings to each interaction — all of these things *matter*. Instead of narrative prosthesis as a hermeneutic lens, we might more aptly turn to Rosemarie Garland-Thomson's epistemology of the misfit.

> *Fitting* and *misfitting* denote an encounter in which two things come together in either harmony or disjunction. When the shape and substance of these two things correspond in their union, they fit. A *misfit*, conversely, describes an incongruent relationship between two things: a square peg in a round hole. The problem with a misfit, then, inheres not in either of the two things but rather in their juxtaposition, the awkward attempt to fit them together. When the spatial and temporal context shifts, so does the fit, and with it meanings and consequences. Misfit emphasizes context over essence, relation over isolation, mediation over origination. Misfits are inherently unstable rather than fixed, yet they are very real because they are material rather than linguistic constructions. The discrepancy between body and world, between that which is expected and that which is, produces fits and misfits [Garland-Thomson, "Misfits" 592–593].

Bothari thrives in Cordelia and Miles's service because they create the right fit for him. "*Fit,* then, suggests a generally positive way of being and positioning based on an absence of conflict and a state of correct synchronization with one's circumstances" ("Misfits" 593). As Aral points out, Bothari's mind isn't strong enough to sustain itself, so he chooses the mirror he likes best and molds himself to that image. Bothari's coping mechanism for dealing with Barrayar's scars on his psyche prefigures Miles's later adoption of a Betan alterego who is similarly disentangled from Barrayaran prejudices.

The treatment for the poison gas Miles is exposed to *in utero* leaves him with brittle bones and diminished, disproportionate stature. He is quick to point out to anyone who will listen that the damage is only teratogenic, affecting his body, but not his chromosomes. His words disrupt the common literary trope of the disabled body as a "deficiency [that] inaugurates the need for a story but is quickly forgotten once the difference is established" (Mitchell and Snyder 210). The first time we see Miles in *The Warrior's Apprentice*, his reluctance to look weak in front of his peers causes him to take one risk too many, and he breaks both legs. His plans to join the Barrayaran Imperial Military Service are completely derailed, setting off a course of events that eventually leads to his creation of the aforementioned Betan alter-ego, Admiral Naismith. However, Miles's body does not inaugurate the story and disappear. It is a constant factor in his decisions and actions. He never forgets that he is more breakable than most, but his primary weakness is the limitations put on him by his culture and class, not his physical frailty. Neither is his body a question that must be answered or explained. The backstory of its peculiarities is simply that — backstory.

As Naismith, Miles acquires the Dendarii Mercenary Fleet and turns them into Barrayar's secret irregular military. He is a military genius, a famed trickster, a worthy adversary. Unlike Miles, who is constantly struggling to prove himself against charges of nepotism because of his father and his physique, Naismith has no family legacy to live up to. Naismith's origins are mysterious. He has a Betan accent, but does not appear to be from Beta Colony. He is a clone, probably from Jackson's Whole, but no one at Jackson's Whole claims to have made him. The Barrayarans suspect he is a Cetagandan creation — a relic of a discarded assassination plot against Aral. Later, Miles discovers his lies have more truth than he would like when a cloned assassin does try to take his place, but the appearance of a real clone-brother as a part of a Komarran plot only helps obfuscate Naismith's cover further. The point, of course, is that Naismith is free where Miles is most bound. He has no home to try to fit into and need only be himself. The Dendarii take their shape from him.

The overriding question for Miles's friends and family and even eventually for Miles himself is which persona he will ultimately choose to maintain. He is not schizoid. This split in personality is not a consequence of a psychic break. It is a split brought on by Miles's inability to be fully himself within the confines of Barrayar's expectations. While his service through the Dendarii earns him a spot in the Barrayaran military, his exploits are all classified. As Lieutenant Vorkosigan, he is limited by his low status within the military hierarchy. As Lord Vorkosigan, he is limited by how his actions might be used against his father. As Naismith, he has no limits — other than those allegiances he chooses to carry over from his other identities. He begins to slip when arguing with superior officers. He tells one supervisor, "'It's just ... things got too important for me to go on playing ensign when the man who was needed was Lord Vorkosigan.' *Or Admiral Naismith*" (*Game* 824). And in a conversation with another, he pleads,

> "Dammit, sir, what would you have of me? The Dendarii are as much Barrayaran troops as any who wear the Emperor's uniform, even if they don't know it. They are my assigned charge. I cannot neglect their urgent needs even to play the part of Lieutenant Vorkosigan."
>
> Galeni rocked back in his chair, his eyebrows shooting up. "*Play the part* of Lieutenant Vorkosigan? Who do you think you *are?*"
>
> "I'm..." Miles fell silent, seized by a sudden vertigo, like falling down a defective lift tube. For a dizzy moment, he could not even make sense of the question. The silence lengthened.

Galeni folded his hands on his desk with an unsettled frown. His voice went mild. "Lose track, did you?"

"I'm..." Miles's hands opened helplessly [*Brothers* 79].

The Dendarii provide a sustaining environment. They allow him to thrive. However, they do not teach him to value his life. While rescuing his clone-brother, Mark, Miles is shot and killed. Though he is frozen and revived, he suffers periodic seizures thereafter. Fearing that the Barrayaran military will shut down his cover, Miles lies and conceals the seizures. His deception leaves the object of a Dendarii rescue mission crippled. Miles is discharged from the military in disgrace. Almost everyone — even his mother — expects him to abandon Barrayar for good and become Naismith for real. He considers it.

Maybe Admiral Naismith was the real one, Lord Vorkosigan put on like a mask. Naismith's flat Betan accent fell so trippingly from his tongue. Vorkosigan's Barrayaran gutturals seemed to require an increasingly conscious effort, anymore. Naismith was so easy to slip into, Vorkosigan so painful [*Memory* 38].

However, Barrayar gives something that the Dendarii simply cannot. Barrayar gives him a purpose larger than himself. When Miles comes up against the Barrayaran perception of his body, he accepts the importance of his status as symbol, even as he refuses to live a life that is *merely* symbolic. Early in his career, he acts as adjudicator for a murder investigation on his father's lands. The victim, Raina, is an infant with a cleft palate. His own family history helps him to figure out that the child was killed by her grandmother. During the denouement, the enraged old woman reveals she had previously killed two of her own babies and had two others who died at birth because of mutations. She screams at Miles,

You [...] *you* are the worst. All I went through, all I did, all the grief, and you come along at the end. A mutie made lord over us all, and all the rules changed, betrayed at the end by an off-worlder woman's weakness. You make it all for *nothing*. Hate you. Dirty mutie ... ["The Mountains of Mourning" (Mountains) 89].

Miles vows to Raina that he will change Barrayar for her and those like her who have no voice (Mountains 100). He has no illusions about what this kind of service means.

"You are doing something for us every minute. Mutie lord. Do you think you are invisible?"

Miles grinned wolfishly. "Oh, Karal, I'm a one-man band, I am. I'm a parade."

"As you say, just so. Ordinary people need extraordinary examples. So they

can say to themselves, well, if he can do *that*, I can surely do *this*. No
excuses."

"No quarter, yes, I know that game. Been playing it all my life."

"I think," said Karal. "Barrayar needs you. To go on being just what you
are."

"Barrayar will eat me, if it can" [Mountains 92–93].

After his dismissal from military service, Miles returns to Raina's grave in an
effort to find meaning. He asks himself, "Had he got so wound up with playing Naismith, and with winning that game, that he'd forgotten what he was
playing for? Raina was one prisoner Naismith would never rescue, down
underground these ten years" (*Memory* 145).

Rosemarie Garland-Thomson proposes that misfitting can be a generative
epistemological stance.

> The moral understandings, subjugated knowledge, or ethical fitting that can
> emerge from what might be called socially conscious, or even theoretically
> mediated, misfitting can yield innovative perspectives and skills in adapting to
> changing and challenging environments. Acquiring or being born with the
> traits we call disabilities fosters an adaptability and resourcefulness that often
> is underdeveloped in those whose bodies fit smoothly into the prevailing, sus-
> taining environment ["Misfits" 604].

If Miles had been born the perfect Vor, his brilliance and class stature might
just as easily have damaged his father's ambitions for reform as helped them.
One can only imagine the threat he would have posed to the emperor, regardless of intent. As a misfit, however, his very existence changes his world.

In "The Mountains of Mourning," Miles tells a story that serves as an
apt metaphor. He says when he was a child, he helped his grandfather foal a
horse, and his grandfather made him hold the horse in his lap because thereafter the horse would always believe that Miles was the bigger of the two.
Similarly, Miles grows up believing that Barrayaran prejudices are more powerful than his own abilities. Naismith proves to him that it's not his abilities
that limit him, it's the way he relates to Barrayar, but only after Naismith is
gone is Miles willing to apply what he's learned. When he begins to relate to
Barrayar differently, when he fully embraces being Raina's champion by bringing the full force of his personality to his life as Lord Vorkosigan, Miles begins
to thrive in an integrated way. His cousin tells him, "You're acting just like
you do when you play Admiral Naismith, except without the Betan accent.
Full tilt forward, no inhibitions, innocent bystanders scramble for their lives"
(*Memory* 235). Miles hadn't even noticed.

Though Miles does eventually lose his way as Naismith, the community
of misfits he forms in the Dendarii is in no way a betrayal of his oath to

Raina. Consider Taura, a young woman he rescues from Jackson's Whole and incorporates into the fleet. Taura is conceived as part of a scientific experiment, an attempt to create a super-soldier by committee ("Labyrinth" 137). Miles is told that she is dangerous mistake, a creature with animal as well as human DNA that needs to be put down. He takes on the job without questioning the description. When he is captured and caged with her, it takes him a little while to realize his mistake. His first impressions of her are animalistic, a consequence of the dungeon environment in which she's been starved and imprisoned.

> The huge rippling shadow struck out of nowhere, at incredible speed. It grabbed the rat by its tail and swung it squealing against a pillar, dashing out its brains with a crunch. A flash of a thick claw-like fingernail, and the white furry body was ripped open from sternum to tail. Frantic fingers peeled the skin away from the rat's body as blood splattered. Miles first saw the fangs as they bit and tore and buried themselves in the rat's tissues [156–7].

Taura, he learns, has an IQ of 135 (161). She was raised in foster care until she was eight, then sent to live in a lab. She is the only one left of her kind. All the others died because of their over-amped metabolisms. Her animality — her claws, her extreme height — over eight feet, her ridged brow and fangs — overrides her humanity for her creators. They see her as less than human, a freak. Her creator attempts to have her killed because he doesn't think her life could possibly be worth living:

> "How free can she ever be, in that body, driven by that metabolism, that face — a freak's life — better to die painlessly, than to have all that suffering inflicted on her —"
> Miles spoke through his teeth. With emphasis. "No. It's. Not" [193].

Taura's experiences in the lab and in her imprisonment have taught her that people lie all the time. When Miles realizes that she is a person and not the mindless monster he was led to believe, he lies to her, too, and tells her that he's come to rescue her and recruit her for the Dendarii. She asks him to prove his good intentions by having sex with her. Miles notes later that she chose a good test. The body can't lie. In order to have sex with her, he has to see her as a woman. When revealing his deception about his reasons for seeking her out, Miles asks Taura what she wants. She says she wants to be normal.

> "I can't give you what I don't possess myself," he said at length. The words seemed to lie in inadequate lumps between them. He roused himself to a better effort. "No. Don't wish that. I have a better idea. Wish to be yourself. To the hilt. Find out what you're best at, and develop it. Hopscotch your weaknesses. There isn't time for them. [...] [T]ell me what 'normal' is, and why I

should give a damn for it. Look at me, if you will. Should I kill myself trying to overcome men twice my weight and reach in unarmed combat, or should I shift the ground to where their muscle is useless, 'cause it never gets close enough to apply its strength? I haven't got *time* to lose, and neither have you" [209–10].

The foundation of Miles's leadership style is giving people the vision to see themselves as they want to be and then giving them the space and opportunity to realize that vision. Taura chooses to join the Dendarii. She finds her fit among the misfits: "She was life-relishing, experience-devouring, living in an eternal Now, and for very good reasons" (*Memory* 32). She and Miles remain occasional lovers for the rest of his time as Naismith, and he comes to love her, thought he never acknowledges her publicly as his lover (*Memory* 35). In some ways, Miles is no more free of prejudice than anyone else.[3] This self-awareness is another reason not to give up on Barrayar. Misfitting is inevitable, even in relation to one's own ideals. It is "the essential characteristic of being human" (Garland-Thomson, "Misfits" 603).

Miles's devotion to Barrayar, his determination to be Raina's champion, could easily slide back into the mold of narrative prosthesis were it not for his double, his clone-brother Mark Pierre. Mark is commissioned and raised by Komarran rebels seeking to assassinate Aral Vorkosigan. As a product of Jackson's Whole, Mark grows up watching his fellow clones used as organ donors or replacement bodies for the wealthy and unscrupulous. His owners take over his care and training only to torture him for years. Since the damage to Miles's body is a product of poison and not, as he is so quick to point out, genetic, Mark's body would have developed to look very different. Mark's is thus sculpted intentionally to match Miles's shorter frame. His body is created so that his head appears overlarge. His bones are broken and replaced to match Miles's injuries. In the course of Miles's adventures with the Dendarii, a lot of bones get broken.

Raised to hate the Vorkosigans almost as much as he hates his makers, Mark is shocked when Miles reacts to discovering the plot against his family by embracing Mark as one of them. Under Betan law — meaning in Cordelia's eyes and thus in Miles's — the men are brothers. Mark is even more perplexed when Miles won't back down on the issue and seems to show a genuine interest in Mark's future.

If backward benighted Barrayar doesn't appeal to you, there's a whole 'nother life waiting on Beta Colony, to which Barrayar and all its troubles is scarcely a wrinkle on the event horizon. Your cloned origin wouldn't be novel enough to be worth mentioning, there. Any life you want. The galaxy at your fingertips. Choice — freedom — ask, and it's yours [*Brothers* 198].

Clearly both tempted and repelled by Miles's offer, Mark kills his maker and flees on his own, only to show up some time later at the Dendarii Fleet. This time, Mark pretends to be Miles in order to launch an attack on Jackson's Whole and free the clones still there.

Just as Miles spends his youth trying to prove himself worthy of his father's legacy, Mark spends his early years as a free agent trying to escape Miles's. Mark wants to be a hero, but he doesn't have Miles's military brilliance, and his grand gesture at Jackson's Whole gets Miles killed. Under these circumstances, with Miles dead and his body nowhere to be found, Mark goes to Barrayar for the first time and meets his parents. Mark is lost, rejected and hated even by the misfit Dendarii. He puts on weight as quickly as possible to avoid being mistaken for his lost brother. Aral, grieving Miles, is uncomfortable with Mark at best. Cordelia, however, tells Mark he fits with his family, regardless of where he chooses to make his home.

> You have an uncle, a grandmother, and two cousins on Beta Colony who are just as much your relatives as Aral and myself and your cousin Ivan here on Barrayar. Remember, you have more than one choice. I've given one son to Barrayar. And watched for twenty-eight years while Barrayar tried to destroy him. Maybe Barrayar has had its turn, eh? [*Mirror Dance* (*Mirror*) 212–3].

Mark is initially Miles's foil, a twisted double who highlights Barrayar's role in Miles's brilliance by virtue of being so different — such an abject failure at everything he attempts, but Mark becomes more. His first step is to rescue Miles, whose corpse has been revived, but not returned home. When this rescue attempt, too, goes awry, Mark is captured and tortured by a sadist who wants to break him simply for the entertainment value. Mark's sense of self is so new and fragile that his personality splits into five distinct intelligences in order to survive his ordeal. Gorge, Grunt, Howl, and Killer all emerge to protect the nascent Lord Mark (*Mirror* 460–461). Mark emerges from the trial remarkably unscathed, as do his four additional personalities, whom he calls *the black gang*. Mark realizes that the all five of them are necessary for him to be whole. He finds a fit on Beta Colony, where counseling and the support of his maternal relatives help him find a functioning balance. He discovers a genius for making money that rivals his brother's genius for making war. He even develops a romantic relationship with Kareen, a friend of the family.

The centrality of place in accommodating human variation becomes apparent when Kareen and Mark pay a visit to Barrayar after having come into their own on Beta Colony. Kareen pulls Mark aside for an unpleasant conversation about the transition.

"But I've been so uncomfortable, since I got back. It's like I can just feel myself, folding back up into my old place in this Barrayaran culture-box. I can feel it, but I can't stop it. It's horrible."

"Protective coloration?" His tone suggested he could understand a desire for camouflage. [...]

"Something like that. But I hate secrets and lies."

"Can't you just ... tell your family?"

"I tried. I just couldn't. Could you?" [...]

"I could tell *my* mother."

"*I* could tell *your* mother. She's Betan. She's another world, the other world, the one where we were so right. It's *my* mother I can't talk to. And I always could, before. [...] I don't understand how it can feel so right there, and so wrong here. [...] Or not right there. Or something" [*Civil Campaign* 103].

Barrayar stifles Mark as it once stifled Miles, but without the mitigating loyalties and inspirational sense of purpose that catalyze Miles's greatness. For Mark, Barrayar is just a foreign and not particularly comfortable place. Mark's doubling with Miles thus undermines Miles's slide into narrative prosthesis by making his relationship with Barrayar an idiosyncratic one between a singular person and his place, a perfect misfitting.

Miles, Bothari, Taura, and Mark are each marked as other because of their physical or mental difference to an inferred normal body. Each comes to terms with that difference when she or he finds a sustaining environment. Though I have focused on these four characters, the Vorkosigan series is rich in human variation, some natural, some traumatic. The aforementioned Quaddies are null-gravity dwellers who have four arms and no legs. Bel Thorne, one of the Dendarii captains, is a hermaphrodite. One of Miles's lovers, Elli Quinn, has her face burned off and replaced after an early battle. What makes Bujold's series stand out from the standard disability-themed literature is its insistence across the board on ability as a contingent state. *Everyone* is disabled in certain contexts. Everyone is enabled in others. Her characters' choices, not their bodies, are what define them. As Miles tells Mark, "You are what you choose to do. Choose again, and change" (*Brothers* 202).

The key difference between Miles's and Mark's bodies is that Miles's bones are brittle and break easily, while Mark's are broken for him by his makers. Every time Miles takes a risk, he does so knowing the likely result is pain. He chooses to move "full tilt forward" anyway. Mark, on the other hand, doesn't understand that he has a choice until much later in life. For the intervening time, he endures. When he is captured and tortured in *Mirror Dance*, he is able to draw on that history of endurance, to choose to survive in a situation that would have almost certainly broken Miles, whose strength lies in forward momentum.

The clone brothers who are nothing alike demonstrate how deeply the concept of variation penetrates the books. It's not just about bodies. Even the concept of realizing one's full potential carries a different meaning for each character. For Miles, it mean bringing his full force of personality to bear on his life and duties as Lord Vorkosigan. For Mark, it's accepting that he is worthy of having a life of his own; embracing his internal multiplicity and letting each of his selves find avenues for fulfillment. For Taura, it's living her short life to the fullest, embracing Miles as her lover whenever she can and staying totally present for each moment. Bothari is odd man out in this list. For him, realizing his full potential is terrifying and undesirable. Bothari finds his contentment by reining in his capacity to do harm, giving his conscience over into the keeping of the one person he trusts.

There is no sentimentality associated with disability in the series. Infants are killed for it. Young women are ordered put to death on the assumption that they'd be better off avoiding the pain of their freakish lives. Instead, the books invoke the breadth of human variation to make a powerful argument for the worth of both individuality and interdependence. As Garland-Thomson writes, "Our experience of living eventually contradicts our collective fantasy that the body is stable, predictable, or controllable, creating misfits for all of us" ("Misfits" 603). Miles and friends live this reality, searching for places and people that will sustain them and allowing their misfits to strengthen and teach them along the way.

Notes

1. The first attempt is against Miles's uterine replicator in *Barrayar*. Miles mentions a second attempt in "The Mountains of Mourning."

2. Bothari appears in *Shards of Honor, Barrayar,* and *The Warrior's Apprentice.* The first two are collected in *Cordelia's Honor;* the latter in *Young Miles.*

3. Though the Dendarii have rules against fraternization, Miles publicly acknowledge Elli Quinn as his lover — "Nobody had to explain or excuse being in love with the beautiful Quinn. She was self-evidently his match" (*Memory* 35). Though Miles and Quinn are not publicly affectionate (*Memory* 23), she is the lover he shows off to others.

Works Cited

Bujold, Lois McMaster. *Barrayar.* In *Cordelia's Honor.* Riverdale, NY: Baen, 1999. 255–590.

_____. *Brothers in Arms.* Riverdale, NY: Baen, 1989.

_____. *A Civil Campaign.* Riverdale, NY: Baen, 1999.

_____. "Labyrinth." In *Borders of Infinity.* Riverdale, NY: Baen, 1989. 103–211.

_____. *Memory.* Riverdale, NY: Baen, 1996.

_____. *Mirror Dance.* Riverdale, NY: Baen, 1994.

_____. *Shards of Honor.* In *Cordelia's Honor.* Riverdale, NY: Baen, 1999. 255–590.

_____. *The Vor Game.* In *Young Miles.* Riverdale, NY: Baen, 1997. 465–827.

_____. *The Warrior's Apprentice.* In *Young Miles.* Riverdale, NY: Baen, 1997. 1–372.
Garland-Thomson, Rosemarie. "Feminist Disability Studies." *Signs* 30.2 (Winter 2005): 1557–1587.
_____. "Misfits: A Feminist Materialist Disability Concept." *Hypatia* 26.3 (Summer 2011): 591–609.
Mitchell, David, and Sharon Snyder. "Narrative Prosthesis and the Materiality of Metaphor." *The Disability Studies Reader,* 2d ed. Lennard J. Davis, ed. New York: Routledge, 2006. 205–216.

The Decay of the Cyborg
Body in Bujold's *Memory*

SYLVIA KELSO

To discuss this topic I want to use two theoretical approaches in a sort of counterpoint. Both may be termed corporeal theory, though the first comes from cyborg studies proper, and the other is most commonly termed Marxist. I will use them to delineate some parameters for my own form of that poly-semantic term, "cyborg," then to consider the interaction of a cyborg figure with the passage of time, and then to discuss the two notable cyborg bodies in *Memory*, Simon Illyan and Miles Vorkosigan himself. Finally, I will look at the cyborg's overall role in the novel.

Chris Hables Gray and Donna Haraway have produced foundation texts in cyborg studies, Haraway with her very well-known "A Cyborg Manifesto," and Gray with the *Cyborg Handbook*. Both offer similar base descriptions of a cyborg: Gray's is any "melding of the organic and machinic" (2), Haraway's, "a hybrid of machine and organism" (149). Both instantly focus on the cyborg's bent for multiplicity, uncertainty and paradox. They each site cyborgs in both the unreal and the everyday: in SF but also in "civilian medical research" (Gray 3), and "not just Robocop [but] our grandmother with a pacemaker" (2). Gray actually distinguishes four sources of "cyborgology," the military, civil medicine, entertainment, and work, notably the computer industry (3).

Similarly, Haraway agrees with Gray that "the cyborg has no origin story" (150) but may be "the Herald of the Apocalypse" (Gray 2). From there, how-ever, Haraway leans increasingly to the abstract, seeing the cyborg as "simul-taneously a myth and a tool[...], a frozen moment and a motor of social and imaginative reality" (qtd. Gray, 1), and then as an "incarnation" that "has no truck with bisexuality, pre-oedipal symbiosis," that is "outside salvation his-tory," that "does not dream of community" as in the "organic family," and that "would not recognize the Garden of Eden" (Haraway, 150–151).

With this defiance of traditional patterns, and the emphasis on "*pleasure* in the confusion of boundaries" (150), Haraway's cyborg was a ground-break-ing theoretical concept, a valuable opening of perceptions for feminist thinkers in particular. Nevertheless, it is a long way from the corporeal, everyday cyborg that she and Gray also insist on. "Grandma with a pacemaker" does not seem likely either to lack dreams of family community, or fail to recognize the Garden of Eden.

Gray does construct rough and useful categories of cyborg technology: restorative, as in returning lost functions, or normalizing, as in grandma's pacemaker. These evidently derive from medicine. There are also reconfiguring technologies, making "creatures equal to but different from humans" (3), and enhancing technologies, which produce the more than human cyborg. The former come, at the moment, from SF, but the latter are, as Gray says, the very real "aim of most military and industrial research" (3). Finally, entertainment-based cyborgs, in particular, may portray degrading cyborg technologies, presenting humans as virtual reality addicts, or even the de-individualized Borg (3). Such categories are handily fluid in practice, two or three often operating on an individual cyborg. The Borg warriors, first introduced in the second season of *Star Trek: The Next Generation,* are a fine example.

Haraway claims that "a cyborg exists whenever two kinds of boundaries [between human and animal and human and machine] are simultaneously problematic" (qtd. Gray 1). With these Borg warriors technology simultaneously reconfigures, enhances, and degrades to a point that blurs the boundaries of machine, insect and human. The warriors are reconfigured, different from if equal to humans, but they are enhanced by their modifications, notably in the eyes and hands: however, single-eye extensions also destroy the appearance of "normal" binocular humanity, while the enhanced machine hands pervert the traditional criterion of humans as toolmakers. At the same time the armored bodies move the figure toward insectile, or even a form of the undead, since the rib-shapes can suggest either a skeleton or an insectoid thorax. This last effect is increased by the smooth, apparently bare and vulnerable "belly" which makes the thoracic armor suggest a wing-case. This physical appearance anticipates the "degradation" of lost psychic individuality supposedly experienced by these cyborgs.

Even the Borg do not address one conspicuous absence that Grandma with a pacemaker reveals in both theorists' articulations: cyborg "incarnations" may have no origin, or be outside history, or signal the end of history, but they themselves are tacitly seen as perfect and immortal. Grandma, though, is subject to the inevitable fate of an organic body in time: decay, which leads to death. The pacemaker is a restorative, even a normalizing technology. But what happens to a cyborg body when the machine element breaks down?

In contrast to Haraway and Gray, a decaying, time-embedded body is a key concept in the theories of Mikhail Bakhtin. His corporeal theory, so to speak, focuses on what he terms the grotesque body, an adjective which in common usage would also apply to the Borg warriors. To a 19th Century critic "the grotesque starts when [...] exaggeration reaches fantastic dimensions" (cited Bakhtin, *Rabelais,* 315). So the Borg warriors exaggerate the human criteria of excellent vision and toolmaking hands, and the armor that implies human impregnability, to a point where "grotesque" carries not merely the sense of fantastic, but its contemporary nuance of abnormality, deformation, and repulsion.

Bakhtin, however, valorized his grotesque body, developing it in resistance to what he formulates as the "classical body" of the post–Renaissance aesthetic canon. Similarly, Klaus Theweleit extracted from German fascist culture a male/female opposition recoded as impermeable/pregnable, making the impregnable male body a central tenet of Western masculinity (Theweleit 1: 244–49; 2:40). This hard, dam-like body could be contaminated by symbolic dirt, slime, or bog (1: 385–402), and was opposed to the abject of pulped male or female enemy bodies (1: 194–95; 2: 17–20).

Like Theweleit's male body, Bakhtin's "classical body" is smooth, closed, isolated, and, notably, ageless. His grotesque body, unlike Theweleit's, is a positive construction, which emphasizes "apertures or [...] convexities [...] ramifications and offshoots: the open mouth, the genital organs, the breasts, the phallus, the potbelly, the nose." This body is seen in "copulation, pregnancy, childbirth, the throes of death, eating, drinking, defecat[ing.]" It is "ever unfinished, ever creating," not shown in an ageless period equidistant from birth and death, but most often depicted on the thresholds of birth or death; and its central and positive principle is change (*Rabelais,* 26–27).

These two forms of corporeal theory produce fruitful views of both Illyan and Miles in *Memory.* As Bujold readers will know, Simon Illyan is a long-term mid-level character in the Vorkosigan series, novels grounded in the militaristic and at times old-fashioned society of Barryar, which even before the Barrayarans acquire space colonies is ruled — usually — by an emperor. Illyan begins as a lowly lieutenant in the Barrayaran military, who rises to a position both feared and envied as the head of ImpSec, Imperial Security. Much of his power derives from an experiment devised by a powerful and unscrupulous emperor: he has been fitted with an eidetic memory chip. Conveniently skipping questions of storage space and bio-engineering capabilities, this chip has allowed Illyan to remember *everything.*

The advantages of a perfect human data-gathering device are obvious, and would make Illyan an enhanced cyborg, in Gray's terms. But the downside is actually degrading. Beside military data and imperial secrets, Illyan must also remember trivia, horrors, all the day-to-day ephemera that most of us can jettison. He has no choice. Well down the series, in the aptly named

Memory, Illyan's chip begins to decay, and an ambiguous cyborg enhancement/degradation becomes degradation in a far more literal sense.

Here terms from Gray and Bakhtin run in counterpoint. Gray uses "degradation" in the basic dictionary meaning, principally, "to lower the character or quality" of something (OED). But in Bakhtinian theory, the grotesque body is intrinsically based in "the material bodily principle," which Rabelais combined with folk humor to form what Bakhtin terms "grotesque realism." And its "essential principle [...] is degradation." To Bakhtin, degradation is "the lowering of all that is high, spiritual, ideal, abstract," back to "the sphere of earth and body" (*Rabelais,* 18–19 and passim.) Bakhtin's obvious example is Don Quixote: the Don's high chivalry is "degraded" by physical reality, not just through his mistakes over windmills and serving girls, but by the presence of Sancho Panza, with his gross appetites and big belly (20–22). In this case, degradation is not so much a lowering of character as a way to reach a more truthful perception of life.

Paralleling the Don's ideals, Illyan's cyborg enhancement was at the highest level: his chip was invisible, functioning physically in his brain, the highest organ in both literal and metaphorical senses, and mentally, in an inhuman perfection of recall. For Bakhtin the head is topographically in the upper bodily spectrum (21); and since Illyan's body has no visible machinic elements, no protrusions or convexities or obvious openings to the outer world, Bakhtin might call him a "classical" cyborg.

But as the chip degrades, Illyan is reduced to a bodily form below the level of "normal" men. First, a man once "infinitely reliable" (Bujold, *Memory,* 188) begins to forget dates and times in a manner suggestive of incipient Alzheimer's; then his incisive oral presentations weaken (185–86).Then he begins confusing past and present in ever more alarming cycles. These are particularly startling to Miles, as Illyan begins phoning him in a panic about security operations completed years since (190). At last Illyan grows incoherent in a general briefing, has to be forcibly sedated when he resists attempts to take him to a doctor, and is then confined under physical restraint (195–7).

In fact, this decay is not "natural" to either component of Illyan's body. He has been the victim of an attempted coup; his cyborg body, closed first by his chip's site in his most protected bodily area, and then warded by the security ramparts of ImpSec headquarters, has been opened by enemy action. He has inhaled poisonous airborne spores (technically, a "prokaryote" [306]) which settle in his nose and throat and migrate to attack his chip's circuits.

For Bakhtin, "the nose and the mouth play the most important part in the grotesque image of the body" (*Rabelais* 316), but "the mouth [...] dominates all else" (317). The mouth is the body's most obvious opening, into which food goes, from which more degrading products such as vomit emerge. That Illyan inhales his poison brings both important aspects of the grotesque face into play, and transforms him to a fully Bakhtinian body, one whose orifices and protuberances both connect it to and bring it undone by the outer world.

Eventually Illyan's chip is removed in a risky if rapid operation. Though he survives, losing his chip brings a change that operates over several of Gray's cyborg categories. First, he is no longer enhanced, or even a cyborg. At the same time, he has been normalized, but by *removal* of his machinic element. In Bakhtin's terms, he has been degraded to more material levels, firstly by the process of the actual loss, and now by the consequence. He has lost his rank and status as head of ImpSec. Moreover, his memory is now even less trustworthy than a normal human's. He has to re-learn the world almost like a child. His discovery of a "map" — an aid-memoire he never needed with the chip — is a particularly poignant moment in this process (419).

Interestingly, Illyan's change also literalizes another key aspect of Bakhtin's theory. For Bakhtin, "one of the fundamental tendencies of [the grotesque body] is to show two bodies in one: the one giving birth and dying, the other conceived, generated and born" (*Rabelais* 26). Bakhtin reads this in cosmic terms; but when his chip fails, Illyan as an individual experiences both metaphorical death and birth: the old Illyan "dies," and a new Illyan is born, inhabiting the same body as before.

We now have some interesting theory-based answers to the question: What happens when the machinic element of a cyborg body decays? In Gray's terms, in this case, it appears that "decay" need not be negative, "enhancement" might prove a degradation in disguise, and "normalizing" may mean losing all cyborg elements. Through this lens, the cyborg body displays not only ambiguity but a fluidity, at least in crossing Gray's categories, that begins to match Haraway's conception.

Through the Bakhtinian lens, "degradation" is a less absolute term. Here losing the chip produces, from one angle, a positive improvement in life, because it changes the static classical body into one that is open, changing, and moving on. Without the chip and his role in ImpSec, Illyan can have a "normal" life, even to the extent of commencing a love affair. But these changes can still be read as "degradation" against the orthodox advantages of rank and "perfect" function, since Illyan's new forgetfulness is an ambiguous blessing. At the same time, metaphorical life and death switch places in the same body with surprising facility. At the moment of change and decay, the two theoretical frames intersect: the cyborg and the Bakhtinian grotesque body become (momentarily) one.

For Miles Vorkosigan as much as for Simon Illyan, *Memory* is about a drastic, reductive change, whose betterment comes at a Pyrrhic cost. Illyan experiences "death" and "rebirth" in the same body. For the length of the series till *Memory*, Miles has in fact lived two lives in the same body, as Lord Miles Vorkosigan on Barrayar and as the mercenary commander Admiral Naismith elsewhere in space. Ironically but symmetrically, Miles enters *Memory* as Illyan's diametric opposite: the end-product of a lifetime of normalizing cyborg technologies, who at that moment is, perhaps physically and definitely morally, experiencing the first phases of decay.

This is the more ironic because for most of his life Miles has been an exemplary Harawayan cyborg, a pleasurable confuser of boundaries, especially over his two identities, and especially among Barrayar's enemies. Thanks to his physical appearance, he has also been a stubborn solvent of established Barrayaran categories, particularly that most sensitive and fiercely policed binary of "human" and "mutant." And the fact that he must of necessity use wits and daring in place of muscle has made him a resolutely defiant loose cannon among the irregular ranks of ImpSec, where his actions are as likely to appall Illyan, his controlling officer, as to move him to praise.

Miles's technological involvement actually begins before birth, in what Haraway might call a re-written origin myth. Embryonic damage from a nerve-gas attack on his parents means that in *Barrayar* his embryo must come to term in a uterine replicator (161–165, 370–378). His very existence is therefore due to a machine, and as Gray says of all cyborgs, he is not only the end-product of "incredible institutional support," but "part of a system" (2). In this case, the "system" is the military machine of Barrayar, which acquired the replicator from a more sophisticated planet's technology, and it is in the Barrayaran military that Miles will live most of his life.

The consequences of the nerve-gas damage dominate Miles's infancy and early childhood: post-natal spinal surgery, hip surgery, and bones so brittle a humerus snaps during post-natal examination (*Barrayar* 373). More orthodox normalizing cyborg technology appears in the connective story for *Borders of Infinity*, when Miles is hospitalized for all his major bones to have plastic replacements (1–7, 101–102 et passim). But finally, in *Mirror Dance*, Miles's combat luck runs out. He is literally killed in action and has to be resurrected in a cryonic repair facility. This time, on top of nerve damage from "cryostasis," he needs an entire suite of artificially regrown organs, heart, stomach, and lungs (355). Miles now repeats physically, and even more extremely than Illyan, Bakhtin's metaphor of the grotesque body as two in one, simultaneously dying and being born.

Emerging from death, via a second childhood and adolescence, Miles also has to recover memory and identity (*Mirror* 395–396). Again, this second life, reliant on heavy support and extreme technology, makes Miles both a restored and normalized cyborg par excellence. But he has acquired a lethal flaw, a tendency to random, black-out convulsions, and this corporeal degradation rapidly produces a more deadly moral decay. Frantic to return to ImpSec, Miles's channel to his Naismith identity, which, according to his mother, is his hold on sanity in the restraints of Barrayar (558), Miles does not mention the convulsions during his final medical clearance (547–548).

The rapid and dire consequences of this deceit form the beginning of *Memory*. While leading a rescue raid with the Dendarii, Miles has a convulsion and laser-amputates the rescuee's legs (1–6). To top it off, he falsifies his report to ImpSec. When the truth emerges, Illyan gives him a medical discharge (85–92). But in effect, Miles has been cashiered: expelled from ImpSec, from the military, and from his second identity. In Haraway's terms, his confusion of boundaries and creation of pleasurable ambiguities have reached a disastrous singularity. In Gray's terms, his restorative cyborg repairs have produced a physical, ethical and status degradation, with no sign, at this point, that such degradation will function in the Bakhtinian sense.

The central story of *Memory* is Miles's recovery from this nadir. After Ivan and Duv Galeni force him out of sheer passive despair (94–98), Bujold thriftily supplies the motive power for his renewed thinking, interaction with Barrayaran society, re-entry into ImpSec, and eventually, complete redemption and a higher status than ever before, by involving him in Illyan's decay.

After Galeni consults him over the first signs of this (184–189), Miles is forced first to initiate and then to become a leading figure in the investigation of Illyan's collapse. At first suspicious, then protesting at Illyan's treatment, he first suspects sabotage, then appeals to the Emperor to defeat the stonewalling new head of ImpSec. Given the over-riding authority of an Imperial Auditor (225–226), it is Miles who makes the perilous decision to have the chip removed (241–254), finds the personnel to track down the sabotage (263–264), organizes the hunt to find the means of its delivery (337–338), and personally identifies (380–385) and plans the trap to capture the perpetrator (395–396).

The last step in Miles's own moral regeneration is when the villain offers to return his role as Admiral Naismith in exchange for a scapegoat for Illyan's sabotage. After long agonizing, Miles refuses. Rejecting his literal alter ego, Miles Vorkosigan chooses to be "*myself*" (386). The last physical reclamation is the discovery/invention of a device that will let him manage his convulsions, or at least, provoke them at a suitable time (436–438). If his faulty cyborg body is not completely mended, its flaw is at least under a form of control.

At this point, Miles appears to have far exceeded Illyan's gains and losses, in Gray's terms at least. Where Illyan's normalizing meant the loss of a cyborg enhancement along with his prior status, and a somewhat diminished "normal" life, Miles's cyborg body has been restored, and its flaw at least partially remedied. And where Illyan lost his command status, Miles has just hop-stepped right over the military promotion chain, to reach a level only a handful of other Barrayarans share. Nevertheless, for Miles too there are negative sides to the change.

The major loss is the excision of Miles's Naismith identity. In Haraway's terms, he has virtually ceased to be a cyborg. He can no longer confuse identities, pleasurably or otherwise. He is no longer Illyan's loose cannon, and his physical form has become largely accepted, so he can no longer upset crucial Barrayaran categories. Moreover, within Lord Vorkosigan's permanent identity he is limited to the community of an "organic family," loss of his several if sequential galactic lovers, and the constraints that come with the role of his father's heir. If he does not recognize the Garden of Eden, salvation history, as in a determined linear life pattern with a fairly certain end, is no longer quite outside his ken.

Through Bakhtin's lens, the very escape from degradation figured in Gray's terms means that Miles has not, like Don Quixote, achieved a newer, truer sense of reality. He has rather had to truncate a number of possibilities in his fluid, ambiguous dual cyborg existence. It is a simpler, not necessarily a truer, reality that remains.

Miles and Illyan's changes occur in a freefall space that centers, both metaphorically and literally, within ImpSec, and whose chaos evokes Bakhtin's other influential concept, the carnival. To Bakhtin, the carnival, the traditional pre–Lent space of free-for-all activity and display, offers a "temporary liberation from the prevailing truth and from the established order" (*Rabelais* 10), that issues particularly in "the peculiar logic [...] of the 'turnabout'" (11) or reversal. This includes "uncrowning" in particular, as the head of the usual hierarchy is dislodged for the length of the carnival, and a king of clowns elected in his place.

For Miles this turnabout functions less accurately than for Illyan: the chaos that Miles himself produces among the Dendarii is only the opening bracket of the novel, before the action moves to Barrayar. It also leads to his permanent uncrowning as Admiral Naismith, and his successor will by no means be a king of clowns. On Barrayar, the pattern is more complex. Miles is uncrowned in earnest with his cashiering from ImpSec, where he was unofficially being considered as Illyan's heir. He is eventually reinstated, however, as a supreme trouble-shooter and problem-solver, when he becomes an Auditor, so Miles-as-Lord-Vorkosigan has been recrowned in at least half his identity.

In Illyan's case the uncrowning is not only obvious but permanent; moreover, the usurper who has engineered Illyan's fall is appointed King of Misrule in his place (*Memory* 197–200). But while Miles's moral degradation has produced a minor dislocation in the ranks of ImpSec, and thrown his own life(s) into chaos, Illyan's degeneration flings the entire institution into uncovenanted confusion. The Head of the institution has suddenly not merely lost his personal self-control, but uncovered unprecedented possibilities for treachery and mayhem within the innermost citadel of Barrayar. Established order appears to go by the board, prevailing truth is cast in doubt.

But unlike the actual carnival, for Illyan as for ImpSec, while this loss of truth and order may be temporary, it is neither joyous nor a liberation. Nor is it a covenanted, recurring change, but a single unexpected event. Indeed, the disorder may be read simply as the loss of equilibrium which Todorov considered a pre-requisite for the movement of any narrative (75–76). The story progresses through crisis and resolution to another equilibrium, not necessarily, or indeed, not usually the original form. In this case, certainly, neither Miles nor Illyan's new equilibrium is the same. But after the explanation of Illyan's collapse, and the unmasking and removal of the usurper villain, ImpSec, like society after carnival, reverts to the old status quo.

In the '80s, when Bakhtin was a new theoretical discovery and his own work was being discussed, carnival was read as a potentially revolutionary agency (Morson 237), or even an agency that for Bakhtin *had* to be liberating (Bernstein, 291). In the 21st century, positive views of carnival are often made a prologue to using the concept as a theoretical tool, as I have here. Such views tend to ignore Bakhtin's own limits on the nature and potential of carnival (Blackledge and Creese, Iddings and McCafferty). Though Bakhtin repeatedly calls both grotesque realism and the carnival positive, joyful, liberating, even as late as his work on Dostoevsky he never suggests that carnival is more than a temporary liberative space. Nor, though Bakhtin read Rabelais as believing that "the father's new flowering in the son [takes place] on a higher degree of mankind's development" (*Rabelais* 406), does Bakhtin himself claim that carnival change must be either lasting or for the better. Indeed, his opening definition specifically makes it temporary, an excursion from, but not a shifting of the status quo.

In this strictly Bakhtinian sense the chaos in *Memory* may be read as carnivalesque, in that the status quo of ImpSec, and metonymically, of Barrayaran society in general, does not alter. But beyond the demands of narrative per se, as Todorov read them, the re-assertion of the status quo here may also have generic roots. *Memory* is actually a hybrid of SF with the thriller/mystery, and mysteries and thrillers, like their forebear, the detective story, demand a re-assertion of the status quo: solution of the mystery, unmasking, capture and/or punishment of the villain, and a firm closure. Only an open ending of some sort — the villain is never known, the villain escapes justice — would produce real change in the form, and such a change would probably vex readers to the point where the particular novel would fail, or else have to be degraded: that is, denied classification in that genre.

One significant aspect, however, is absent from *Memory*'s carnival space: for Bakhtin, laughter is essential to both the carnival and grotesque realism. Carnival laughter is festive, universal, and, it is important to note, ambivalent (*Rabelais* 17–18). In grotesque realism also "[l]aughter degrades and materializes" (20). But though Bujold can make masterly use of the comedy of chaos, as in the immemorially disastrous dinner scene from *A Civil Campaign* (160–182), while the chaos is extreme, laughter is conspicuously absent from *Memory*.

This may be due to the overall tenor of the book. Most of the earlier Vorkosigan books could fit fairly comfortably into the genre/form that Bakhtin proposed for Dostoevsky: one of the serio-comic genres, in which genuine and important issues are confronted during the passage of an adventure novel plot garnished with eccentricities and extravagances that Bakhtin traces directly to the influence of the carnival (*Dosteovsky*, 101–138). Not quite similarly, most of the Vorkosigan books are fast-moving adventures, drastic events occur, more than one eccentric appears, serious issues are confronted, but over-the-top comedy is often hovering very close.

Memory is another matter. Both Miles and Illyan's changes in this novel are drastic and reductive, and the rewards ambiguous. It is hardly surprising, in terms of content, that this novel should lean more to the tendency of the SF genre as a whole, which rarely tends to humor, especially of the over-the-top grotesque realist type. SF is more often about deadly serious aggrandizing projects to save the world, if not the universe. Nevertheless, one must ask, without carnival laughter, can this novel be claimed to present either an example of Bakhtin's grotesque body, or of a carnival space?

Like the outcome of Illyan and Miles's changes, the answers are ambiguous. Comic tone or not, Illyan and Miles exhibit several aspects of the positive grotesque body: cyborg decay gives them a metaphorical death and rebirth in the same physical form. Their "decay" does have a positive aspect, and the chaos of each collapse does lead to a personal improvement of sorts. On the other hand, ImpSec displays the equally ambiguous nature of the Bakhtinian carnival: the rule of misrule and chaos is temporary, and ends with a renewal of prevailing truth, order, and the status quo.

Laughter or not, then, the ambiguity of Bakhtinian concepts persists, and ambiguity is an aspect Bakhtin repeatedly ascribes to the carnival and its mirth. Such ambiguity, refusal to permanently categorize, in fact, work that may be read as itself unfinished and contradictory, has been argued as a central feature of Bakhtin's thought. But there is another figure in this text to whom ambiguity, contradiction, and evasion of categorical boundaries are regularly imputed, at least by Haraway. Has the place of laughter has been taken by the cyborg in this text?

Beyond their similar qualities, the cyborg's structural pre-eminence in *Memory* matches that of laughter in a truly serio-comic text. We begin with both Miles and Illyan as high-ranking cyborgs, who in Illyan's case must lose an enhancement to become "normal." Miles has to lose his second identity, and with it a good deal of his cyborg qualities, at least on Haraway's terms, but he ends as an even higher-ranking figure, who has once again become a normalizing cyborg. Cyber-technology is the agent of most of the important changes to these characters' lives. And though Illyan is a mid-level character, the decay of his cyborg body precipitates the novel's major crisis; it is through solving the mystery of that decay and catching its perpetrator that Miles can redeem his opening and catastrophic mistake, achieve his own equilibrium, and bring the entire novel to a close. If the cyborg is not as all-prevalent as laughter in a carnivalesque text, its cyborg figures are certainly essential to the novel as a whole.

WORKS CITED

Bakhtin, Mikhail. *Problems of Dostoevsky's Poetics*. Manchester: Manchester University Press, 1984.

_____. *Rabelais and His World*. Trans. Helene Iswolsky. Bloomington: Indiana University Press, 1984.

Bernstein, Michael André. "When the Carnival Turns Bitter: Preliminary Reflections Upon the Abject Hero." *Critical Inquiry* 10.2 (Dec. 1983): 283–305.

Blackledge, Adrian, and Angela Creese. "Meaning-Making as Dialogic Process: Official and Carnival Lives in the Language Classroom." *Journal of Language, Identity and Education* Issue 4 (Sept. 2008): 236–53.

Bujold, Lois McMaster. *Barrayar*. Riverdale, NY: Baen, 1991.

_____. *Borders of Infinity*. Riverdale, NY: Baen, 1989.

_____. *A Civil Campaign*. Riverdale, NY: Baen, 1999.

_____. *Memory*. Riverdale, NY: Baen, 1996.

_____. *Mirror Dance*. Riverdale, NY: Baen, 1994.

Gray, Chris Hables, ed. *The Cyborg Handbook*. New York: Routledge, 1995.

Haraway, Donna J. "A Cyborg Manifesto: Science, Technology, and Socialist-Feminsim in the Late Twentieth Century." In *Simians, Cyborgs and Women: The Re-Invention of Nature*. New York: Routledge, 1991. 149–181.

Iddings, A., and S. McCafferty. "Carnival in a mainstream kindergarten classroom: A Bakhtinian analysis of second language learners' off-task behaviors." *Modern Language Journal* 91.1 (2007): 31–44.

Morson, Gary Saul. "Who Speaks for Bakhtin? A Dialogic Introduction." *Critical Inquiry* 10.2 (Dec. 1983): 225–243.

Todorov, Tzvetan, and Arnold Weinstein. "Structural Analysis of Narrative." *NOVEL: A Forum on Fiction* 3.1 (Autumn 1969): 70–76

From Iberian to Ibran and Catholic to Quintarian

Bujold's Alternate History of the Spanish Reconquest in the Chalion Series

DAVID D. OBERHELMAN

The fantasy fiction of Lois McMaster Bujold frequently takes place in an alternate reality that, while it has its roots in a historical context, nevertheless has some carefully orchestrated similarities to and differences from the primary world which the reader inhabits. *The Sharing Knife* series, for example, is set in a world that resembles the lands of the Native Americans of the Great Lakes Region, and *The Spirit Ring* takes the autobiography of the historical Italian artist Benvenuto Cellini along with other historical sources such as Georgius Agricola's *De Re Metallica* and weaves them in to a narrative of magic that is at once like and unlike Europe of the Renaissance. Bujold's efforts at constructing an alternate reality in her fantasy is nowhere more pronounced than in the *Chalion* novels: *The Curse of Chalion* (first published by Eos in 2001) and *Paladin of Souls* (2003) along with the related novel, *The Hallowed Hunt* (2005).

Like her other historical fantasy series, the *Chalion* books, especially the first two (since *The Hallowed Hunt* focuses on the Weald, another region in Bujold's invented map roughly corresponding to medieval Germany) posit an alternate universe in which the Ibran Peninsula on the outskirts of a late medieval quasi–European continent becomes the locus of religious conflict between the dominant Quintarian religion with its fivefold pantheon of the Father, the Mother, the Daughter, the Son, and the Bastard — the divine representative of all that is "odd," the out-of-season, including the homosexual and all that is contrary or other — and the heretical Quadrene faith of the Roknari Archipelago that repudiates the Bastard and his oddity or difference in its strict dualistic, master-slave philosophy. In this series Bujold takes the *Reconquista* or the Reconquest, the seven hundred-year conflict over territory between the Catholic Spanish states on the Iberian Peninsula and the Islamic principalities of Al-Andalus — the so-called Moorish states that held a foothold on the southern tip of Europe—as the basis for her own reflections on the relationship between the divine and the human, and on holy war and its justification. The Spanish Reconquest which led to the final defeat of the last Islamic stronghold in Granada in 1492 was accompanied by a wave of religious fervor or even fanaticism that led to the forced conversion or expulsion of the remaining Muslims and Jews and then to the terrors of the Inquisition. The Chalionese Reconquest, in contrast, heralds the rise of a more pluralistic, open-ended faith that accepts or incorporates rather than banishes or subjugates difference. Thus by creating her own fantastic retelling of the account of the Catholic Monarchs Ferdinand II of Aragon and Isabella I of Castile along with other reinventions of figures and events from the tumultuous history of Spain in the 1400s, Bujold is able to explore the theological implications of ethnic conflict and show how the divine, political, and personal spiritual realms are comingled and ultimately inseparable in both the Chalionese secondary reality and our own primary reality.

Bujold's approach to alternate history involves the introduction of small, carefully regulated change into the historical context in order to maintain a resemblance between the invented secondary world of her fiction and the primary world, a resemblance that allows her to study how incremental differences affect not only the social realm but even the metaphysics of the universe itself. She writes of the small and highly controlled changes she made in the Renaissance world with its notions of magic to create the universe of *The Spirit Ring*:

> My own view of historical cause and effect is chaotic in the mathematical sense. We have root causes that are too slow to measure but have visible effects—you know, the butterfly wing thing—so that if you even make small changes, the ultimate result would be enormous changes. Part of the fantasy of it is the idea that you can make any changes and not have a totally different world. That's like cheating, to have [*sic*] close to our own history and yet allow it to be different ["Answers" 220].

The "cheat" of positing a close yet different history and world reflects Bujold's concern with balance, the maintaining of equilibrium, that undergirds the cosmic order in her novels; the butterfly effect must be contained so that despite the alternated elements (such as the substitution of the religions of five and four deities for Catholicism and Islam), the two worlds will still parallel each other enough for the contrasts to be pronounced.

The specific historical context Bujold adapted for her Chalion series is the late medieval Spanish clash with the Muslim states occupying the southern end of the Iberian Peninsula. As she commented in a 2001 interview, one of the sources of inspiration for *The Curse of Chalion* was

a course I took a few years ago at the local university on the history of
medieval Spain, about which I had known almost nothing. I emerged from it,
reeling slightly, clutching a huge armload of incandescent incidents and chewy
characters, with no very clear idea what I wanted to do with them. I knew I
didn't want to do alternate history or historical fantasy, so I set it all aside
while working on other projects ["Interview"].

Her initial impulse was not to do an alternate history, but as she goes on to
say, the Spanish material became linked to a nascent story of a long-suffering
civil servant, what evolved into Cazaril's story, and thus her Ibran Peninsula
with its own religious conflict and version of the Reconquest took shape.
Bujold developed a map for her invented world, flipping the map of the Iberian
Peninsula so that the Roknari, the invaders corresponding to the Muslims,
came from the north (the Roknari Archipelago) and states of Chalion, Ibra,
and Brajar — the alternate versions of the Spanish kingdoms later united into
the Spanish Empire (respectively, Castile and León, Aragon, and Portugal) —
were at the southern end of the map.[1] From there she went on to populate her
Chalionese universe with many figures based loosely or indirectly on figures
from Spain in the 1400s and beyond.

The secret marriage of Iselle of Chalion to Bergon of Ibra formed the
basis for her alternate history; as she notes in the same interview, it is "a
real historical incident that will be recognized instantly by any student of
the early life of Isabella of Castille [*sic*]" ("Interview"). From there Bujold
developed the other characters in the royal family of Chalion in the image
of the other members of the royal family of Castile and León; for example,
as she noted in an interview for the New Zealand Press Association, "the
idea for the character of Teidez in *The Curse of Chalion* came from Isabella
of Spain's ill-fated younger brother Prince Alfonso, and the notion of the
encounter with the menagerie from a footnote about Alfonso in an academic
biography about his elder half-brother Enrique IV" ("Mike Houlahan").
The anonymous Wikipedia entry for *The Curse of Chalion* gives a fairly exhaus-
tive, if entirely unattributed, enumeration of the parallels, indicating the
extent to which Bujold's fans have taken her statements and their own inves-
tigations to ferret out the many links between Chalion and the historical
Spain:

> Iselle's mother Ista, heroine of the sequel *Paladin of Souls*, is based on Isabella
> of Portugal. Iselle's father Roya (King) Ias is based on John II of Castile,
> whose favorite Alvaro de Luna inspired Bujold's Arvol dy Lutez. Iselle's half-
> brother Orico represents Henry IV of Castile, who was called "the Impotent,"
> and her full brother Teidez corresponds to Alfonso de las Asturias. The geog-
> raphy is likewise based on that of the Iberian Peninsula in the 15th century —
> but mirrored, north for south. Chalion is Castile; Ibra is Aragon and Valencia;

South Ibra is Catalonia; Brajar is Portugal; the Roknari princedoms are Al-
Andalus; and Darthaca is France.

For *Paladin of Souls* Bujold drew implicit comparisons between the conflicts
with the Roknari princedom of Jokana with Castle Porifors with the legendary
clashes in the Spanish epic *El Cid*. She also comments on "Mad Queen Joan,
Isabella's unfortunate daughter, who dragged her husband Phillip the Fair's
embalmed corpse around half of Spain for a while. She was the jumping-off-
point for the character of Cattilara" ("Women's Hero").[2] The quasi–Spanish
names and lexicon of the world of Chalion (featuring invented words such as
roya for "king," *royacy* for "kingdom," etc.) further underscores its indebted-
ness to the chronicles of the Spanish kingdoms as they were trying to unite
the peninsula under Christian rule.

The books therefore set up many one-for-one correspondences between
people, places, and events in Spain leading up to 1492 and those in Bujold's
world. Yet she is not writing a straightforward historical *roman à clef* in which
the annals of Isabella and her family are merely retold under the guise of different names. Given Bujold's recognition that small changes in any alternate
history are fraught with the potential to multiply and reproduce in butterfly
wing fashion unless kept under control, any specific alternation in the historical or cultural context takes on great significance within the accounts. In
the case of the *Chalion* novels, the most dramatic single change is the recasting
of the Catholic–Islamic religious struggles at the heart of the Spanish Reconquest into the Quintarian–Quadrene struggle between the gods themselves as
embodied in their human agents, the "saints" in the incarnational theology
of the invented universe. In interviews Bujold has drawn attention to the centrality of the religious issues at stake in her story: she explains, "I had acquired
a lot of fascinating historical background on medieval Spain, a wonderfully
lurid but under-utilized place and period, but I knew I didn't want to do an
historical fantasy, which would be too constrained for the religious issues I
also wanted to explore" ("Lois McMaster Bujold"). She observes that the key
which helped her decide how to make use of that historical background came
in her reflections on the nature of magic, particularly the death magic that
figures so prominently in the two novels' plots, and the relationship of the
gods to humans in that universe, and how the dispute over the number of
their ranks — five versus four — gave her inspiration. As she comments in
another interview, "In figuring out what the explanation and underpinning
of such an event must be in Chalion's curiously balanced theology, I discovered
a lot about my world's possibilities and its magic's — and gods'— powers and
limitations. Once I had that explanation in hand, I was able to go on and
weave the concept seamlessly into the whole story" ("Interview").

The kernel around which the alternate history of the *Chalion* books grew thus lies in the nature of magic and the gods' power, and Bujold contrasts that world to the nature of divinity in the faith of late medieval Spain that emerged out of the Crusader zeal of the Reconquest. A brief consideration of the territorial and religious nature of the seven hundred years of confrontations in Iberia can help bring out the issues Bujold foregrounds in recasting the nature of the Chalionese cosmos. Islamic Berber and Arabic armies from North Africa first invaded the Iberian Peninsula in 711, overrunning much of the loosely allied lands held by the Christian Visigoths of Hispania.[3] The Christians were reduced to a small pocket in the northern part of Iberia, and Islamic rule took hold in Al-Andalus. The Muslims secured their hold on the peninsula by establishing their own political institutions, especially that of the Caliphate of Córdoba. Efforts to reclaim lost land by the Christians began as early as 722 when King Pelayo of Asturias, one of the remaining Visigothic petty kingdoms, began fighting for the cause of *salvie Spanie*, the salvation of Spain (O'Callaghan 697).

Indeed, the concept of Reconquest and reunification was a Christian invention following the Islamic invasion, an attempt to restore an ideal state that had previously never existed (Lomax 1–2). Fuelled by the returning Crusaders who had fought the Arabs in the Holy Lands, the next several centuries witnessed an ongoing tug of war between the Catholic states and the Muslim "Moorish" confederacy, but the conflict revolved around the axis of religion. As famed Spanish historian José Goñi Gaztambide has observed in his seminal work on the medieval Iberian battles, the Catholic bishops, popes, and councils issues many series of bulls and indulgences promising remission of sin to those who took up the cause of the Reconquest; in effect, the Reconquest became *una guerra santa indulgenciada* ("an indulgenced holy war") against Islam on the far western edge of Europe (Goñi Gaztambide 46). Cordova fell in 1031, and following the demise of the caliphate, Al-Andalus was subdivided into a group of small principalities or *tā'ifas* that over the next few centuries fell in succession to the armies of the advancing Spanish kingdoms. Granada was the last remaining Islamic territory by the thirteenth century, and lasted until Ferdinand and Isabella's final campaign in 1492.

Iberia in the 1300s and 1400s, the era Bujold used as the inspiration for her *Chalion* books, was marked by a gradual replacement of the Muslim culture in the reclaimed lands by the dominant Christian faith of the Spanish kingdoms. Granada was, in effect, a vassal state of the neighboring Castile and León, but Muslims in the recaptured lands often converted and consequently integrated themselves into Spanish society. Some historians have argued that the period before the fall of Granada was one in which there existed a détente of sorts in the holy war, a stretch of religious tolerance and pluralism, in which not only Catholic and Muslim peoples co-existed, but the Jews — the other large religious minority in the peninsula — enjoyed some measure of tolerance in Iberian culture.[4] Even among the "Moors" there was a modicum of tolerance towards the Christian inhabitants of Al-Andalus, although that view has been criticized for being overly romantic (Benthall 17n3).

This hiatus in the conflict ended during the reign of King Enrique IV of Castile, Isabella's half-brother. Following Isabella's marriage to Ferdinand of Aragon, the surreptitious marriage pact that united two of largest Iberian kingdoms, and the subsequent death of Enrique in 1474, the queen came to the throne with a renewed desire to drive the Muslims as well as the Jews out of Christian lands. As Elizabeth Lehfeldt notes of that moment in Spanish history, "the peninsula was desperate for a monarch who would rule with a firm and moral hand and deliver it from the religious and political presence of the Muslims (a wish felt even more keenly throughout Europe after the fall of Constantinople in 1453)" (32). The Catholic Monarchs reignited the flames of the holy war in their campaigns against the last Muslim outpost, and after the defeat of Granada in 1492, the forced conversion of Muslims and subsequent expulsion of the Jews became, as Isabella's recent biographer Nancy Rubin Stuart has argued, one of the darker aspects of her piety (7). Indeed, after 1492, the year Isabella and Ferdinand also funded Christopher Columbus on his voyage of discovery, the Spanish Empire emerged with its own legacy of conquest and imperialism. Spain from that time through the era of the Counter-Reformation was a nation marked by a growing religious intolerance and even persecution though the actions of the infamous Spanish Inquisition, the tribunal created to stamp out heresy and remove all deviation from faith (Netanyahu xv–xvi). The tortures and abuses inflicted by Tomás de Torquemada and the other Inquisitors reflect their refusal to accept religious or ethnic difference (Judaism and later Protestantism) and, especially under Hapsburg Spain after the reign of Ferdinand and Isabella, all alien elements including the French, homosexuals, and other deviants.[5] Thus one of the tragic results of the Reconquest was the violent reaction against difference and otherness that marked Spanish Catholicism for over a century.

Given the complicated heritage of religious conflict and traditions of tolerance versus intolerance that marked the Spanish Reconquest, Bujold's decision to mine that vast historical record for her fantasy is quite telling, for the subtle change she makes in the nature of the contending faiths in her universe produces very different theological, philosophical, and social realities for the Quintarians. Central to Bujold's conception of the Quintarian faith with its five gods—five being a prime number that is not divisible by two and thus cannot be reduced to oppositional pairs—is how it tolerates remainders, otherness, whereas the "heretical" Quadrene faith of the Roknari which excludes the Bastard is predicated upon such pairs of two in which one element always dominates the other. As she explains in an interview,

> I wanted Chalion's Temple to carry out many of the vital social functions performed by real religions in our history, but I also wanted to come up with a theology that was non-dualistic, as I think dualism is a mistake. Although we can imagine good and evil as pure extracts as a thought experiment, they are never actually found that way in reality. So the five gods of Chalion were selected as a number that could not be divided evenly, because the moment you give human beings more than one of anything, they immediately try to set things in some hierarchy of value and position themselves on the "best" side, whether that actually makes any sense or not. Best for what? Of course, this immediately suggested a Chalionese heresy, where people re-invent dualism by selecting the most ambiguous of the gods to be the "evil" one, and they're off and running again ["Mike Houlahan"].

Bujold's alternate history of the Reconquest is therefore predicated upon the notion that the Quintarian battle against the Quadrene represents a holy war, one waged by the human agents acting on behalf of the gods, ultimately to establish a more tolerant, pluralistic social order versus the rigidity and slavery of the Roknari. In that sense, Bujold reverses the historical trajectory of the Spanish Reconquest, a campaign that arguably led to the hardline Catholicism of the Spanish Empire with rigid theological dichotomies (heretics versus the faithful) enforced by its own tribunal, and uses her unlikely saints—Cazaril and the Dowager Royina Ista—to be her god-touched crusaders in the fight for a more open-ended belief system that accepts and celebrates difference.

The Curse of Chalion establishes the historical parallels between the conflicting states and faiths on the Ibran Peninsula and those of the familiar Iberian Peninsula in the Middle Ages. Bujold depicts her alternate world as one on the verge of the Reconquest, and since the divine confrontation is always rendered through human actors in that universe, she effectively pits her Quintarian hero against the dead but still potent Golden General of Roknar, the legendary Roknari leader and favorite of the Father of Winter who had united the Quadrene forces in the northern peninsula for a major offensive again the Quintarian royacies. The novel takes place after the defeat of the Golden General through the Roya Fonsa's use of death magic which resulted in the curse hanging over the royal house of Chalion. The narrator describes the early years of the Roknari invasion and the contemporary political landscape of the peninsula in terms that any student of Spanish history would immediately recognize:

When the Roknari had first invaded from the sea, they had overrun most of Chalion, Ibra, and Brajar in their first violent burst, even past Cardegoss, to the very feet of the southern mountain ranges. Darthaca itself had been threatened by their advance parties. But from the ashes of the weak Old Kingdoms and the harsh cradle of the hills new men had emerged, fighting for generations to regain what had been lost in those first few years [*Curse* 109].

Chalion and Ibra — the Castile and Aragon of this world — as well as Brajar (i.e., Portugal) are at the beginning of the novel ready to advance upon the remaining Roknari principalities. As Cazaril tells the lady Bertiz, all that is needed is a union of two main Quintarian royacies to bring about an end to the Quadrene presence on the continent:

Chalion alone could not defeat all five princedoms, and even if by some miracle it did, it has no naval expertise to hold the coasts thereafter. If all the Quintarian royacies were to combine, and fight hard for a generation, some immediately strong and determined roya might push it through and unite the whole land. But the cost in men and nerve and money would be vast [*Curse* 132].

With these broad strokes, Bujold sets the stage for the Iselle-Bergon marriage and focuses the reader's expectations so that these Quintarian Monarchs, like their Catholic counterparts, herald a new momentum in the Reconquest and mark a turning point in the longstanding war with the Roknari. This larger historical and political framework supporting the Castillar Lupe dy Cazaril's story in *The Curse of Chalion* allows Bujold to contrast the holy war of the Spanish and the Muslims with that of the Quintarians and Quadrenes, and consequently rewrite history, or, more specifically, recast the nature of the religious issues at stake.

The first book of the *Chalion* series vividly contrasts the theological and social orders of the Quadrene Roknari and the Quintarians. Cazaril explains early in the book that the Roknari take a radically different view of the Bastard's role in the divine family and, by corollary, all the "oddness" and otherness associated with him:

The Roknari heresy of the four gods makes a crime of the odd loves the Bastard rules, here. The Roknari theologians say the Bastard is a demon, like his father, and not a god, after his holy mother, so call us all devil worshippers — which is a deep offense to the Lady of Summer, I think, as well as to the poor Bastard himself, for did he ask to be born? [*Curse* 84].

The Roknari's repudiation of the Bastard, the patron of human experiences that do not fit into the fourfold familial and seasonal structure of the Father, Mother, Son, and Daughter, reflects their cultural hatred of all that does not fit into a hierarchical system. Indeed, even their complex language has different modes of address and grammatical forms to denote levels of subservience between speakers within their equally complex and nuanced social strata: the slave-master, servant-lesser servant, master-warrior, slave-scholar, and others. The Quadrene faith is most violently opposed to the homosexual love that defies the male-female dualism that dominates their view of the sexes. Umegat, the exiled Roknari divine tending the sacred menagerie of Chalion, reveals that his male lover, a closet Quintarian, was castrated and lost his thumb, "the fifth finger that was the Bastard's" (*Curse* 223), as well as his tongue, thus becoming a martyr. These tortures, ones often associated with the vicious excesses of the Inquisition in Spanish history, reveal the extent to which the Roknari seek to eradicate all that does not fit into their unrelenting binary logic. Yet the irony of the Roknari vilification of the Bastard and what he represents is immediately apparent in Cazaril's back story. His enslavement on a Roknari gallery and his decision to save Danni, later revealed to be Bergon of Ibra, from rape by the oar-master on the slave galley reveals the hypocrisy underlying the Quadrene intolerance. But Cazaril plays an even great part in the ongoing holy war with the Roknari invaders.

Cazaril serves a vital function in the narrative, for he is the protagonist in his own tale of redemption and also the fulcrum in the ongoing war of Reconquest that pits him, and the Quintarian cause, against the hypocrisy and atrocities of the Quardrene. The main plotline of the novel focuses on the related personal conflict between Cazaril and the dy Jironel brothers and how, through the aid of the Daughter of Spring, one of Quintarian gods, the god-touched castillar is able to survive the spell of death magic he cast and remove the demon and Dondo's soul from his body. Bujold effectively weaves the tale of this personal conflict into the larger tapestry of Chalionese Reconquest narrative, for the miracle that frees Cazaril also breaks the curse of the Golden General over the royal family of Chalion, and Cazaril's own experience of slavery with the Roknari becomes instrumental in the brokering of the marriage agreement between Iselle and Bergon, the very boy he saved from slavery and abuse at the hands of the Roknari. Indeed, Cazaril functions as one of the crusaders campaigning against the Roknari, and indirectly challenges (and conquers) the legacy of the Lion of Roknar himself. His role in the Reconquest may be in many respects greater than that of the Quintarian Monarchs of this alternate history, for Cazaril effectively completes Fonsa's magical confrontation with the Golden General. Although the general was a Quadrene "avatar incarnate" (*Curse* 226), and the leftover curse a product of his god-touched force of will that poisoned Chalion, Cazaril becomes the Quintarian saint who retroactively defeats the mightiest of the Quadrenes and in the process unites the opposition against the Roknari. His victory, for

Bujold, represents the triumph of freedom and self-sacrifice (Cazaril "dying" three times for the Chalionese royal family) over Roknari brutality and enslavement, and it is also a spiritual victory for the five gods over the heresy of dualisms. It is in the next *Chalion* novel, *Paladin of Souls*, that Bujold presents the next wave in this crusade against the Quadrenes — the struggle between Ista, the Bastard's own saint, and the Golden General's sorceress daughter Joen, the quintessence of the Quadrene will to subjugate others.

Ista's main story, like Cazaril's in the first novel, is intricately bound up with the larger theological and historical events of the Chalionese Reconquest against the Quadrene, specifically the battle against Jokana, the petty Roknari princedom adjacent to Castle Porifors that serves as the Granada of this alternate world. Like Cazaril, she turns out to be a god-touched saint — in her case touched by the Bastard himself, the "paladin of souls" who confers some of his own champion's ability to free souls from demons to the widowed queen — and in the course of her main struggle to save Lord Illvin from Cattilara's demonic magic tethering him to his deceased brother Arhys she enters into the fray of the ongoing holy war of Reconquest against Joen and her other demon-ridden victims. Ista takes up the fight against the Golden General and his family by fighting them both in body and on the spiritual plane, using her power to remove possessing demons to emerge as a full-fledged warrior for the Bastard and the whole Quintarian cause. Thus Bujold makes the mother of her Isabella figure the one who, like the zealous Castilian queen in Spanish history, begins the final assault against the invaders, both the spiritual invaders of human souls and the physical invaders on the Ibran Peninsula.

The threat of Jokana to the northern provinces of Chalion looms over the novel from the initial capture of Ista and her other pilgrims, and comes to center stage late in the book when Joen leads an attack on Castle Pontifors with an unusual force, a company of demon-possessed sorcerers. The connection between Joen and the Illvin-Arhys-Cattilara plotline becomes evident in the Golden General's plan to use a powerful demon against the Quintarian forces. The Quadrenes, lacking the Bastard's divine powers of control, could not manage the demon, and it jumped into the general's daughter. That the general had hoped to capture a divine of the Bastard to help him free his daughter indicates the hypocrisy at the heart of the Quadrene faith (as it is later said of Joen, "a bad Quadrene is not the same thing as a good Quintarian" [*Paladin* 350]), and it also represents the extent to which the Roknari will use their oppressive beliefs to defeat their enemies by any means necessary. Joen thus functions as a demonic time bomb that, when her father's curse is broken (by Cazaril's actions in *The Curse of Chalion*), can suddenly erupt onto the scene as political and supernatural threat to the Chalionese. As the co-regent for her grandson Prince Sordso she reveals herself to be the true heir to her father's theological duplicity and oppression.

Joen's own embittered soul allowed her to overcome the demon inside her and bend it to her will. The demon that inhabited both Umerue and Cattilara reveals this hidden history:

> "Joen was frantic," said the demon. "She believed"—or convinced herself—"that the old demon was a legacy from her great father, given to her in secret to rise up in just such an unhappy hour and save his grandson from traitors. So she kept it in secret and began learning from it. The old demon was pleased to have such an apt pupil, and taught her everything, thinking it would soon turn the tables and mount her. It underestimated the iron strength of her will, tempered through four decades of swallowed rage. It became even more her slave" [*Paladin* 350].

The diminutive, withered Joen thereby proves herself to be the embodiment of Quadrene belief in hierarchy and subjugation, for she even enslaves a demon and then goes on in turn to force demons into others in order to enslave them, creating her sorcerer army. She even enslaves her own Sordso, the son in whose name she was rallying the Quadrene forces. Ista's thoughts sum up the extent of Joen's depravity: "What Joen did to her enemies might be named war; what she did to her own people was sacrilege" (*Paladin* 420).

The final contest between Ista and Joen occurs on a spiritual battlefield while the siege of Porifors rages in the physical world. Armed with the Bastard's power and her own openness to change, Ista attempts to reach out to Joen and encourage her to give up her manic possessiveness, for as she communicates to the "Mother of Jokana," "*You torment and demolish the very souls you most desire to make grow and love you. You possess truer gifts, stunted though they have been. Let go, find them instead, and live*" (*Paladin* 422). Joen is literally swallowed up by Ista as a result of her refusal to "let go" and give up her quest to master the souls of others as well as the Ibran Peninsula. The novel ends with Ista, despite her romantic possibilities with the newly liberated Illvin, taking up the Bastard's cause and pledging to fight demons and to undertake the mission of Reconquest. As she tells the Learned dy Cabon, the divine of the Bastard who aided her throughout her journey, "We will likely be riding into the Five Princedoms. If you truly aspire to martyrdom, as your early sermons to me implied, you may still have a chance" (*Paladin* 438).

The first two novels of her *Chalion* series end with the world poised on the brink of great change. Bujold's next novel of the Quintarian gods, *The Hallowed Hunt*, breaks with the pattern by concentrating upon another part of her invented Europe and by setting the action in an earlier time period. She has discussed her inspiration for that novel in the medieval history of

Germany, but there too, as in her two *Chalion* books, Bujold explores the juxtaposition of different belief systems in a time of cultural upheaval — the uneasy transition from the older faith based on animal spirits to the Quintarian faith.[6] *The Curse of Chalion* and *Paladin of Souls* take on an era in southern European history that is fraught with great religious and political controversy, particularly now in the twenty-first century looking back at those events, but Bujold carefully avoids linking the Quintarian faith to Christianity and the Quadrene faith to Islam just as she resists making Iselle and Bergon exact replicas of the Catholic Monarchs. What she does instead is use the familiar outline of the Spanish Reconquest and the complex religious issues that arose in it and from it to serve as the scaffolding upon which she builds her own meditations on religious tolerance, acceptance of otherness or oddity, and respect for the difference that is inherent in the human experience.

NOTES

1. See the map of Chalion on *The Bujold Nexus* fansite at http://www.dendarii.com/map.html.

2. Bethany Aram offers a balanced assessment of the *locura* ("madness") of Juana of Castile in "Juana 'the Mad's' Signature: The Problem of Invoking Royal Authority, 1505–1507."

3. The term *Morisco* or "Moor" was inexactly applied to both the North Africans, Berbers from modern Morocco, and other Arabs who formed the bulk of the invasion force (Harvey 1). This imprecise nomenclature endured, however, and "Moor" came to represent all the inhabitants of Muslim faith in the Iberian Peninsula.

4. See Stanley E. Payne's discussion of Spain and Islam in *Spain: A Unique History* for the complex religious landscape of late medieval Spain with its three competing religions that co-existed for several centuries under a truce of sorts that kept the cold war from regaining momentum (54–71).

5. Carter Lindberg gives a detailed account of the Reformation and the reaction by Catholic Europe, particularly the Spanish Inquisition, in *The European Reformations*.

6. Bujold addresses the struggle of competing religions from Northern European culture in the early Middle Ages that inspired her work: "In the case of *The Hallowed Hunt*, elements from more northern European history provided the seed crystals. I wanted to access some of that fascinating, dark, complex pre–Christian 'great northern thing' that so entranced Tolkien, among others. Research reading included the Finnish epic *Kalevala*, the German classic *The Nibelungenlied* (read in 12 hours while stuck at LAX due to a delayed flight to New Zealand), two biographies of Charlemagne, and a great deal of material on the dark ages Christian conversion of those parts" ("Lois McMaster Bujold").

WORKS CITED

Aram, Bethany. "Juana 'the Mad's' Signature: The Problem of Invoking Royal Authority, 1505–1507." *Sixteenth-Century Journal* 29.2 (1998): 331–358.

Benthall, Jonathan. "Confessional Cousins and the Rest: The Structure of Islamic Toleration." *Anthropology Today* 21.1 (February 2005): 16–20.

Bujold, Lois McMaster. "Answers." In *Dreamweaver's Dilemma: Short Stories and Essays.* Framingham, MA: NESFA Press, 1995. 197–225.

_____. "Interview in Barnes & Noble F&SF Newsletter Exploration." Corrina Allen, interviewer. July 2001. *The Bujold Nexus.* 12 April 2012. http://www.dendarii.com/explorations.html

_____. "Lois McMaster Bujold and *The Hallowed Hunt.*" 21 May 2005. *Blogcritics.* 29 Dec. 2011. http://blogcritics.org/books/article/lois-mcmaster-bujold-and-the-hallowed/.

_____. "Mike Houlahan of the New Zealand Press Association Talks to Lois McMaster Bujold." 1 April 2003. *The Bujold Nexus.* 12 April 2012. http://www.dendarii.com/int-nz.html.

_____. *The Curse of Chalion.* New York: HarperTorch, 2002.

_____. *Paladin of Souls.* New York: HarperTorch, 2005.

_____. "Women's Hero Journey: An Interview with Lois McMaster Bujold on *Paladin of Souls.*" June 2009. *Women Writers: A Zine.* 12 April 2012. http://www.womenwriters.net/june09/paladin_interview.html.

"The Curse of Chalion." 29 December 2011. *Wikipedia.* 12 April 2012. http://en.wikipedia.org/wiki/The_Curse_of_Chalion.

Goñi Gaztambide, José. *Historia de la bulla de la cruzada en España.* Vitoria: Editorial del Seminario, 1958.

Harvey, L. P. *Islamic Spain: 1250–1500.* Chicago: University of Chicago Press, 1992.

Lindberg, Carter. *The European Reformations,* 2d ed. Malden, MA: Wiley-Blackwell, 2010.

Lehfeldt, Elizabeth. "Ruling Sexuality: The Political Legitimacy of Isabel of Castile." *Renaissance Quarterly* 53.1 (2000): 31–56.

Lomax, Derek W. *The Reconquest of Spain.* London: Longman, 1978.

O'Callaghan, Joseph F. "Reconquest and Repopulation." In *Medieval Iberia: An Encyclopedia.* Ed. E. Michael Gerli. New York: Routledge, 2002. 697–700.

Netanyahu, B. *The Origins of the Inquisition in Fifteenth-Century Spain,* 2d ed. New York: Random House, 2001.

Payne, Stanley E. *Spain: A Unique History.* Madison: University of Wisconsin Press, 2008.

Stuart, Nancy Rubin. *Isabella of Castile: The First Renaissance Queen.* New York: ASJA Press, 2004.

(Absent) Gods and Sharing Knives

The Purposes of Lois McMaster
Bujold's Fantastic Ir/Religions

JOHN LENNARD

Lois McMaster Bujold is by most standards an extremely successful author of science fiction and fantasy. Besides winning many prizes, she is published in hardback, mass-market, digital, audio, and omnibus editions; sells well in all Anglophone markets (though least in the UK), and has had more than a dozen novels translated into each of Spanish, Italian, German, French, Polish, Russian, Japanese, Croatian, and Chinese (and some into Bulgarian, Romanian, Serbian, Hebrew, Dutch, Czech, Lithuanian, Estonian, and Finnish). A pioneer with publisher Baen in the promotional use of the Internet,[1] she inspires lively discussion in online communities dedicated to her work,[2] and much English and Russian fanfiction[3]—but her academic standing remains slight. She appears in Clute's & Nicholl's *Encyclopedia of Science Fiction* (1993) and Mann's *Mammoth Encyclopedia of Science Fiction* (2001), and a brief entry in the seventh edition of the *Oxford Companion to English Literature* (2009) notes her generic skills, but prior to this volume there has been only a handful of essays,[4] and she goes unmentioned in survey work by such scholars of SF as Broderick, Luckhurst, and Melzer.[5]

In some ways academic reluctance to engage with Bujold is predictable. Her best-known series, fourteen novels and four novellas concerning Lord Miles Vorkosigan of Barrayar[6] (1986–2004, 2010), began by mixing military space opera with superior political romance and Greek tragedy, and via astonishing generic engineering issued in the SF comedic novel of manners; throughout, the "Vorkosiverse" posits and variously displays ideals of military and neo-feudal service, aristocratic honor, absolute imperial rule, and extended conversation — which is to say that Bujold is equally unpalatable to the critical left and devotees of the technosublime. As a white Mid-Westerner she fails to serve the agendas of minority writing attached to her close contemporary Octavia E. Butler (1947–2006), while as an independent post-war woman unimpressed by feminist orthodoxies and deeply interested in the mal/practice of parenthood she has been far less amenable than the older

Ursula Le Guin (b. 1929) and Joanna Russ (1937–2011) to recruitment in the gender wars. But if such ideological filters are removed, academic failures to recognize Bujold's literary talent and superb teachability seem glaring.

My concern here is with Bujold's non– (largely post–) Vorkosigan work — three volumes in the "Chalionverse" series[7] (2001–05) and a four-decker novel, *The Sharing Knife* (2006–09), fantasies marking a development in her writing. There are many thematic continuities with the science-fictive Vorkosiverse — romance, parenthood, the distinction of reputation from honor[8]— but after more than fifteen years and a dozen novels Bujold's shift from far-future, relatively high-tech science fiction to historicized, low-tech fantasy, including shifts of publishers and from extra-terrestrial settings to distinctly European- and North American–derived geographies, offers a clear disjuncture. And intriguingly, both fantasy series (and her one fantasy standalone) centrally raise questions of theology that are rarely more than deep background in the Vorkosiverse.

Bujold's first fantasy, *The Spirit Ring* (1992), is a heroic *Bildungsroman* drawing on the *Autobiography* of the great Renaissance silversmith Benvenuto Cellini and Germanic faerie lore — but though a success on publication[9] it has been largely eclipsed by the popularity of the Vorkosigan series, to which (with hindsight) it stands in suggestive contrast.

The early Vorkosiverse novels were *inter alia* a late–Cold War product whose Barrayarans — green-uniformed and predominantly of Russian stock — are typically atheists given to ancestor-worship. One protagonist, Miles's mother Cordelia, a Betan immigrant to Barrayar, is a Presbyterian of some future variety[10] and there are narratives of grace to be discerned, but equally a Soviet-era overlay of godlessness.[11] Occasional comments touch directly on religion and theology, such as Emperor Ezar's deathbed observations that he has always thought theists more ruthless than atheists and finds atheism a simple but comforting faith (*Shards of Honor* 284), but if Barrayar's pervasive atheism is never narratively trumpeted there are persistent and striking contrasts between how things work there and (say) the kind of self-serving political theology Bob Dylan satirized when he sang that "the country was young / With God on its side" (Dylan). In striking contrast, the overtly Italian-Swiss Renaissance world of *The Spirit Ring* admits not only a potent, all-embracing church but gives it an inquisitorial arm — and in making magic as real as revenants and kobolds sharply distinguishes that arm from psychologized understanding of real-world inquisitors and torture-burnings in European history. Nor is it merely local scene-setting: the mixed-race and rapidly orphaned protagonist, Fiametta, has irrational powers of sufficient strength to make her licensed toleration by the Church a matter of life and death —

increasingly so as exigencies of survival and maturity drive her to do what she must. But it is equally true that the religious issues raised, if pervasive, never dominate, partly because Bujold was then a necessary rather than comprehensive world-builder, leaving much to productively uncertain implication, and partly because the dénouement is so richly eclectic (drawing on mythic sources from Ovid to the Golem of Prague, adding a startling twist, *and* successfully concluding Fiametta's romance) that no one theme emerges as the tonic. There is nevertheless a sufficient association of Bujold's fantasy with the metaphysical, in a manner alien to the sciences of the Vorkosiverse, that the world of Chalion should not have surprised Bujold's readers as much as the mailing-list discussions suggest it seems to have done.

Within a few pages, the protagonist of *The Curse of Chalion* [*Curse*] (2001), Cazaril, taking shelter in a ruined mill, finds a well-dressed corpse in unusual company:

> Five candle stumps, burned to puddles, blue, red, green, black, white. Little piles of herbs and ash, all kicked about now. A dark and broken pile of feathers that resolved itself in the shadows as a dead crow, its neck twisted. A moment's further search turned up the dead rat that went with it, its little throat cut. Rat and Crow, sacred to the Bastard, god of all disasters out of season: tornadoes, earthquakes, droughts, floods, miscarriages, and murders ... *Wanted to compel the gods, did you?* The fool had tried to work death magic, by the look of it, and paid death magic's customary price [5–6].

In Chalion gods are explicitly present, their interventions recognized in theology, law, history, and practical experience. To attempt death magic is the crime of attempted murder, but to succeed is to buy another's death with your own, a "miracle of justice" subtler than Mosaic Law. Readers soon learn that the corpse is that of a merchant, his "victim" an infamous duelist who slew his son and evaded law by intimidating witnesses and bribing a judge; and like the efficacy of the bereaved father's prayer and self-sacrifice *in extremis*, the pantheon that becomes visible around the Lord Bastard offers a ringing critique of Christian and other religious ideologies.

Bujold's pantheon is genuinely a Holy Family — Father of Winter, Daughter of Spring, Mother of Summer, and Son of Autumn equally guiding the annual round, with the Bastard (child of the Mother and a great-souled demon) gathering to Himself all that is out of season. Each has associated colors, activities, stages of life, graces (justice, birth, healing, friendship, balance), corporeal signifiers resembling *chakras* (forehead, mouth, heart, belly, groin), and digits (the Bastard being the thumb).[12] Sexism remains a feature of Chalionese society, especially among the aristocracy, but any notion of female exclusion from priesthood or sacred capacity would be ludicrous, and the ultimate equality of all is underwritten by the one, small miracle granted everyone at the end of their lives, an indication at every funeral of which deity has taken up the dead person's soul. In Chalion itself (one polity among several on a peninsula, with other realms on the continent behind) that miracle is typically unequivocal behavior by a sacred temple-animal, and the religious status of animals becomes increasingly central to *Paladin of Souls* (2003) and *The Hallowed Hunt* (2005), as it transpires that animals possess souls and may (like humans) be god-touched or demon-ridden. Successive novels explore relations with a particular deity — *Curse* with the Daughter, *Paladin* with the Bastard, *Hunt* with the Son — and Bujold has suggested in interview that the series may be completed as a quintet with novels engaging the Father and Mother ("Lois Bujold: Bookfest 04").

The theology of the Chalionverse is a subtle and complex dance of matter and spirit writ large in action. Bujold accepts a common humanist critique of monotheist religions, that one may fairly suppose a deity who is any two of omniscient, omnipotent, and benevolent, but not all three; and deletes omnipotent. Her deities know all and are infinitely merciful, the Bastard being "god of last resort, ultimate, if ambiguous, refuge for those who had made disasters of their lives" (*Curse* 159) — but They may not "reach in [to the world] except through living souls," which can deny Them passage or open wide and "in renouncing action, [make] action possible" (199). As this suggests (and many details confirm), elements of traditional theologies, Christian to Buddhist, are incorporated, with twists of Bujold's own (notably, that matter, "remember[ing] itself so very clearly," is "an amazement to the gods" [412]). The constructed situation produces a common ethos, radically unlike that of the contemporary U.S., where *none* doubt the gods' existence but those few who truly *are* god-touched find it wholly disconcerting, a humbling experience they prefer to keep private. When an envious divine tells the now-sainted Cazaril (a saint being one who "hosts a miracle") that "The Lady of Spring must love you dearly," his rejoinder is wry: "As a teamster loves his mule that carries his baggage [...] whipping it over the high passes" (277). And when a soldier-friend believes the "gods are on our side, right enough. Can we fail?," Cazaril's retort is sharp: "Yes. [...] And when we fail, the gods do, too" (369). Many theological doctrines and rhetorics are thus critiqued, including any necessary personal possession of or by the divine (as in "Born Again" theologies), human domination rather than stewardship of the natural world, the cultivation of piety through fear of eternal punishment, and all individual assertions of preferentially knowing or understanding divine will that are not underpinned by empirically evident miracles.

The Chalionverse thus necessarily represented for Bujold a shift not only in genre but to some extent in technique and style. Some SF&F writers, like Tolkien, are "icebergs," publishing only a fraction of the material they imagine but able to provide answers to almost any question; Bujold, contrariwise, was a "searchlight," imagining only what necessarily fell within protagonists' experience. This served the adventure-driven narratives of the Vorkosiverse well, but in its minimalist world-building tended to preclude the mythic resonances that so enrich Tolkien. Chalion and its surrounding polities, however, are rendered far more explicitly, in geography and general culture, than anywhere in the Vorkosiverse. Deep echoes and refractions of real-world history and geography are involved, the Chalionese peninsula being plainly a version of Iberia: various parallels with its Mediaeval and Early-Modern history, including a version of the Moorish occupation and Reconquista, and in *The Hallowed Hunt* expansion to west-central Europe with Charlemagne's wars as cultural backstory, collectively create a historically known level of technoculture and densely particular cohesion.[13] But so too is Bujold's invented Quintarian theology, with its (supposed) texts, inset sermons, and embracing implications; and its mis/understandings within the fiction open a distinct path to the mythic. For readers, as for Cazaril, the death of his primary antagonist, apparently consumed by fire after dealing Cazaril what should be a fatal belly-wound, is a complex irony involving a lesser antagonist, the death-demon who slew him, and a peculiar series of miracles that saw soul and demon encapsulated like a pregnancy in Cazaril's stomach, but for those who see only the final outcome the antagonist is simply "struck down" for "impiety." Cazaril, saved from death by a further miracle, calls this "a good story [that] will do for most men" (419), but readers know the nascent myth is simplistic, attributing to the gods powers of direct intervention They do not have; that the antagonist died more of theological stupidity than impiety, his free will ignorantly determining his fate; and that (in an entirely practical sense) the gods are far subtler than we and it behooves us to remember it.

Myth (from μυθος, "word, speech") is literally that which is spoken as distinct from written, and Bujold (as in the vignette of roundabout but miraculous justice ending *Curse* as the poor merchant began it) very intelligently plays off within the series the politics of the un/spoken, un/known, and written. Critiques of authoritarian and gender politics are common in SF&F, long addicted to dystopias, and theology a stronger theme than non-readers of the genre might suppose,[14] but Bujold's fusion in these novels of an overt concession of supernatural destiny with fiercely practical refusal of the super-heroic — ordinary human agency is *always* needed — is unusual. In interview, discussing *Paladin of Souls*, she has referred to Joseph Campbell's famous Jungian study, *The Hero with a Thousand Faces* (1949), remarking that the "Hero's

Journey is just the wrong shape for the Heroine" and describing her choice of a post-maternal heroine as consciously engaging with the inadequacy of the maiden-mother-crone triad to modern female life-expectancy and experience ("Women's Hero"). In this sense she comes close to explicit avowal of rewriting received myth on a broadly feminist basis, but the absence of narrow ideology and the restless intelligence of her protagonists and narration fuses critical and spiritual self-awareness with emotional and moral apprehensions, rendering myth not as pagan supposition but as post-literate wisdom.

Bujold also took a considerable risk, literary and otherwise, by providing her theological creation with its own schism, between (from her protagonists' points-of-view) Quintarian orthodoxy and the Quadrene heresy, which asserts the Lord Bastard to be a demon, refusing Him worship and persecuting His divines. In details and cultural consequences this echoes Shia–Sunni and Protestant–Catholic divides, as well as that between Christian and Islamic monotheisms, but is sufficiently distinctive and theologically cross-wired to be itself, catching at readers' instinctive dubiety of a Lord Bastard while drawing sharp attention to His merciful inclusiveness and human pursuits of persecution. Most obviously, worship of the Bastard makes Quintarianism tolerant of homosexuality, a love out of season, while in Quadrene lands it remains unable to speak its name and those convicted suffer mutilation and execution. The Lord Bastard is the seasonless least of the gods, yet His signifier on the hand is the thumb — weaker than the fingers but touching all to provide grip; He is also the god of balance and vile jokes ("Lord Bastard, you *bastard*," as exasperated Ista says to His face in *Paladin*, provoking only a grin [170]), and if Quintarian societies remain as troubled as all humanity Quadrene polities are distinctly worse, associated historically and theologically with an overweening imbalance in favor of the Father.

The primary plot of *The Curse of Chalion* turns on a partial righting of that imbalance, extended in *Paladin of Souls*, while a different historical imbalance and theological persecution through genocidal massacre in earlier Quintarian history informs *The Hallowed Hunt* (the model being Charlemagne's Massacre at Verden in 782 C.E.). As both imbalances generated ultra-patriarchal military tyranny spawning immaterial wrongs that haunt the gods, while righting them involves self-abnegation and generates civil peace and salvations of the lost, the series can also be read as offering original myths of our present social and political evolution that pass beyond commentary and analysis to wisdom about attitudes, beliefs, and endurance. In one of the solicited cover blurbs for *Paladin* Diana Paxson observes that "we learn that [...] it's okay to argue with the gods" — *with*, not *about* — and the cranky interaction of Bujold's protagonists with gods who gnaw and harry them to merciful ends raises the series far above the run of the genre. Sundered in Their nature from the physical contests and sexuality in which Homeric gods amorally indulge themselves, Bujold's deities lack stiff-necked Olympian pride and recurrent fury, being instead wonderfully possessed of irony and (at least in the Bastard's case) low humor; perhaps most strikingly, all those so far closely encountered have laughed or wept with human interlocutors, going beyond even Shakespeare's apprehension of weeping angels "who, with our spleens, / Would all themselves laugh mortal" (*Measure*, 2.2.126–7). Bujold's gods' infinite love, compassion, mercy, and grace for souls are in the best traditions of liberal Christianity, but Their emotional range, familial complementarity, apparent motivations, and limitations inform a vision far removed from sectarian ego and devoid of any punitive hell, genuinely respectful of Free Will in the fullest sense.

The Chalionverse does not abandon the political awareness and action of the Vorkosiverse, but adds to them, with the supernatural and the social functioning of theism, an implicit critique of religiosity that includes satire without ever lessening itself into a satirical mode. Near the end of *Curse* the ex-saint Cazaril borrows from another ex-saint a volume of linked moral, spiritual, and bawdy narratives that is clearly Chaucer's *Canterbury Tales*,[15] while *Paladin of Souls*, in form explicitly a pilgrimage into grace, begins with protagonist Ista encountering a version of the traveling pilgrim-company, including the Wife of Bath and the Nun's Priest (6–11) — so the Chaucerian model of self-transcending satire is plainly relevant. But so too, especially where Ista's final antagonist in *Paladin* is concerned, are Freud and Klein, and the hideous vision of demonic maternity Ista eventually faces and with divine help defeats would be a classic misogyny if Ista was not, in complex balance, herself a mother who has known both the triumph and the loss of a grown child. Socio-psychologically, Bujold's dynamic of damned and redeemed postmaternity includes an indictment of over-controlling parenthood both kind and unkind, a suffocating, velvet prison and a vicious hell of projected inadequacies; literarily, the combination of high adventure, richly comic mockery, resonant theologies, and monstrous gothic dream is highly unusual.

The matter could be pursued in feminist terms but broader humanism seems better advised. Bujold remarked in a written exchange with the Australian academic and novelist Sylvia Kelso,

> I have no desire merely to replace a Patriarchy with a Matriarchy, thanks. Each is equally prone to slip into toxic, soul-destroying forms.
>
> "Where had anyone experienced a matriarchy for test-comparison?" you may logically ask. In fact, most of us have, as children. When the scale of our whole world was one block long, it was a world dominated and controlled by

women. Who were twice our size, drove cars, had money, could hit us if they wanted to and we couldn't ever hit them back. Hence, at bottom, my deep, deep suspicion of feminism, matriarchy, etc. Does this mean putting my mother in charge of the world, and me demoted to a child again? No thanks, I'll pass ... ["Letterspace" 404–05].

Neither Bujold's cheerful irreverence nor her attention to maternity should disguise the gender neutrality and human inclusiveness of "children," "us," "our." Some fans, especially among those self-identifying as feminist and/or in some measure queer, have objected in webposts (and private discussions) to the hetero-normativity and reproductive imperative that attend her uses of romance, but despite those strong features of her fiction its more fundamental divide is not between the sexes but between parents and children — the war of generations or, more accurately, the struggle of genetics and selfhood as a propagating, comedic form of the recurrent struggle between fate and the individual.

It is also notable that scientific training, professional experience at the sharp end of healthcare, and motherhood lead Bujold to a strongly biological mode of analysis. Aral Vorkosigan thinks "all true wealth is biological" (*Mirror Dance* 278)[16] and his creator further postulates that "all true story is biological" and "cultures are to biology as cuisines are to hunger" ("Sherwooding"; also see "Interview" with Lester). Thus in the Vorkosiverse Miles's constant wrestle with his gene-complements and damaged body is central, with the tension between taking responsibility and accepting infantilization. Similarly in the Chalionverse, whether in the structure of the Holy Family and differing genetics of the Bastard, Chalionese temple animals, Cazaril's bizarre pregnancy, Ista's age and the contrast of her motherhood with Joen's, Horseriver's accursed state, or the largest understanding of all life (including gods) as emergent properties of matter,[17] the perspectives Bujold offers embrace biology and ethology, countering religious claims of human distinction and personal grace with truths of genetics, metabolism, and heritable behaviors. Where Christianity asserts a highly unnatural paradigm of fatherhood, Bujold supplies a more natural form of divine increase and half-siblings; where religions of the Book assert the unique supernatural destiny of man, Bujold supplies a vision of spiritual as much as natural continuity between *Homo sapiens* and all life within the biosphere; and where many religions encourage political stasis and philosophical conservatism, Bujold ensures that her created theology is dynamic, extending the drives of physics and chemistry, matter and life, into the divine.

Each volume of *The Sharing Knife* seems simple on first reading — an episodic tale of a couple on a journey, using close third-person narration tied to the protagonists' points-of-view and separating them only during intense but limited action sequences. They meet, marry, and undertake a physical and spiritual journey from what have been their respective homes and cultures to a new home and emergent, compounded culture for themselves and their children. True, the physical journey is a great loop, and true also that along the way they repeatedly save and ultimately change the world — but by comparison with the Vorkosiverse, where up to five points-of-view have been used in one novel, the continuous narrative is straightforward, in the manner of travelogue; and by comparison with the pantheistic complexities and divine humors of the Chalionverse the simplicity of the heroic tests the protagonists face is striking. Yet Bujold remarked in interview, "*The Sharing Knife* may be my subtlest work yet," and it is certainly the hardest to write about compactly (interview with Moridin).

First, therefore, some facts. In *Beguilement* (2006) Fawn Bluefield, a pregnant 18-year-old farmer's daughter running away from home, traumatically loses her baby but meets and marries Dag Redwing, a much older (but longer-lived), one-handed Lakewalker widower; the novel ends with Fawn's second, legitimate departure from reconciled parents. In *Legacy* (2007) the couple travel to Dag's home, but depart when their intercultural and intergenerational romance is rejected by his close family and camp authorities. In *Passage* (2008) they travel by way of a honeymoon down two great rivers to the sea, and in *Horizon* (2009) return overland to a new home, explicitly aiming to extend personal union of bodies and minds to a greater cultural fusion; an epilogue shows Fawn safely delivered of a child and wider cultural reform beginning.

Structurally, the novels might be regarded as paired diptychs. *Beguilement* and *Legacy*, uniting the couple and setting them adrift, are closely continuous, as are *Passage* and *Horizon*, bringing them back to harbor, while between *Legacy* and *Passage* there is a jump of a few days and a hundred miles.[18] Bujold's initial concept extended only to the first two novels, by intent paired romances, the first ending with the woman's choice of the man over her family and the second with the man's choice of the woman over her rival, in this case his job (bound up with family and culture) rather than another woman.[19] The third and fourth novels equally pair, as outward and homeward legs of a journey and as romances — this time in the older literary sense of (vernacular) tales of travel and adventure rather than the narrower subgeneric sense of tales of courtship (though several of those are worked in). Yet if each volume is sturdy and shapely enough to stand alone, and the diptychs perceptible, the general title names a single, four-decker novel rather than a quartet, and the relevant model (allowing for his double-stranded narrative) is clearly Tolkien's *The*

Lord of the Rings, available in one, three, six, or seven volumes but utterly a single work.

The principal danger that Dag and Fawn face (with all in this "wide green world"—a recurrent phrase in dialogue and narration) is what Farmers call *blight bogles* and Lakewalkers *malices*. To understand the ontology of these preternatural entities requires a special *groundsense* that only adult Lakewalkers possess, *ground* being to all physical things, including life, much as we might suppose spirit to be to body—essentially infusing yet other than it. The roots of the idea reach back from a contemporary Gaian vision of the biosphere cradled in its complementary physical environment to deist visions of God as the Book of Nature (and in U.S. context to Emerson and Thoreau)—but in Bujold's creation groundsense serves to divide Farming and Lakewalking cultures, while ground itself unifies everything within or in contact with the biosphere, from humans to rocks. To "rip" ground from something, or otherwise adjust other ground with one's own, as Lakewalkers can, may be quotidian *groundwork* between comrades, a skilled craft of healing or making, an act of seeming magic, or murder—and a malice is an entity, hatching unpredictably from the earth in random locations, that acts as a massively aggressive cancer of ground. Ignorant of mortality, malices seek to incorporate all ground into their own, at first as blindly as the most helpless neonate but, as larger and more intelligent living things (including Farmers and Lakewalkers) are ripped of their grounds, with exponentially increasing intelligence as they undergo successive molts from sessile to mobile, rising up an evolutionary chain. Beyond innate and absolute destructiveness the process has peculiar horrors, for malices also perform groundwork to create slaves, reshaping seized animals into quasi-human *mud-men*[20]; they can also enthrall human minds and have a particular taste for pregnant females, whose uterine groundwork of making offers them an especially rich and informative diet.

Unchecked, every malice that hatches—as half-a-dozen or more do each year—has the capacity to consume the world. Where a malice is other life cannot be, animal or vegetable, and once life has been consumed the physical world is groundripped, even rocks slumping to dust; such *blighted* land remains for centuries inimical to life. And the *only* thing that can stop a malice, by teaching it mortality, is a *sharing knife*—a strictly Lakewalker artifact, carved and groundworked from donated human bone (femurs and humeri are best) and subsequently *primed* with a death, a human ground donated to the knife in the moment of dying by its blade, gifted to lie dormant in its bone until the knife is driven into a malice, when death is shared and the malice dissolves into poisonous but inert dust. Lakewalker groundsense in life is necessary if the donated death is to have the *affinity* to share properly, so only Lakewalker bones and deaths are used; only Lakewalkers wield sharing knives; and only Lakewalkers truly understand what they and malices do.

This sharing of a death, and so a life, is as central to all four volumes as their general title implies, and the necessary funerary customs of Lakewalkers (with the misunderstandings that arise among Farmer communities) suggest one rich area of Bujold's dovetailed narratives. The importance of sharing death with malices swiftly, before they grow wise and strong, makes Lakewalkers nomadic, with seasonal camps dotted around patrol areas, and creates a culture dominated by the effort of supporting constant patrolling throughout thousands of square miles of settled, cultivated, or wilderness land. Lakewalkers are crippled by the burden of unending paramilitary effort yet at odds, politically and culturally, with the far more productive and populous Farmer economies they protect, while the absolute necessity of what they do, enforced on individual and collective psyches by every malice encountered and slain, every knife carved and primed, every shared death mourned and praised, keeps all bound tightly to a narrow round in that wide green world.

In one sense Lakewalker society is literally hidebound, its people as deeply set in rigid ways as the inhabitants of Peake's bitterly satirical *Titus Groan* (1946) and *Gormenghast* (1950), but the more potent literary source is Tolkien. Bujold's engagement with *The Lord of the Rings* is largely conscious, for she encountered it at a critical point in her development and has repeatedly (though not uncritically) praised Tolkien's achievement:

> [*The Lord of the Rings* is] the work to which I've returned most persistently, since I first read it in 1965 [interview with Bonnie Norman].
>
> Is [*The Lord of the Rings*] a perfect book? No, doubtless not. No human thing is. Is it a great book? It is in my heart; it binds time for me, and binds the wounds of time [Carl, "Conversation" 33].

There is so much (sub–)Tolkienesque imitation or influence in Anglophone fantasy that any serious engagement with Tolkien is simultaneously an engagement with the tropes and topoi of hundreds of standalones and trilogies — so he may be taken as at once himself and a generic exemplar subject to critique and (in Adrienne Rich's sense) revisioning. And while I assume here that Tolkien's work, specifically *The Lord of the Rings*, are the subject of direct engagement and revisioning, discussions on the mailing-list show that a reader need not know Tolkien's work to see the fantasy tropes that are present and understand how Bujold reworks them.

This matters, for that revisioning and its consequences are comprehensive. As a primary example, Lakewalkers clearly reimagine Aragorn's Númenórean Dúnedain, or Rangers, patrolling fallen Arnor against encroachment by Sauron's creatures and will. Like Rangers, Lakewalkers inherit a lifelong, unthanked task of battle, expending greater lifespans in defending all at great cost, only to be repaid with dark suspicions of their difference and willful ignorance of their nobility and sacrifice. Equally a traveling, martial people, they have the same field-, wood-, and warcraft as Rangers — as well as, through groundsense, potentials to heal in ways far beyond Farmers' herblore, as Aragorn has through his hidden Númenórean kingship. But the Lakewalkers' struggle is far bleaker than that of the Rangers. Tolkien once remarked that his "Ring of Sauron is only one of the various mythical treatments of the placing of one's life, or power, in some external object, which is thus exposed to capture or destruction with disastrous results to oneself" (*Letters* 279), and such possible destruction provides a framework of hope mediated in Tolkien's narrative through prophecy and the antique knowledge of elves, wizards, and ents. Rangers, that is, struggle in hope, buoyed by received wisdoms promising deliverance and assisted by beings and artifacts of ancient, sometimes supernatural provenance; Lakewalkers struggle without hope of deliverance, knowing a single failure will end the world, and their only artefacts of power are worked from their own bones and sacrifices. The knowledge of sharing knives and groundsense are forms of genetic inheritance, but the enclosing, religiose framework of *The Lord of the Rings* (the coming Age of Men in the fullness of Eru's time) is utterly lacking in *The Sharing Knife;* nor do Lakewalkers have any certain knowledge of the past that led to their present, even their legends being fragmentary. Bujold uses that encompassing bleakness and agonized uncertainty to promote the quotidian, homely, and co-operative hope Dag's and Fawn's union comes to offer. Cazaril, in *The Curse of Chalion*, suspected that "prayer [...] was putting one foot in front of the other. Moving all the same" (349), a truth Dag and Fawn enact; but the commonest Lakewalker oath is "absent gods," and there is no more sign of active divinity in *The Sharing Knife* than in *King Lear.*

In SF&F terms the novel could be labeled dystopian, for there are, here and there in its world, traces of a lost civilization whose catastrophic collapse was presumably linked to the coming of malices, and whose scattered survivors produced Farmer and Lakewalker cultures. But here matters become epistemologically and ontologically complex, for just as Lakewalkers blend with their Rangerly aspects signs of Amerindian somatotype and tribal tent-culture, so the setting is plainly Bujold's native Mid-West, from a great northern "Dead Lake" encompassing all the Great Lakes, where the sunken ruins of "Ogachi strand" can be seen in place of Chicago, to the rivers of *Passage's* journey, the Grace and Gray, which correspond to the Ohio and Mississippi.[21] Dag and Fawn re-enact the flatboat round of the late eighteenth and early nineteenth centuries from the upper Ohio to New Orleans, returning overland on the angle — Bujold's "Tripoint Trace" paralleling the Natchez Trace and extending through the Appalachians. An "Author's Note" in *Passage* credits several historical sources, including *A Narrative of the Life of David Crockett, by Himself* (1834), and one implication of the dystopian backstory is an echoic sense of a long post-catastrophic North America that has in isolation recovered culturally to a point equivalent to *c.*1800.

Analogies cannot be forced — there are no buffalo herds or gunpowder (though stamped metal crossbows have just been invented), and the great trade-triangle, flatboats down, keelboats or land-caravans up, is an internal circulation, largely lacking the East-Coast markets and wholly without the overseas trade New Orleans historically served — but neither can correspondences with geography and history be ignored. This "wide green world" is not our world but the novel is in one aspect a vision of a far future grossly depopulated, impoverished, and endangered by what North American humans now are or will become — but recalling historical forks in the road and teetering on the brink of a new industrial age. As Farmer numbers grow, stretching Lakewalker resources to breaking-point and creating proto-cities that accumulate capital and creativity, there is for historically informed readers a pressing awareness of a nascent Cincinnati and Pittsburgh, of what the steamboat and cotton gin meant for the Mid-West and its native life, animal and vegetable — an ecological awareness fuelled by the Gaian concept of ground and the potential correspondence of malice-blighted land with both irradiated land (as at the Nevada Proving Grounds) and lands like those between Chicago and Buffalo that are industrially soiled to the point of ruinous sterility.

Such triangulation of known past and supposed future, criss-cross bearings on the reading present, is not uncommon in SF&F, and may be a basic aspect of the genre, but Bujold's construction is as subtly complex as her narratives seem straightforward. Myths of the Western Frontier and their underlying truths are constantly activated and as constantly alienated: homesteaders strike out into unsettled territory, copper-skinned tribal warriors merge with weather-beaten Rangers, and exploitative proto-industrialists raping the land are echoed by malices blighting all life; as the heroic journey through trial and loss to understanding and gain is at once the historical riverman's round from Ohio to the sea and back, and the romance journey of an odd couple into happy parenthood. If all meanings were equally at play the result might be chaotic, but Bujold's technique allows the mythos of the Lakewalkers to be seen with Tolkien's Rangers and tribal Amerindian society (and their respective literary and historical freights) equally serving as the distance-points of her picture, referential foci implicit in the perspective but lying outside the frame.[22] *Any* detail of narrative or conversation, any fragment of legend or backstory, may press with fabular force on present attitudes and practices, disputes and contradictions, and the potency of the whole increases exponentially as successive installments lock into place.

The incremental volumes have strong linking structures and patterns. In each, one particular evil is overcome — malices of increasingly advanced intelligence in *Beguilement*, *Legacy*, and *Horizon*, a murderous Lakewalker renegade in *Passage*— and in parallel Dag's capacity of healing groundwork matures in symbolic acts of reconstruction or healing using the renascent ground of his lost hand, successively of a glass bowl, a sharing knife, a human knee and appendix, and a human womb, child, and spine. In each someone is wrenched from a familiar, stifling home into a company pilgrimage of hope — Fawn, Dag, Fawn's brother Whit, and a Lakewalker medicine maker, Arkady — that collects other strays, Farmers (including rivermen) and Lakewalkers alike. In each, forms of purely human malice are encountered in the sins of falsehood and lust, jealousy and pride, despair and envy, indifference and selfishness; and in each deepening understanding of the potentials of groundwork, by protagonists and readers alike, induces a new pertinence of philosophy, broadly, in turn, Gaian, Emersonian, Marxist, and Augustinian, while all sins and philosophies are in some measure present throughout. The Gaian goes with ground and groundwork, the Emersonian with the relation of individuals to history, the Marxist with the imminence of capitalized industry (signified in a new mint), and the Augustinian with the fundamental divide of sessile and mobile, which applies to malices as they mature and to sedentary farmer and nomadic Lakewalker cultures.

Given Bujold's knowledge of first-millennial history and the dystopian politics and theologies with which Augustine grappled following the sack of Rome in 410 c.e., many Augustinian resonances might be traced, especially in structural oppositions; but the profoundest engagement of *The Sharing Knife* is with his insistence (in book 13 of the *De Civitate Dei*) that death is penal. Amid the fragmented materials of Lakewalker legend are conjectures from which a Christian theology of punitively inherited sin and death might be constructed, the lost civilization in its overweening pride failing, birthing malices, and leaving its descendants cursed to fight them — but Dag's (and others') normative use of "absent gods" as oath or exclamation, the lack of any certain connection between lost past and altered present, and the corresponding absence of any theology, collectively frame a wholly distinct understanding of mortality. As the bones of ancestral Lakewalkers are recovered, carved into knives, primed with a heart's death, and taken into the working, wide green world as tools against the all-encompassing death latent in every malice, a union of the grounds and purposes of dead and living is created that goes far beyond Barrayaran ancestor-worship and stands in sharp contrast to modern Western norms of predatory death, mortal terror, and hasty cremation. Self-sacrifice, donating body and spirit in death, is an ultimate end for individual Lakewalkers, without promise of personal post-mortem survival or divine reward but with well-grounded hope of utility to the living, as individual kin or co-workers and as collective humanity — an ideal Bujold compares with real-world practices of organ, blood, and body donation.[23]

Within that encompassing validation, moreover, Bujold weaves a particularly memorable tale connecting Fawn's lost and surviving babies. The miscarried babe, whose conception and faithless father initially drove Fawn to flee home, is not lost to natural causes. She is captured by a mud-man and taken to its malice, her fetus's ground being ripped from it and her *in utero* — but, Dag arriving and the malice being itself slain in the next instant by Fawn wielding Dag's sharing knife, the fetus's ground is accidentally transferred to an unprimed sharing knife Dag also carries, against his own potential need to suicide if mortally wounded.[24] That newly primed knife, a bone from Dag's long-dead wife containing a Farmer death (without a birth), functions to unite Fawn and Dag but also to precipitate Dag's alienation from the rigidities of Lakewalker culture and his investigation of groundwork, a trope that becomes that of the craft-apprentice discovering fundamental truths that stultifying teachers have long forgotten or misinterpreted. The knife's utility is a painful conundrum, for the innocent Farmer death it contains lacks the affinity to make it capable of teaching a malice mortality, but Bujold wonderfully solves the puzzle (in *Legacy*) in its use to destroy with Dag's ground-assistance a surviving fragment of a slain malice, an isolated *involution* the malice had deployed as a mud-man nursery. The peculiarities of the knife's death-without-a-birth and the malice's birth-beyond-a-death balance movingly, while emotional and material connections between Dag's dead wife's bone and Fawn's dead child-by-another greatly deepen their union and bless it with a redemption as profound as it is purely human.

A second sharing knife links *Passage* and *Horizon*. Its origin is unknown (it is among the booty of the renegade Lakewalker's gang), but Dag redoes its groundwork and offers the captured renegade the chance to share his death-by-execution as atonement. Taking an exceptional step into public action Dag also explains exactly what he is doing, and why, to Farmers (largely rivermen) he led against the renegade's gang, an act of disclosure intensely disturbing to all but critically breaching mutual isolations; the resulting knife, like the one that bore the fetal ground, is anomalous in origin and nature. Correspondingly, it is used against a malice, after Dag's temporary incapacitation in *Horizon*, by the newly pregnant Fawn and her brother, without Lakewalker assistance — a feat by groundsense-less farmers that spells revolution for Farming and Lakewalking beliefs, cultures, and societies, and more proximately ensures Fawn's survival to bear her and Dag's child. The two anomalous sharing knives superbly thematize and orchestrate, in paired succession, the central myth of co-operative survival and growth that Bujold expounds — Dag and Fawn jointly conceiving, bearing, and midwifing a secular human deliverance that impassions life, compensates for loss, and redeems sacrifice.

A further strand of the theme concerns the *beguilement* for which the opening volume is named. Though Lakewalkers use groundsense and donate ground reinforcements to help and heal themselves, they are strictly forbidden and deeply inhibited from healing Farmers, partly because they fear to excite demand they could not meet but primarily because Farmers are left beguiled, violently craving further ground-interaction. Dag's discovery that emergency groundwork on Fawn after her miscarriage has *not* beguiled her, that mutual love transcends the problem, leads him to discover the cause, that Lakewalkers do not beguile one another because they automatically *exchange* ground, but in treating Farmers their own assumptions and bigotry prevent the exchange, leaving Farmers beguiled by their own newly excessive grounds. All that is necessary to avoid beguilement or to unbeguile is to be open to accepting ground from another, to abandon pristine self-closure — but for Lakewalker and Farmer cultures this is an axis of revolution, and in the new culture Dag and Fawn envision the genetic power of Lakewalkers will be set to work healing Farmers (rather than hoarding medical "magic"). Dag's explorations of groundwork also find a way of giving Farmers a degree of protection from ground-ripping, and in the new culture Lakewalkers will work towards maximally enabling Farmers to protect themselves and to help in the still necessary, unending work of patrolling to discover and slay every last malice that emerges.

That malices are unchanged, their fatal immortality unchecked save as it has always been checked, knife by sharing knife, is the last expression of Bujold's subtlety. The novel charts a hopeful revolution in culture and strategy but struggle and war continue, and there is no possibility of any revolution in tactics; each malice must be pierced by a knife, and neither constant patrolling nor mortal danger in close-quarter combat can be qualified. Farmer society may be on the verge of revolutionizing living standards but production of sharing knives cannot be industrialized, and nothing lessens Lakewalkers' obligation to donate bones and hearts' deaths to the unending war of survival. By comparison, for all Tolkien's elegiac tenor and long theological view of evil, *The Lord of the Rings* climaxes in unquestionable eucatastrophe (a word he coined in his essay "On Fairy-Stories"), the destruction of Sauron by "two humble Hobbits" as a divinely joyous moment of saving the world.[25] Conversely, in *The Sharing Knife* the world is, as Dag insists, saved every time a malice is slain — once each in *Beguilement* and *Legacy*, twice in *Horizon*— and yet the struggle is unaltered. For all Tolkien's insistence on the heroic capacity of humble hobbits, and his potent Christian parable (born of experiences in 1914–18) of little men stepping forward into greatness at the hour of need, his heroes are rendered finally mythic and transcendent, privileged travelers into the Uttermost West; while Bujold's ordinary farmgirl and weary old patroller who repeatedly save and begin to transform their world remain to parent children, plant crops, tend the sick, and love ordinary life in the malice-riddled lands of the Mid-West.

This is a point Bujold has addressed directly, responding to a comment posted after one of Jo Walton's Tor blogs on the series that regretted the absence of any final eucatastrophe:

> Not only was [the Ultimate Defeat of All Evil] not the story I was telling, it was the story my entire 1600 page story was arguing *against*.
> Most epics are, in one way or another, war stories, and [*The Sharing Knife*] was an epic all about waging peace. (As is romance, as is much comedy.) Which put it seriously at odds with several centuries of Western narrative tradition, I noted while wrestling with it all. I was asked recently in an interview why so little democracy is ever shown in the F&SF genres, and it occurred to me that democracy, too, resists the usual narrative expectations, or at least, habits, because it, too, is all about waging peace. Democracy as an argument that goes on endlessly, and never reaches closure...?
> It wasn't just the minor aspects of Tolkien (and the genre he spawned) I was taking on, here. How successfully, it's not for me to know, but there you go. There is a trick to deliberately thwarting reader expectations — you have to deliver in the end something as good or better than the reward that was withheld. Which is harder than it sounds — those narrative habits are so ingrained *because* they work, over and over. And over. (Quite like the romance template, I must observe. Which points to something biological, under all the social camouflage.)[26]

Considering its setting and parable of quotidian democratization in the face of absolute evils one could argue for *The Sharing Knife* as a profoundly North-American response to *The Lord of the Rings* that works through its distinctive geographical, historical, and literary reference, and through systematic negation of the religious beliefs and assumptions of supernatural destiny that perfuse the highly Catholic Tolkien's huge legendarium. Grappling in its heroic medievalism with the worst of the twentieth century, *The Lord of the Rings* was (until J.K. Rowling exploded Harry Potter upon an unsuspecting world) the most widely shared popular fantasy of modern times, for good but also dated (historically specific) and in some ways pernicious reasons. Critiques of

Tolkien's conservative Catholic misogyny and support for hierarchy are well-known, those of his (supposedly) anti–Modernist Georgianism and (in the hostile view) pastiche antiquity familiar to literary critics — but explicit responses to his Europeanism, Christian religiosity *per se* (as politically and philosophically harmful), and eucatastrophic-yet-elegiac redemptions (as self-deluding), are very much rarer. And what replaces Tolkien's theological structures and underpinnings is, again, biology — not a reaching out to that which is beyond and other, but a reaching within for that which is wholly human and fundamentally animal. Even the quasi-mystical powers of groundsense that Lakewalkers enjoy are understood in genetic terms (halfbreeds having unpredictable and limited abilities, not the absolute choice afforded Tolkien's half-elven), and the entire struggle, strictly limited to the wide but not high biosphere, is always conducted in terms of flesh and blood. As in the Chalion-verse feminist readings are possible but biological ones comprehend them and extend more widely still, the elements of feminism, from the narrative presence of Fawn's menstrual cycle and pregnancies to the strong affirmations of domestic work, being themselves part of a cultural understanding rooted in the realities of biochemical life.

Resonant equally with tropes of fantasy and history — Emerson on self-reliance, Twain on the tremendous romance of Mississippi boating, Faulkner on wilderness, Martin Luther King's Civil Rights dream, the evils wrought and celebrated under banners of theology and industry, and the unending intrapatriarchal struggles for personal dominance that maculate history — *The Sharing Knife* is indeed Bujold's "subtlest work yet," deserving both critical attention and to be taught as widely as possible for its intrinsic merits and profound capacities to provoke thought.

Bujold's associations of religion with fantasy and irreligion with science fiction is odder than it first seems. The sub-genres are not of course wholly distinct, and neither is Bujold's polarization: Cordelia Vorkosigan reads the Vorkosiverse in terms of grace and the glory of God, while the (supposed) deities of the Wide Green World are notable only for their frequently remarked absence. Yet it remains true that to enter the Vorkosiverse is largely to set theology and metaphysics aside, while to enter any of Bujold's fantasy worlds is to be faced, early and often, with problems and issues that actively require, if not a theological attitude, then at least an attitude to theology.

What is striking is the extent to which the foregrounding of religious issues is associated with critique. Whether in relation to Fiametta's vulnerability to her church, the saint-harrying gods of the Chalionverse, or the absent gods of the Wide Green World whose apparent legacy of malices is a constant threat to all life, theology no sooner appears than it undergoes searching scrutiny. Given the acidic dysfunction of politico-religious discourse in the U.S., Bujold's single most important market, the mode of fantasy may offer a degree of cultural protection that harder SF treatments of, say, a future Christianity would not — and certainly the evidence of the mailing list suggests that a wide range of believers, including some with fairly fundamentalist understandings of Christian dogma, can read Bujold without moral difficulty. More positively, one could say that whereas a novel like Mary Doria Russell's *The Sparrow* is concerned with the human impulse to faith only as represented and conditioned by the Society of Jesus, Bujold's fantasies do not engage with any particular sect but rather with human capacities of belief and faith, and hence remain open to all readers.

Bujold's fantastical theologies are always accompanied by biological understandings and constructions of narrative. Fiametta's resolution of her problems turns (in a way that should not be spoiled) on lactation; the gods of the Chalionverse can act only through the living, whose bodies with their frailties and fluids are a constant presence; and all Lakewalkers have to oppose malices are the sharing knives made of their own bones and deaths. Bujold's notion that "cultures are to biology as cuisines are to hunger" is borne out in her work, and much that might be separately identified in criticism (including feminism, practice of comedy, and narrative analyses of sociopolitics) can be subsumed into that pervasive concern. Her protagonists' ages matter as much as their genders; at root the drives to union of comedy and reproduction are the same; and the technologies she invents in any detail — uterine replicators, cryonics, groundsense — are intrinsically of or open to bioscience and deployed in ways specifically highlighting biological issues and imperatives.

The access of religious and theological concerns in Bujold's fantasy exposes them to a biological critique, that in the Chalionverse poses against the masculinities, patriarchies, anthropomorphisms, and irrational rigidities of real-world religious dogma and institutions a strongly ethological and holistic view of the human animal; and in *The Sharing Knife* insists upon the intrinsic depth and range of that animal's resources, even when faced with an overwhelming anti-biological foe. Bujold's ways of narrating and analyzing biology, presenting bioscientific critique, were developed in the Vorkosiverse through uterine replicators, the contrast of Miles's teratogenic and Mark's surgical and chemical damage, the great genetic experiment of the Cetagandan empire, bioengineered Quaddies and Taura, and many more such tropes and topoi; but their great flowering has been in the post–Vorkosiverse fantasies, where they have been deployed not against but to encompass a pervasive mode of human thought and society that tends strongly to manipulate rather than understand biology, and that in contemporary U.S. politics is as polarized from it as God from Darwin. That Bujold has nevertheless been largely ignored by scholars of SF&F as a politically incorrect conservative is an irony I imagine she appreciates without much caring for.

To line up the Vorkosiverse, *The Spirit Ring*, the Chalionverse, and *The Sharing Knife* is thus to consider in outline an increasingly remarkable literary career characterized by exceptionally skilled generic engineering and sustained themes of responsible parenthood, personal honor, and public service. As much as the older Le Guin and Russ, the closely contemporary Butler as an African American pioneer in the genre, and the somewhat younger author of young adult fantasies, Tamora Pierce (b. 1954), a less literary but also academically underrated talent,[27] Bujold has forged a distinctively and powerfully female but also individual path in SF&F, very creatively manipulating popular genres and sub-genres and deploying seemingly conservative ideologies that conceal radical critiques to what are, broadly speaking, integrationist, feminist, and richly humanist ends. Her concerted literary effort to move beyond a Christian paradigm and certain of its implicit values without discarding its wisdom or ideal ethics, though pursued in the Vorkosiverse, could not in that creation find full expression, but in the fantastical polytheist theology of Chalion and post-deist humanism of *The Sharing Knife* Bujold has achieved in great measure an imaginative, moral, critical, and spiritual vision of our mortality and social needs from which any might and all could profitably learn.

NOTES

1. Bujold's official mailing-list (to which she regularly posts) dates to 1994; *A Civil Campaign* (1999) was the first novel promotionally "snippeted" by Baen Books; and with *CryoBurn* (2010) she joined the Baen authors to have a CD with almost her complete backlist included with a new hardback.

2. In addition to the mailing-list, there are discussion communities at http://community.livejournal.com/lmbujold/ and http://bar.baen.com/ ("Miles to Go").

3. See http://www.dendarii.co.uk/FanFic/, http://community.livejournal.com/bujold_fic/, and http://www.fanfiction.net/book/Miles_Vorkosigan/. For Russian fic see http://lavka.lib.ru/bujold/ and http://www.barrayar.slashfiction.ru/.

4. See bibliography under Carl & Helfers, Duchamp, Haehl, Kelso, Lennard, Lindow, Merrick & Williams, Smith, & Wehrmann.

5. She is not cited in Broderick's *Reading by Starlight* (1995), Luckhurst's *Science Fiction* (2005), or Melzer's *Alien Constructions* (2006).

6. A fifteenth novel, *Captain Vorpatril's Alliance*, was published in the fall of 2012.

7. Fans also refer to the "Five Gods Universe" (5GU).

8. Formally made in *A Civil Campaign: A Comedy of Biology and Manners* (293).

9. It came second in the 1993 *Locus* readers' poll for Best Fantasy Novel of the year.

10. Cordelia's theism is evident in the narratives; Presbyterianism is specified by Bujold in the FAQ answer, "It's clear that Cordelia is religious...."

11. See my essay "Of Marriage and Mutations."

12. There is an overview at "Religion in the Chalionese Universe" on Wikipedia.

13. The extraordinary tale of Queen Joanna and the corpse of Philip I the Fair is of particular importance to *Paladin of Souls*, and the massacre of pagan Saxons at Verden in 782 to *The Hallowed Hunt*.

14. For a brief overview, see Farah Mendelsohn, "Religion and Science Fiction."

15. "'It's a fine conceit,' said Umegat. 'The author follows a group of travellers to a pilgrimage shrine, and has each one tell his or her tale in turn. Very, ah, holy.' 'Actually, my lord,' the dedicat whispered, 'some of them are very lewd'" (*Curse* 439).

16. I omit two ellipses (the phrase being spoken by Aral in breathless cardiac extremis).

17. See Bujold's "Science Fiction, Fantasy, and Me," her keynote address at the 2008 UPC Awards in Barcelona.

18. *Beguilement* and *Legacy* were grouped in an SFBC omnibus (2007).

19. See the Bujold email quoted in Nikohl K. & John Lennard, eds., *A Reader's Companion to* A Civil Campaign 234–5. By generic convention Fawn's rival should be Kauneo, Dag's long-dead first wife, but Bujold productively inverts that trope.

20. "You understand how mud-men are made, right? The malice places a live animal in the soil, and alters the creature's ground to impel its body to grow into a human form. [...] Ground is the underlying truth of the world. The malice turns it into a lie, or at least, into something else, and the matter labors to match it" (*Horizon* 326).

21. To avoid the necessity of multiple river-crossings the courses of the Cumberland and Tennessee Rivers are changed, being combined into the "Hardboil" and given a confluence with the Gray (Mississippi) rather than the Grace (Ohio).

22. There is wide interpretative possibility: Jo Walton, writing for the Tor website before *Horizon* was published thought Lakewalkers resembled "Rangers with something of the spirit of cowboys" rather than Amerindians ("Western Fantasy"). I owe this reference to Katherine Collett.

23. Email to the author, May 2010; cited with permission.

24. There are Lakewalker legends of paired patrollers finding themselves facing a malice with only an unprimed knife — so one must suicide to provide a priming.

25. In his lengthy 1951 letter to Milton Waldman, Tolkien said that in the "scene where all the hosts of the West unite to do honour and praise to the two humble Hobbits, Frodo and Sam, we reach the 'eucatastrophe' of the whole romance: that is the sudden joyous 'turn' and fulfilment of hope, the opposite of tragedy, that should be the hallmark of a 'fairy-story' of higher or lower tone, the resolution and justification of all that has gone before. It brought tears to my eyes to write it, and still moves me, and I cannot help believing that it is a supreme moment of its kind." (The passage is quoted from Hammond & Scull's *The Lord of the Rings: A Reader's Companion*, p. 748, rather than Tolkien's *Letters*, as this source reprints the entire letter including the *précis* of *The Lord of the Rings*.)

26. Jo Walton, "Tussling with Tolkien," comment no. 5. The plain-text formatting has been silently emended. I owe this reference to Katherine Collett.

27. Bujold has not read Pierce's work (email to the author, May 2010, cited with permission), but several moments in *The Sharing Knife* demonstrate a convergence, notably the childlike confusion of the mud-bat Dag slays (*Horizon*, p. 346) and the deaths of "killing devices" powered by slain children in Pierce's *Lady Knight* (2002).

WORKS CITED

Birch, Dinah, ed. *The Oxford Companion to English Literature*, 7th ed. Oxford: Oxford University Press, 2009.

Broderick, Damien. *Reading by Starlight: Postmodern Science Fiction*. London: Routledge, 1995.

Bujold, Lois McMaster. *The Curse of Chalion*. New York: Eos, 2001.

_____. "Women's Hero Journey: An Interview With Lois McMaster Bujold on *Paladin of Souls*." Alan Oak, interviewer. June 2009. *WomenWriters*. 9 March 2012. http://wome nwriters.net/june09/paladin_interview.html.

_____. "An Interview with Author Lois McMaster Bujold." Bonnie Norman, interviewer. November 2008. *A Working Title*. 12 March 2012. http://awthome.wordpress.com/2010/ 02/08/an-interview-with-author-lois-mcmaster-bujold/.

_____. "Interview: Lois McMaster Bujold." Jeff Lester, interviewer. September 2011. *Lightspeed*. 12 March 2012. http://www.lightspeedmagazine.com/ nonfiction/feature-intervie w-lois-mcmaster-bujold/.

_____. "Interview with Lois McMaster Bujold." Moridian, interviewer. 20 May 2010. *ShadowDance*. 12 March 2012. http://heretherebeshadows.blogspot.com /2010/03/inter view-with-lois-mcmaster-bujold.html.20 May 2010.

_____. "It's clear that Cordelia is religious..." Lois Bujold Mailing List Plot FAQ. The Bujold Nexus. 9 March 2012. http://www.dendarii.com/ bujold_faq.html#cord-religion.

_____. "Lois Bujold: Bookfest 04." 9 Oct. 2004. *Library of Congress Webcasts*. 9 March 2012. http://www.loc.gov/today/cyberlc/feature_wdesc.php?rec=3586.

_____. *Mirror Dance*. Riverdale, NY. Baen, 1994.

_____. *Paladin of Souls*. New York: Eos, 2003.

_____. "Science Fiction, Fantasy, and Me." Keynote address at the 2008 UPC Awards in Barcelona. Nov. 2008. The Bujold Nexus. 16 April 2012. http://www.dendarii.com/bar celona.html.

_____. *Shards of Honor*. Riverdale, NY: Baen, 1986.

_____. *The Sharing Knife: Horizon*. New York: Eos, 2009.

_____. "Sherwooding on genre, gender, representation." 11 Aug. 2011. Email to the Official LMB mailing-list. 12 April 2012. http://lists.herald.co.uk/ pipermail/lois-bujold/2011-august/080062.html. Quoted with permission.

Campbell, Joseph W. *The Hero with a Thousand Faces*, 2d ed. New York: Bollingen Foundation, 1968.

Carl, Lilian Stewart, and John Helfers, eds. *The Vorkosigan Companion: The Universe of Lois McMaster Bujold*. Riverdale, NY: Baen, 2008.

Clute, John, and Peter Nicholls. *The Encyclopedia of Science Fiction*, rev. ed. New York: St Martin's Griffin, 1995.

Duchamp, L. Timmel. "Pleasure and Frustration: One Feminist's Reading of Lois McMaster Bujold's *A Civil Campaign*." 2000. *L. Timmel Duchamp*. 9 March 2012. http://ltim mel.home.mindspring.com/campaign.html.

Dylan, Bob. "With God On Our Side." 1963. *BobDylan.com*. 3 March 2012. http:// www.bobdylan.com/songs/with-god-on-our-side.

Haehl, Anne L. "Miles Vorkosigan and the Power of Words: A Study of Lois MacMaster Bujold's Unlikely Hero." *Extrapolation* 37.3 (Fall 1996): 224–33.

Hammond, Wayne G., and Christina Scull. *The Lord of the Rings: A Reader's Companion*. Boston: Houghton Mifflin, 2005.

Hartwell, David, and Kathryn Cramer, eds. *The Space Opera Renaissance*. New York: Tor, 2006.

K., Nikohl, and John Lennard, eds. *A Reader's Companion to* A Civil Campaign. 2011. *The Bujold Nexus*. 9 March 2012. http://www.dendarii.com/accc.html.

Kelso, Sylvia. "Lois McMaster Bujold: Feminism and 'The Gernsback Continuum' in Recent Women's SF." 1992. *The Bujold Nexus*. 9 March 2012. http://www.dendarii. co.uk/FanFic/gc3.html.

_____. "Loud Achievements: Lois McMaster Bujold's Science Fiction." 1998. *The Bujold Nexus*. 9 March 2012. http://www.dendarii.com/reviews/kelso.html.

_____. *Three Observations and a Dialogue: Round and About SF*. Seattle: Acqueduct Press, 2009. (Includes "Letterspace" and "Loud Achievements.")

_____, and Lois McMaster Bujold. "Letterspace: in the chinks between published fiction and published criticism." In *Women of Other Worlds: Excursions through Science Fiction and Feminism*. Helen Merrick & Tess Williams, eds. Nedlands: University of Western Australia Press, 1999. 383–409.

Lennard, John. "Of Marriage and Mutations: Lois McMaster Bujold and the Several Lives of Lord Miles Naismith Vorkosigan." In *Of Sex and Faerie: Further Essays on Genre Fiction*. Tirril: Humanities E-Books, 2010. 70–111.

Lindow, Sandra J. "The Influence of Family and Moral Development in Lois McMaster Bujold's Vorkosigan Series." *Foundation: The International Review of Science Fiction* 83 (Autumn 2001): 25–34.

Luckhurst, Roger. *Science Fiction*. Cambridge: Polity Press, 2005.

Mann, George, ed. *The Mammoth Encyclopedia of Science Fiction*. New York: Carroll & Graf, 2001.

Melzer, Patricia. *Alien Constructions: Science Fiction and Feminist Thought*. Austin: University of Texas Press, 2006.

Mendlesohn, Farah. "Religion and Science Fiction." In *The Cambridge Companion to Science Fiction*. Edward James and Farah Mendlesohn, eds. Cambridge: Cambridge University Press, 2003. 230–40.

"1993 Locus Awards." 1993. *The Locus Index to SF Awards*. 9 March 2012. http://www.locusmag.com/SFAwards/Db/Locus1993.html.

Peake, Mervyn. *Gormenghast*. London: Eyre & Spottiswood, 1950.

_____. *Titus Groan*. London: Eyre & Spottiswood, 1946.

Pierce, Tamora. *Lady Knight*. New York: Random House, 2002.

"Religion in the Chalionese Universe." 26 Nov. 2011. *Wikipedia*. 9 March 2012. http://en.wikipedia.org/wiki/The_Fivefold_Pathway_of_the_Soul.

Shakespeare, William. *Measure for Measure*. In *The Riverside Shakespeare*, 2d ed. G.B. Evans et al., eds. Boston: Houghton Mifflin, 1997. 584–621.

Smith, Erica H. "Runaway Roses and Defiant Skellytums: Thoughts on Plants, Gardens, Horticulture and Botany in the Vorkosiverse." 12 May 2007. *LiveJournal*. 9 March 2012. http://hedda62.livejournal.com/214169.html.

Tolkien, J.R.R. *Letters*, 2d ed. Humphrey Carpenter, ed. Boston: Houghton Mifflin, 2000.

_____. *The Lord of the Rings*, 2d ed. Boston: Houghton Mifflin, 1994.

_____. "On Fairy-Stories." *The Monsters and the Critics and Other Essays*. Christopher Tolkien, ed. London: George Allen & Unwin, 1983. 109–61.

Walton, Jo. "Western Fantasy: Lois McMaster Bujold's *Sharing Knife* Books." 2 January 2009. *Tor.com*. 9 March 2012. http://www.tor.com/blogs/2009/01/western-fantasy-lois-mcmaster-bujolds-sharing-knife#11206.

_____. "Tussling with Tolkien: Lois McMaster Bujold's *The Sharing Knife: Horizon*." 23 February 2009. *Tor.com*. 12 April 2012. http://www.tor.com/blogs/2009/02/lois-bujolds-the-sharing-knife-horizon.

Wehrmann, Jurgen. "Jane Eyre in Outer Space: Victorian Motifs in Post-Feminist Science Fiction." In *A Breath of Fresh Eyre: Intertextual and Intermedial Reworkings of Jane Eyre*. Margarete Rubik and Elke Mettinger-Schartmann, eds. Amsterdam: Rodopi, 2007. 149–65.

Appendix
Bibliography and Awards

Bibliography

The most complete and detailed bibliography can be found at *The Bujold Nexus*, http://www.dendarii.com/biblio.html. Here I list each series in its internal chronological order, followed by original date of publication.

VORKOSIGAN SERIES

"Dreamweaver's Dilemma" (1996)
Falling Free (1988)
Shards of Honor (1986)
Barrayar (1991)
The Warrior's Apprentice (1986)
"The Mountains of Mourning" (1989)
The Vor Game (1990)
Cetaganda (1995)
Ethan of Athos (1986)
"Labyrinth" (1989)
"The Borders of Infinity" (1987)
Brothers in Arms (1989)
Linking sections of *Borders of Infinity* (1989)
Mirror Dance (1994)
Memory (1996)
Komarr (1998)
A Civil Campaign (1999)
"Winterfair Gifts" (2004)
Diplomatic Immunity (2002)
Cryoburn (2010)
Captain Vorpatril's Alliance (2012)

CHALION SERIES

The Hallowed Hunt (2005)
The Curse of Chalion (2001)
Paladin of Souls (2003)

THE WIDE GREEN WORLD SERIES

The Sharing Knife, Vol. 1: Beguilement (2006)
The Sharing Knife, Vol. 2: Legacy (2007)
The Sharing Knife, Vol. 3: Passage (2008)
The Sharing Knife, Vol. 4: Horizon (2009)

STAND-ALONE BOOKS

The Spirit Ring (1992)
Women at War (1995), edited with Roland J Green

Major Awards

The most complete and detailed list of awards, including nominations, can be found at *The Bujold Nexus*, http://www.dendarii.com/awards.html.

1989

Falling Free: Nebula Award for best novel of 1988.

1990

"The Mountains of Mourning": Nebula Award for best novella of 1989. Hugo Award for best novella of 1989.

1991

The Vor Game: Hugo Award for best novel of 1990.

1992

Barrayar: Hugo Award for best novel of 1991. 1st, Locus Poll for best SF novel of 1991.

1995

Mirror Dance: Hugo Award for best novel of 1994. 1st, Locus Poll for best SF novel of 1994.

2002

The Curse of Chalion: Mythopoeic Award 2002 for Adult Fantasy Literature.

2004

Paladin of Souls: Hugo Award for best novel of 2003. 1st, Locus Magazine poll for best fantasy novel of 2003.

2005

Paladin of Souls: Nebula Award for best novel of 2004.

2007

Ohioana Career Award.

2009

Romantic Times Achievement Award for Sci-Fi/Fantasy.

2011

Skylark Award, New England Science Fiction Association.

About the Contributors

Virginia **Bemis** taught literature and composition at Ashland University, retiring as an associate professor in 2011. She teaches online at Catherine of Siena Virtual College. She continues research in popular culture and disability studies and is also a disability rights advocate. She is working on a book on representations of disability in comics and graphic novels.

Janet Brennan **Croft** is head of access services and an associate professor of bibliography at the University of Oklahoma libraries. She is the author of *War in the Works of J.R.R. Tolkien* (Praeger, 2004) and several book chapters on the Peter Jackson films; has published articles on J.R.R. Tolkien, J.K. Rowling, and Terry Pratchett in *Mythlore, Mallorn, Tolkien Studies,* and *Seven*; and is editor of two collections of essays: *Tolkien on Film* (Mythopoeic Press, 2004) and *Tolkien and Shakespeare* (McFarland, 2006).

Andrew **Hallam** received his B.A. in creative writing from the University of Denver and an M.A. from Colorado State University with a thesis on allegory in Umberto Eco's *The Name of the Rose*. At the University of Denver he continued research into allegory and wrote a dissertation on *The Lord of the Rings* to receive his Ph.D. An adjunct faculty member at the Metropolitan State University of Denver he works full-time with the developmentally disabled in Lakewood, Colorado.

Sylvia **Kelso**, of James Cook University of North Queensland, Australia, is an editorial board member for *Femspec*, and contributing editor for *Paradoxa: Studies in World Literary Genres*, for which she edited a special volume on Ursula K. Le Guin. She has published articles with *Science Fiction Studies, Journal of the Fantastic in the Arts, Foundation,* and *Extrapolation,* and has a Ph.D. on the interaction of feminism(s) with SF and Gothic fiction.

Regina Yung **Lee** is a doctoral candidate in comparative literature at the University of California, Riverside, where she studies speculative fictions, feminist theory, the films of Jia Zhangke, and francophone literatures. She first encountered Cordelia Naismith Vorkosigan in her early undergraduate days, and has been an ardent supporter ever since.

John **Lennard** taught at the universities of London, Cambridge, and Notre Dame, the Open University and the University of the West Indies. He is now an independent scholar and a partner in Humanities-Ebooks. His publications include *The Poetry Handbook* (1996; 2d ed., Oxford University Press, 2005), *The Drama Handbook* with Mary Luckhurst (Oxford, 2002), and two essay collections, *Of Modern Dragons* (HEB, 2007) and *Of Sex and Faerie* (HEB, 2010).

Sandra J. **Lindow** is a teacher, writer and editor and lives in Menomonie, Wisconsin. Her critical work *Dancing the Tao: Le Guin and Moral Development* was published by Cambridge Scholars of Newcastle on Tyne, England, in 2012. Her seventh book of poetry is also in the publication process.

David D. **Oberhelman** is a professor of humanities at the Oklahoma State University Library. He holds a Ph.D. in English from the University of California, Irvine, and a master's degree in library and information science from the University of Pittsburgh. A specialist in Victorian and fantasy literature, he co-edited with Amy H. Sturgis *The Intersection of Fantasy and Native America* (Mythopoeic Press, 2009) and wrote *Dickens in Bedlam* (York Press, 1995).

Shannan **Palma** received her Ph.D. in women's, gender and sexuality studies from Emory University, winning the 2012 Kore Award for Best Dissertation on Women and Mythology for her work on fairy tales as myths about gender in popular culture. Her expertise is in the ways people use myth to simplify complex experiences of identity and desire.

Amy H. **Sturgis** has a Ph.D. in intellectual history from Vanderbilt University and specializes in science fiction/fantasy and Native American studies. She is the author of four books and the editor of six others, most recently *The Intersection of Fantasy and Native America* (Mythopoeic Press, 2009). Recent essays appear in *The Philosophy of Joss Whedon* (University Press of Kentucky, 2011), *Fringe Science* (Smart Pop Books, 2011), and *Star Trek and History* (forthcoming, 2013).

Linda **Wight** is a lecturer in literature and film at the University of Ballarat, Australia. Her Ph.D. dissertation examined masculinity in science fiction texts recognized by the James Tiptree, Jr., Award for doing something new with gender. She focuses especially on literary constructions of physical disability and the significance of the inviolable male body.

Index